D1190873

The last taboo

MANCHESTER
1824

Manchester University Press

The last taboo

Women and body hair

edited by Karín Lesnik-Oberstein

Manchester University Press

MANCHESTER AND NEW YORK

distributed exclusively in the USA
by Palgrave

Published by Manchester University Press
Oxford Road, Manchester M13 9NR, UK
and Room 400, 175 Fifth Avenue, New York, NY 10010, USA
www.manchesteruniversitypress.co.uk

Distributed exclusively in the USA by
Palgrave, 175 Fifth Avenue, New York,
NY 10010, USA

Distributed exclusively in Canada by
UBC Press, University of British Columbia, 2029 West Mall,
Vancouver, BC, Canada V6T 1Z2

British Library Cataloguing-in-Publication Data
A catalogue record for this book is available from the British Library

Library of Congress Cataloging-in-Publication Data applied for

ISBN   0 7190 7500 9   *hardback*
EAN   9780 7190 7500 1

First published 2006

15 14 13 12 11 10 09 08 07 06   10 9 8 7 6 5 4 3 2 1

Typeset
by Servis Filmsetting Limited, Manchester
Printed in Great Britain
by The Cromwell Press Ltd, Trowbridge

Dedicated with love to Hoyte

Contents

Figures

Contributors

Daniela Caselli is a lecturer in twentieth-century literature and culture at the University of Manchester. She is the author of *Beckett's Dantes. Intertextuality in the Fiction and Criticism* (Manchester: Manchester University Press, 2005). She has published articles on Beckett, Djuna Barnes, critical theory and modernism. She is at present working on a monograph on Djuna Barnes.

Neil Cocks is Head of English at Southeast Essex College. In 2000, he completed a PhD on the history of the nineteenth-century boy's school story. He has previously published on issues of gender and sexuality in articles on Kipling's '*Stalky and Co.*: hunting the Animal Boy' (*Yearbook of English Studies*, vol. 32, 2002) and 'Writing, death and absence in *Tim* by H. O. Sturgis' (*Nineteenth Century Contexts*, 26(1), 2004). He is currently working on a book about contemporary pedagogical theories.

Mary Ellen Croteau is the artist who created the art object (*Hair Book* (1992)) from which the image for the cover of this book was taken. She is a multimedia artist who has exhibited extensively in the US as well as in Europe, Asia and South America. She has lectured internationally, has been widely reviewed and has won numerous awards for her artwork. She has an MFA from Rutgers University. Calling her work 'cultural critique', Croteau uses a variety of media, from painting and photography to sculpture and installation, 'to lay bare the underlying bias in our social icons'. Mary Ellen Croteau's artwork can be viewed at www.maryellencroteau. womanmade.net.

Jacqueline Lazú is an assistant professor of Modern Languages at DePaul University in Chicago. She has written numerous articles on Latino and Caribbean theatre, cultural and literary criticism. Lazú is also a playwright, and her most recent play *The Block/el bloque: a Young Lord's Story* is based on extensive research that she has conducted on the political activities of street gangs and nationalist groups in Chicago in the 1960s. She is currently completing a book on the history of Puerto Rican theatre and performance in the United States, with the assistance of a Woodrow Wilson Foundation Fellowship.

Karín Lesnik-Oberstein is a senior lecturer in the School of English and American Literature, University of Reading, and director of the School's 'Centre for International Research in Childhood: Literature, Culture, Media (CIRCL)'. Her major publications include *Children's Literature: Criticism and the Fictional Child* (Oxford: Clarendon Press, 1994), and, as editor and contributor: *Children in Culture: Approaches to Childhood* (London: Palgrave, 1998); 'Children in Literature', Special Section of *The Yearbook of English Studies*, vol. 32 (Leeds: MHRA, 2002), and *Children's Literature: New Approaches* (London: Palgrave, 2004). Her research focuses on inter- and multi-disciplinary critical theory.

Alice Macdonald completed her MA at the University of Warwick. Her other publication is an article on 'Performing gender and nation in *¡Ay Carmela!' Tesserae, Journal of Iberian and Latin American Studies*, 4(1) (June 1998), 47–59. Her current research interest is the semiotics of hair in cinema.

Laura Scuriatti is an assistant professor of Literature at the European College of Liberal Arts, Berlin (Germany). She has published articles on H. G. Wells, Ford Madox Ford, Mina Loy and contemporary art. She has also edited an anthology of contemporary German literature. Her current research interests are gender and the avant-garde, and European modernism.

Stephen Thomson has been a lecturer in the School of English and American Literature at the University of Reading since 1999. His main research interests are childhood, nineteenth-century science narrative, and comparative literature. Recent publications include essays on Derrida in the *Oxford Literary Review*, and Beckett in *Samuel Beckett Today/Aujourd'hui*. He is currently at work on a book on sleepwalking.

Louise Tondeur is a lecturer in creative writing at the School of Arts of Roehampton University in London. She has published two novels with Hodder Headline (London): *The Water's Edge* (2003) and *The Haven Home for Delinquent Girls* (2004). Louise is also completing a Ph.D. on hair.

Sherry Velasco is Professor of Hispanic Studies in the Department of Spanish and Portuguese, University of Southern California, Los Angeles. Her areas of specialisation are early modern Spanish prose and theatre, and early modern women's narrative, and her interests are in the areas of gender studies, queer theory, and visual cultural studies. Sherry Velasco is the author of three books: *Male Delivery: Reproduction, Effeminacy, and Pregnant Men in Early Modern Spain* (Nashville, TN: Vanderbilt University Press, 2006), *The Lieutenant Nun: Transgenderism, Lesbian Desire, and Catalina de Erauso* (Austin, Texas: University of Texas Press, 2000), and *Demons, Nausea, and Resistance in the Autobiography of Isabel de Jesús 1611–1682* (Albuquerque, NM: University of New Mexico Press, 1996).

Sue Walsh is a lecturer in the School of English and American Literature, University of Reading. Her publications include 'Animal/child: it's the "real" thing' (*Yearbook of English Studies*, vol. 32, 2002), and ' "Irony? – but children don't get it do they?" The idea of appropriate language for the child in narratives for children' (*Children's Literature Association Quarterly*, 28(1), 2003). She has a book forthcoming on Kipling's children's literature and post-colonial theory.

Carolyn D. Williams is a senior lecturer in the School of English and American Literature, University of Reading, and has published chiefly on topics related to sexuality and the body. Her current research interests include Boudica narratives and boundaries between human and animal in early modern culture. A fair-skinned brunette, she gets through a lot of razors.

Acknowledgements

I first formulated the idea for this book with one of my very first students, Juliette Mapp. Esther Beugeling then helped me to develop further some of my initial thinking. My very dear friend Harriet Kline worked with me on formulating and proposing earlier versions of this volume, with her usual insight and intelligence. Another very dear friend, Janice Rooke, cheer-led the book throughout with the interest and enthusiasm she always brings to all my work. Too many people to name individually, including many of my ever-supportive and most kind past and present colleagues in the School of English and American Literature at the University of Reading, supplied contacts, information, references and encouragement through the years: many thanks to all of them. Thanks to Terry Lovell and Emma Francis at the University of Warwick, and Erica Burman, Dani Caselli, and the Women's Studies Centre at Manchester Metropolitan University, for inviting me to guest-lecture on my research about body hair, and to all the staff and students at the lectures for their interest and suggestions. Several people from the world of publishing supported this project in helpful ways: Tim Farmiloe, Anne Beech and Dee Mortensen; Matthew Frost and the team at Manchester University Press actually made it happen. The contributors to this volume have been amazing. I am deeply grateful for their heartfelt commitment to this project, their generosity and thoughtfulness, and their sheer patience. All my dear friends have lived with this project for many years: their belief in it, and in me, has been crucial, as ever. My beloved family has supported me while I worked on the book as absolutely as they always do: all my love to Bobe, Sarit, Saskia, Martijn, Zev and Ayal. This book is dedicated with love to Hoyte.

1 The last taboo: women, body hair and feminism

Karín Lesnik-Oberstein

The vast majority of women in Western culture, as well as in many other cultures, remove the hair on their bodies.[1] The hair on the top of women's heads is valued and admired, spoken, written and sung of as one of the ultimate signs of femininity. It is portrayed in movies, paintings, photographs and on television, and there is a large and profitable industry devoted to styling, colouring, and extending or replacing head hair. Body hair,[2] on the other hand, is described as 'unfeminine', 'excess hair', 'superfluous hair' or 'unwanted hair'. On the whole, it is only mentioned in advertising for hair-removal products, or in women's magazine articles discussing hair-removal techniques. It is rarely portrayed in movies, paintings, photographs or on television.[3] As Alice Macdonald discusses more extensively in Chapter 4 of this volume, 'Hairs on the lens', even when there are any references to women shaving, such as in some American sitcoms, the women are almost never shown with body hair. This is similar to the situation with regard to advertising images of women removing body hair. The images are of women mimicking the removal of hair from already hairless bodies (or the 'unshaven' sections are hidden under a mass of shaving foam, for instance), or of the resulting hairless body. A large and profitable industry is devoted solely to removing women's body hair in any way possible: shaving, plucking, depilatory creams, bleaches, waxing, sugaring, electrolysis, laser treatment, medication. Head hair has been the subject of academic studies in literature and the social sciences, but there are almost no academic studies on body hair.[4] There is only a more extensive medical literature around women's body hair defined as 'excessive', and as an abnormality or aberration, called 'hirsutism'. The only other writing on it is a fairly prolific amount of pornographic material, in magazines or on the Internet, on women's body hair as fetish, or on shaved women as fetish.

Any consideration of women's body hair, in short, is clearly regarded as a legitimate subject of only medical and cosmetic interest, with the two aspects being extensions of each other, as both have the aim of removing the hair. Otherwise, women's body hair is seen as, apparently, either too ridiculous and trivial – or too monstrous – to be discussed at all.[5] In this sense, women's body hair is truly configured as a taboo: something not to be seen or mentioned; prohibited and circumscribed by rules of avoidance; surrounded by shame, disgust, and censure. It is in this sense too that this book refers to it as 'the last taboo'. In a Western capitalist society which sees itself (either with pride or self-condemnation) as having broken most established taboos (mainly around sexuality and the body), women's body hair remains an area of silence and blankness. It is the polarity of the ridiculous triviality and threatening monstrosity of women's body hair, expressed in its near-complete invisibility or absence both in language and visual imagery, which is the topic of this book. Is body hair in every sense so utterly irrelevant that there is absolutely nothing to be said about it other than brief and repetitive instructions on how to remove it? In this age where every topic is milked for its commercial or academic interest, why has, apparently, nothing at all been considered to be worth saying about body hair? In short, why does body hair appear at one and the same time meaningless: there is nothing to be said about it or shown about it, and as too meaningful – too disgusting/horrible/private – to be permitted mention? In Chapter 3 of this volume, 'A history of pubic hair, or reviewers' responses to Terry Eagleton's *After Theory*', Louise Tondeur addresses, for instance, Eagleton's claim that contemporary academic research in the areas of literary or critical theory has lost political relevance when he states that 'Not all students are blind to the Western narcissism involved in working on the history of pubic hair while half the world's population lacks adequate sanitation and survives on less than two dollars a day.'[6]

I want to start thinking about why possibly body hair is seen as either – or both – too silly (too trivial) and too dangerous (too monstrous) to consider, by comparing the treatment of body hair with the extensive attention paid to another aspect of women's bodies: body weight. There are thousands of popular and academic books on women and body weight, dieting, eating-disorders, and body image. Interestingly, many of these books claim to be discussing women's bodies in totality, but almost all of these include no mention of body hair whatsoever. Since books on dieting or weight control can be seen as parallel to articles on hair removal, in that they accept a presented goal, and therefore address themselves primarily to how to achieve this goal, I will not consider them extensively here. Instead, I want to focus on feminist analyses of body weight as a problem for women: as an oppressive patriarchal ideal, which regulates and controls, or produces (the terminology will depend on theoretical orientation), the female body. Yet body hair is not mentioned in this light. Even more interestingly, when it is mentioned at all, it is usually portrayed as a concern solely for 'extremist' feminists. In fact, it is one of the ways in which (popular or academic) feminists may define, and distinguish themselves from, 'extremist' feminists: 'extremists', then, are, apparently (there are several versions) man-haters and/or separatists, lesbians (seen negatively), bra-burners, women who wear no make-up, do not shave and see themselves as 'victims' of the patriarchy, and – often presented as the most damning charge of all, especially by popular writers on feminism – are not 'fun'. As Rosalind Coward suggested, in 1992:

> While many women identified with feminism's economic goals, they were anxious to distance themselves from a sexual antagonism to men and from a sexual revolution which they saw as undermining their 'femininity'. The feminist vision of a new sexuality came to be seen as the fevered imaginings of man-haters. Through the 1980s we heard men and women telling us how it was quite natural to want to be sexy for men. Only 'uptight lesbian feminists' had a problem with that.[7]

However, according to most writers on feminism, body weight is not involved in a split between 'fun' and 'not fun' feminists. It is accepted as both an area of serious concern for feminism, and by the same measure it is used as a legitimisation of the continued seriousness and relevance of feminism itself in the late twentieth and early twenty-first centuries: as long as women can so visibly be seen still to be controlled, damaged or even killed by their attempts to comply with a patriarchal ideal, feminism cannot quite so easily be seen as superfluous or superficial by those who would wish to claim it as such. Body weight, and women's bodies defined by that focus, then, are a major site of contestation for feminism. The attempts to reclaim the female body from the cult of ever-increasing thinness are a central focus for both popular and academic feminist analyses. Body hair does not even merit a mention, let alone any consideration as a subject of contestation. In this context, body-hair's absence may be interpreted as a result of being 'not seen', because, again, being both too trivial to discuss – it does not kill women as anorexia or bulimia do – but also as being too dangerous: might feminism be undermined by laying itself open to charges of triviality, grim rigidity or monstrous ugliness ('not fun')?

It will already be apparent that there are several issues at play here: firstly, and most importantly, as a gender issue, women's body hair plays a different role to body weight. Central to this argument is that 'fat' women are portrayed as undesirable or unattractive, but nonetheless still as female. In fact, both in patriarchal and in feminist terms, women's involvement with issues of body weight has come to figure as an important aspect of 'femininity'. 'Hairy' women, on the other hand, are monstrous in being like men, or masculine. Amie Braman, for instance, reports of her study 'Women and body hair: social perceptions and attitudes' that:

> I found that people perceived the woman with body hair as less sexually attractive, sociable, intelligent, positive, and happy than the woman without body hair. At the same time, they saw the woman with body hair as more active, stronger, and more aggressive. These are typically masculine traits that are

generally viewed as positive in this culture. They are not viewed as particularly feminine, however, and thus take on negative connotations here.[8]

Joan Ferrante adds that:

the perceived undesirability of hair growth departing, even slightly, from what is defined as feminine is rooted in constructs of gender . . . Case studies by Ross *et al.* (1965) indicate that superfluous facial and body hair on women triggers anxiety about sexual identity, since such hair is one of the obvious symbolic characteristics that differentiate the male from the female. Moreover, the authors find that many women are unable to discuss the problem because of the threatening symbolic implications of any amount of hair beyond what is culturally considered the female distribution. In sum, superfluous hair is viewed by women as a confusion of symbolic categories, blurring the boundaries that separate woman from man . . . [Hirsute] subjects [in a North German study, Zerssen and Meyer (1960)] believe they possess a characteristic of the male, they do not run true to a normal female type, and they are defective females. Because of their perceived stigmatization they have an intense and exaggerated concern that their perceived deviation will be noticed and they will be rejected.[9]

It is in this that the 'monstrousness' of 'hairy' women consists: they transgress the boundaries of gender, as 'fat' or 'thin' (despite accusations of 'boyishness') women are not presented as doing. This, then, is the area wherein the danger of women's body hair lies. As Freud suggests, in discussing 'The taboo of virginity', taboos rest on the fear of 'some danger . . . a generalized dread of women is expressed in all these rules of avoidance.'[10] Feminist analyses have, however, largely ignored body hair as a legitimate site of contestation, and in doing so, I am suggesting, are participating – whether they like it or not, and whether they intend it or not – in a patriarchal taboo, enforced through the threat of ridicule and trivialisation (how could you devote attention to something so silly?), or of total dismissal (the all-too familiar: 'you are monstrous, or mad').

These issues alert us to what I will argue is the importance of making women's body hair visible, both as an issue and as visible on/of the body. For what I want to enter into is an analysis of the problem of protest, resistance or contestation becoming absorbed into, and used by, the dominant discourse. Along the lines of argument of the French philosopher and historian Michel Foucault, I will suggest that the problem of women and body weight has become as much a means for the patriarchy to define and control 'femininity', as a site of resistance to patriarchy. Feminist theorist Judith Butler formulates this Foucauldian-inspired view as follows: 'Feminist critique ought also to understand how the category of "women," the subject of feminism, is produced and restrained by the very structures of power through which emancipation is sought.'[11] I want to be clear, then, that my arguments here are not based, theoretically speaking, on some plea for either a return to the 'natural body' (or on the idea that that is even a possibility), or on a plea to 'award' women's (certainly present) suffering over body hair and its removal an 'equal' status with the problems around body weight (or parallel related and relatable issues such as cosmetic surgery). Instead, I am agreeing here with arguments such as that of Judith Butler and Donna Haraway that bodies are not 'born' (do not exist as 'natural' 'underneath' culture), but are created as meaning, including gender. Butler writes:

> But if there is no subject who decides on its gender, and if, on the contrary, gender is part of what decides the subject, how might one formulate a project that preserves gender practices as sites of critical agency? If gender is constructed through relations of power and, specifically, normative constraints that not only produce but also regulate various bodily beings, how might agency be derived from this notion of gender as the effect of productive constraint? If gender is not an artifice to be taken on or taken off at will and, hence, not an effect of choice, how are we to understand the constitutive and compelling status of gender norms without falling into the trap of cultural determinism? How precisely are we to understand the ritualized repetition by which such norms produce and stabilize not only the effects of gender but the materiality of sex? And can this repetition, this rearticulation, also constitute the occasion for a critical reworking of apparently constitutive gender norms?[12]

And, as Elizabeth Grosz sums up:

> The subject cannot remain neutral or indifferent to its own body and body-parts. The body is libidinally invested . . . The human subject is capable of suicide, of anorexia, because the body is meaningful, has significance, because it is in part constituted both for the subject and for others in terms of meanings and significances . . . This significatory, cultural dimension implies that bodies, egos, subjectivities are not simply reflections of their cultural context and associated values, but are constituted as such by them, marking bodies in their very 'biological' configurations with sociosexual inscriptions.[13]

As such, I – and the other contributors to this book – am participating here in a critical analysis of the stories told about women's bodies (and men's, necessarily in such a constructivist consideration, as I will go on to discuss further later), and endorse the importance of such analyses to identifying or locating possibilities for the re-formulation of women's identities. As Foucault suggests,

> Critique doesn't have to be the premise of a deduction which concludes: this then is what needs to be done. It should be an instrument for those who fight, those who resist and refuse what is.[14]

Therefore I do not wish to be understood to be simply advocating that not removing body hair will return women's bodies to some a priori 'natural' 'female' self (see Sue Walsh's Chapter 9 in this volume on 'Bikini fur and fur bikinis' for further analyses of ways in which certain ideas of the 'natural' underpin meanings of body hair). I do wish to suggest that addressing the silence around a mass practice by women may reopen questions about the relevance of feminism and feminist practice on the, potentially, widest scale. It is not, then, a question of my wanting to 'convert' women to not removing body hair (or not wearing make-up or undergoing cosmetic surgery: issues which are popularly related to one another), because, as such, this would only have a predictable outcome as the 'story' stands at present. It would be (in fact is) doomed to total political, social and cultural – if not necessarily personal – ineffectiveness, dismissed or marginalised as 'eccentric' (mad), 'ugly' or 'ridiculous' (see Carolyn Williams's Chapter 6 in this volume for a charting specifically of literary narratives about body hair and gender, many of which include, or refer to, such ideas). But, by examining the taboo for how and why it functions, we may create, or make visible, these areas as sites of possible contestation. Asserting the possibility of after all asking questions about such taboos as body hair may disrupt some of the silence, invisibility and closure of collusion (even, or especially if, unintended) with capitalist patriarchy. The near-absolutely silenced may attain a force from resisting its very silencing. As 'presence' it constitutes, and is constituted as, 'madness', but to use this madness may be a route. That it subsequently – as with body weight – can be co-opted by existing power-structures for their own purposes, does not detract from the potential force of the eruption of the oppressed, or, as Freud puts it, the return of the repressed. As Annette Kuhn quotes Biddy Martin, 'feminist critical practice "can be a fundamentally deconstructive strategy which questions the possibility of universals or absolute meanings and exposes the constitution of power at stake in their assertion." '[15]

Attendant on this issue is a challenge too to some (mostly popular) feminism to consider more carefully its formulations (referred to earlier) around 'fun' feminism and 'victim' feminism. The whole idea of make-up and clothing, or other ritual decorative practices, as constituting in any simple way 'celebrations' of 'femininity', serves to close down important questions around the coercive practices of social ridicule and social exclusion for those not willing or able to participate in this 'celebration', never mind around the more general question of how women (or anyone) come to believe that they have freely 'chosen' to engage in certain practices. As Susan Bordo writes:

> normalisation, to be sure, is continually mystified and effaced in our culture by the rhetoric of 'choice' and 'self-determination' which plays such a key role in commercial representations of diet, exercise, hair and eye-colouring and so forth. 'You get better or worse every day,' cautions Glen Frye on behalf of Bally Matrix Fitness, 'The choice is yours.' (Yes, you are free to choose to be a lazy, self-indulgent slob?) 'The body you have is the body you inherited, but you must decide what to do with it', instructs Nike, offering glamorous shots of lean, muscled athletes to help us 'decide' . . . The commercial texts . . .

participate in the illusion . . . that our 'differences' are already flourishing in the culture as it is, without need for personal struggle and social change – that we are already self-determining, already empowered to look in the mirror and see what is right, instead of what is wrong. The exposure of such mystifications, which should not be impeded by too facile a celebration of resistance, must remain central to a feminist politics of the body.[16]

Who, indeed, is celebrating what? Are women then 'celebrating' the patriarchal creation of themselves? I would argue so. Although undoubtedly these 'celebratory' feminists would claim they would defend – indeed ostensibly do defend – the right of women to avoid wearing make-up or to shave (when it even occurs to them to mention this last practice, which, significantly, is very rarely), in fact their writing participates in the deferral of the very 'victim' status that they imagine they are denouncing – on to the spectre of the grim, non-fun, ugly, aggressive 'extremist'. The wallflower is therefore not liberated from exclusion, but condemned to it forever, by her external 'ugliness', produced and participated in by her as a communication of her own understanding of her worthlessness. And indeed, this is her social and personal worthlessness, a self-confirming circle where image determines worth, and worth image. This status is compounded by 'fun' feminists as now 'not fun' too: an additional condemnation by the very people whom she might have hoped would come to her aid. A (feminist) analysis of oppression confirms that a 'victim' is a person suffering oppression and coercion, not – as 'fun' feminists would have it – a figure who has elected herself to this status as a defeatist martyr. Women suffer too under body hair as stigma. They are seen as monstrous, grotesque, disgusting, aggressive, anti-social or mad; at best: sick, with medical articles talking of the 'management' of hirsutism, and an interesting connection made in some medical research between psychiatric patients and hirsutism. As Joan Ferrante points out:

> For almost a century a significant number of physicians, especially gynecologists, dermatologists, and endocrinologists, have noted the tremendous emotional impact of idiopathic hirsutism upon patients even when amounts of hair are small and medically insignificant . . . Interest in hirsutism by the medical profession stems from two sources – the anxiety women experience with regard to superfluous hair growth and the possibility that hirsutism may be a sign of an underlying endocrine problem. The latter is rare since endocrinologic abnormalities are seen in about one percent of the women who consult a physician about hair growth . . . Most patients, even when amounts of hair growth are slight and medically insignificant, are notably sensitive; the more vulnerable personalities withdraw socially and feel sexually undesirable. The most severely affected have experienced so much shame from ridicule and social rejection they have a morbid preoccupation with hair growth.[17]

Any liberating laughter of feminism, if there is to be such a thing, should not, surely, collude – however unwittingly – with laughing *at*.

Moreover, we may consider further then, that as much as feminism has attempted to help women obsessed by their body weight, it has also encountered a problem in continuing to endorse this area as such a primary focus as a site of contestation for the female body. The cultural circulation and recirculation of the arguments and analyses suggests to me that feminism – from an initial standpoint of analysis and (as) resistance – has now become as much trapped in a participation in what is by now a patri-archally permitted area of protest around the female body. Not for nothing is there a sense of puzzlement that, despite increasing discussion of, pub-lication around, and theories of, the aetiology of eating-disorders, there are also claims of increasing amounts of eating-disorders both within popula-tions, and in terms of geographical distribution. So also, the circulation of this topic as apparently the almost only conceivable way to address the female body,[18] is reflected in the unending circularity of many of the popular arguments around the causes of eating-disorders: are they caused by images of thin models, or are thin models caused by ideals of thinness originating from elsewhere? As Susan Bordo asks: 'just how helpful is an emphasis on creative agency in describing the relation of women and their bodies to the image industry of post-industrial capitalism, a context in which eating disorders and exercise compulsions are flourishing?'[19] Similarly, it is remarkable how many of the feminist arguments around the body, both popular and academic, largely repeat and recycle early analy-ses, notably Susie Orbach's seminal *Fat is a Feminist Issue* from 1978.[20] In other words: the increasing proliferation and circulation – and unending circularity of argument – of issues around body weight and eating-disor-ders, for me points to their present ineffectiveness as a site of resistance, or even to their absorption and co-opting into the economic and discursive structures of patriarchal society. Orbach herself indicates something of these difficulties in her 1988 introduction to the new edition of *Fat is a Feminist Issue*:

> Much to my surprise, the [original, 1978] book struck a powerful chord in hun-dreds of thousands of women. Compulsive eating and its sister conditions – bulimia and anorexia – came out of the closet. Hundreds of self-help groups started up; . . . I began to feel that women were fighting back and contesting the blanket message that they should be thin. I was optimistic that the children being raised now might be free of these disabling body-image and eating prob-lems that had so beset my generation. Ten years on [in 1988], we discover the dismaying fact that 80 percent of San Franciscan girls are dieting because even the scrawny ones believe they are 'overweight' . . . Obsession and preoccupa-tion with the body has increased rather than abated . . . slimness has not declined as an aesthetic; rather it has captured the desire of more and more people and come to represent the longings of more and more women.[21]

Body hair as a site of contestation could in this important sense differ from body weight, in terms of possible meanings which could be developed for it and from it, politically and socially speaking, in that body hair is seen as either removed or not. Unlike 'fat', it is conceived to have a 'point zero' when it is not removed: it is then simply present to whatever degree, while body weight does not reach such a point – unless we count death by either starvation or gross obesity as the terrible alternatives. Dieting is an unending battle which, as has often been pointed out, cannot be won: the goal-posts can be, and are, constantly moved, so that no effort is sufficient. As many feminists have pointed out, this is of great psychological and economic benefit to a capitalist patriarchy: a population of women may be focusing a large part of their energies and desires on their weight and related issues such as (highly profitable) diet foods and exercise, and therefore not (as much) on, for instance, the pursuance of political or economic resistance and change. As Orbach argues: 'In exchange for [women's] desire to transform our lives, we are given back the body and the correct feeding of others and ourselves as the arena in which we should concentrate.'[22] Hair removal participates in this unending economy too: hair has to be removed again and again, and, in fact, it is clearly not in the interest of manufacturers of hair-removal products to produce a once-and-for-all removal system (even the most recent innovations in laser hair-removal, for instance, come with the warning that treatment may need to be repeated every so many years). But, once body hair is permitted to grow, it is not seen – unlike weight – to increase unendingly and unstoppably, as body weight 'threatens' to should it be left 'unregulated'. (Whether or not this would be the case for individual women, it is this 'story' that the 'problem' of body weight relies on.) Therefore body hair which has been permitted to grow does not have to be 'regulated'. I am referring here now to hair growth which specifically falls under the taboo: with 'permitted' hair, e.g. top-of-head hair, eyebrows or pubic hair, 'regulation' is constantly practised to differentiate it from taboo hair; only trimmed pubic hair is permissible, or 'feminine' eyebrows. (For more discussion of this, see parts of Chapter 2 by Daniela Caselli, Chapter 9 by Sue Walsh, and Chapter 8 by Laura Scuriatti, all in this volume.) Again, I am not arguing that what I am suggesting here is 'natural' or 'true' about body hair, but that it is a discourse or narrative which I am expanding upon from the meanings potentially present in the silences around a body hair which is produced as the absence of a potential presence.

In this sense, it is body hair as possibility that I am insisting on here. Choosing to stay or become 'fat' can no longer 'speak' resistance in any clear way. Orbach, in *Fat is a Feminist Issue*, crucially diagnosed the issue of body weight as 'not so much descriptions of body size as . . . emotional categories', and added that:

> I am writing about the need to decode the food and body-image metaphors that have become a woman's language . . . We need to understand what a woman is saying when she uses her body to express difficult emotional issues . . . Because food and the body have become an arena in which women have been allowed

to express themselves, food and the body become a language they communicate with.[23]

Nevertheless, the problematic paradox I have suggested above already presents itself here in Orbach's formulations: this language of the body is the 'arena in which women have been allowed to express themselves'. As with Freud's hysterical women patients (the word 'hysteria' technically means 'to express emotional distress through the body', and was not used by Freud in a derogatory sense about his patients – much misguided anti-Freudianism to the contrary), a 'hidden' language is developed, but once that language is interpreted or read, it may be upheld by the dominant power-structure as the legitimised area of protest. Therefore, body weight still operates as a widespread 'language', but it is now solely a conveyor of meanings to, and *as*, the private self. Women may circulate this anguished communication, but it only circulates back to themselves as anguish or pain, and redoubles in its own self-destructiveness. Socially and politically, the message goes nowhere, except to recirculate through the established magazines and fashion shows. Meanwhile, consumer capitalism enjoys the fruits. It is no wonder that eating-disorders must be negotiated in that 'privatised' sphere: psychotherapy. Anorexia does not, after all, function effectively as a hunger-strike socially and politically speaking – initial feminist claims to the contrary. As Orbach has already indicated, it represents the hunger-strike of private domesticity.

Body hair, on the other hand, is denied the barest possibility of speech or meaning. It does not function as either an image or a language, but as no image or no language. Body hair therefore carries the possibility of becoming a language on the very edge of meaninglessness, wavering between madness and co-opted discourse. Orbach herself (her work, in its importance, again already carrying within it its own difficulties) argues that in order for body weight to disappear as a language, it must first be 'deciphered' and understood, and then forgotten as language. In fact, she is arguing that body weight as an issue can inherently not be resolved by women either becoming 'fat' or 'thin' (enough), but by these perceptions and ideas becoming 'meaningless'. Body hair, by contrast, may be one way to approach meaning as a madness which asserts its right to presence, in order to redraw attention to the myriad ways in which women and bodies are continually always created, never 'natural', or even the same as 'women'. Instead, 'women' and 'bodies' are produced by power-structures and assertions which disguise, suppress, or embed their own presence and purpose. That this – or any – madness may potentially always be co-opted in turn, is part of this recognition: that meaning, and the body, will never become stable, ended, or 'mastered'. For instance, several contributors to this volume analyse, as yet another specific aspect of this instability of bodies and identities, how body hair may play a role in the construction of the body as a national or racialised body: Daniela Caselli (Chapter 2) and Neil Cocks (Chapter 11) discuss how one nationality may define an 'Other' through the locating of body hair on the 'foreign' (female) body, while Stephen Thomson (Chapter 5), Jacqueline Lazú (Chapter 7) and Sherry Velasco (Chapter 10) consider body hair within French, Nuyorican and Spanish narratives of self-defining nationality or ethnicity.

Finally, I would like to expand a little further my use of the idea of formulating body hair as a 'madness asserting its right to presence', for not only am I following the argument that all bodies are created, also as 'gendered', but that the 'female' body may be described as produced as a specific relationship to 'lack'. Elizabeth Grosz explains:

> If women do not lack in any ontological or biological sense (there is no lack in the real, as Lacan is fond of saying), men cannot be said to have. In this sense, patriarchy requires that female bodies and sexualities be socially produced as lack. This, in some social contexts is taken literally but also occurs at an imaginary and symbolic level, that is, at the level of the body's morphology and the body image.[24]

If it is indeed the case that body hair challenges the boundaries of gender in ways that body weight does not – and that this requires its absolute invisibility – then its visibility does indeed reveal femininity as that which hides within itself the potentially masculine. This link is indicated, for instance, by historian Peter Gay's description of *Punch* magazines' nineteenth-century resistance to women acquiring the vote (another 'masculine' feature): 'Parodying a political female's address to the "electresses" in her district, Punch had the improbable candidate advocate a variety of trivial "womanish" causes, and describe herself as regular in features, with fine teeth: "My hair is dark chestnut; my moustachios are rather lighter." '[25] (for parallel formulations of the moustache as a revelation of the 'masculine' hidden in femininity, see also Daniela Caselli's discussion in Chapter 2 of Wilkie Collins' *The Woman in White*, and Neil Cocks's consideration (Chapter 11) of the critical discussions around the paintings of Frida Kahlo and, for related discussions of bearded women, the chapters by Sherry Velasco (Chapter 10) and Stephen Thomson (Chapter 5)). This revelation of the masculine in the feminine is impermissible – and thus its 'madness' – and precisely this emphasises the threat that is posed by a female body not constituting itself as 'absolute' other:[26] as 'lack' in opposition to the masculine 'presence'. The female body is exhibited as 'lack' in its requirement of constant 'self-creation' as 'feminine' – a body is not 'feminine', culturally and socially speaking, if it has not achieved this status (through make-up, hair removal, dieting, tattoos, or whatever is culturally specified). Male bodies are, in contrast, produced as 'existing' as male, not as achieving 'maleness', although there are several suggestions that this is shifting, in the West at least, with the increase in eating-disorders, body-training, and indeed body-hair removal in men (both homosexual and heterosexual).[27] Indeed, the very fact that I write that those bodies are still, however, '*produced* as existing as male' indicates that this 'existence' is here not thought as itself originary or inevitable ('biological'), but a reading of maleness as a presence in opposition to the 'lack' of femininity.[28] This volume, therefore, in following theories of gender as being produced by, and as, mutually implicated, is inevitably also engaging with body-hair removal in relation to maleness, whether implicitly or explicitly, in the different chapters.

In these senses, it is perfectly logical both that there is a fetish for 'hairy women' and for 'shaven' women (which in this context significantly may refer also to the specific removal not only of 'excess' hair, but of the – arguably increasingly less – 'permitted' pubic hair as well): a fetish is described by Freud as the denial of, or 'substitute for the absent female phallus'.[29] In other words, the fetish, as Donna Haraway explains, is 'an object human beings make only to forget their role in creating it'.[30] This is the central role of fetishisation: to have an object which sexually excites inexplicably but fundamentally. If it were to be revealed as having a meaning and a role (hiding the absence of the female phallus to protect the male from the awareness of his own fear of possible castration) then it could no longer function as fetish. The 'hairy' woman as fetish, then, 'hides' the absence of phallus, while the 'shaven' woman as fetish might find a parallel in Freud's discussion of the ambivalence expressed in some fetishism:

> In very subtle instances both the disavowal and the affirmation of the castration have found their way into the construction of the fetish itself . . . [In one case] analysis showed that it [a piece of clothing which covered the genitals completely] signified that women were castrated and that they were not castrated; and it also allowed for the hypothesis that men were castrated, for all these possibilities could equally well be concealed under the [piece of clothing] . . . Affection and hostility in the treatment of the fetish – which run parallel with the disavowal and the acknowledgement of castration – are mixed in unequal proportions in different cases . . . a parallel to fetishism in social psychology, might be seen in the Chinese custom of mutilating the female foot and then revering it like a fetish after it has been mutilated. It seems as though the Chinese male wants to thank the woman for having submitted to being castrated.[31]

In the light of these formulations around the fetish, I would like to conclude by arguing that my suggestion of making women's body hair visible – open to discussion – might be reformulated as amounting to the revelation of both 'hairy' and 'shaved' women as fetish (or: created). Donna Haraway's description of the fetish has emphasised that it is that which may not be questioned for a role or meaning – which indeed exists by virtue of being protected against questioning. It is in this respect that the taboo on body hair functions: to protect it from question, and to regulate strictly how it is handled. This resistance to questioning has been demonstrated recently specifically by developments in evolutionary psychology, where some research has reclaimed body hair – and other aspects of the 'male' and 'female' (as 'body') – again as 'natural', 'inevitable' or determined, because a product of evolutionary processes. An exchange in the Royal Society's *Biology Letters* concerned an argument that a lack of body hair in women was attractive to men, because it was correlated with a lack of health-threatening parasites and lice in the women. As Robin McKie, the science editor of the *Observer* newspaper, quotes the scientists:

> In this way, hairlessness became a highly desired attribute in humans, a signal that a person was a good mate, particularly for men seeking female partners. [. . .] For men, a signal that a woman was disease-free was especially important because it suggested they would have a better chance of surviving childbirth and so maintain their partner's genotype,' said Bodmer. 'And certainly, everywhere you look in the world, you find that women, no matter what the race or tribe, are significantly less hairy than men.'[32]

Needless to say, why this would be 'particularly' and 'especially' important to men, but not to women, presumably also wanting, within the terms of such arguments, to 'maintain their . . . genotype', is not explained.[33] In fact, much of the statement quoted above seems to be closely related to the comments of Charles Darwin on body hair and gender in his *The Descent of Man*:

> No one supposes that the nakedness of the skin is any direct advantage to man; his body therefore cannot have been divested of hair through natural selection. Nor . . . have we any evidence that this can be due to the direct action of climate, or that it is the result of correlated development. The absence of hair on the body is to a certain extent a secondary sexual character; for in all parts of the world women are less hairy than men. Therefore we may reasonably suspect that this character has been gained through sexual selection . . . [W]e may conclude that it was our female semi-human ancestors who were first divested of hair, and that this occurred at an extremely remote period before the several races had diverged from common stock. While our female ancestors were gradually acquiring this new character of nudity, they must have transmitted it almost equally to their offspring of both sexes while young; so that its transmission, as with the ornaments of many mammals and birds, has not been limited either by sex or age. There is nothing surprising in a partial loss of hair having been esteemed as an ornament by our ape-like progenitors . . . and hav[ing] consequently been gained through sexual selection.[34]

For Bodmer, as cited by McKie, men value less hair (comparative to themselves) in women as a functionally significant indicator of health and greater resistance to hair-loving disease carriers; for Darwin, less body hair, revealing skin, constitutes an 'ornament' for the female in the eyes of the male. If, in relation to Bodmer's claims, only men selected comparatively less hair as an indicator of health, but women did not select men using this criterion, then problems arise. The lessening of body hair is somehow passed on 'almost equally to their offspring of both sexes', but also somehow more so to women, and that type of sexual selection, in Darwin's formulation here, is then both *anticipated* and *produced by* 'female ancestors . . . gradually acquiring this new character of nudity'. 'Ornament', in this sense, is both constitutive of femininity *as* 'femininity' in relation to a 'masculinity' which establishes it and is drawn to it as such,[35] while, at the same time, sexual selection might threaten to be collapsed through the equal passing on of the genetic trait of decreasing hairiness, were it not for the 'almost' in 'almost equally'. This slips in as the indicator of a crucial discrepancy in time-processes, whereby an initial apparently spontaneous 'head start' of women in the process of 'denudation' leads to the lessening of hair being passed on more to women than men. As, indeed, Darwin writes 'With respect to the completion of the process [of denudation] through sexual selection . . . All . . . will admit how ludicrously hideous is the opposite extreme of excessive hairiness.'[36]

In Darwin, then, the judgement in the present of his text of the 'ludicrous hideous[ness]' of 'excessive hairiness', which 'all will admit', produces a past in which women started losing hair before men, and therefore both initiate an aspect of sexual selection through that 'ornament', as well as further producing that ornament through sexual selection, especially, if not exclusively so, for women. In Bodmer's statement, Darwin's notion of the attraction of ornament is replaced by the idea of an ostensibly more 'rational' and functional consideration of disease, but this replacement turns out, in my reading, only to be a displacement: in either case, men are assumed and confirmed as the sexual selectors, and women as the sexually selected,[37] while, simultaneously, less hair in women is the spontaneous origin of such sexual selection.

I hope, then, that by questioning in this book the silence and invisibility around women's body hair – by challenging the taboo on women's body hair – we may have contributed in some ways to maintaining an awareness, for women and men, that it is possible to continue to open up ways of negotiating some of the meanings in their lives, both personal and political.

Notes

1   Statistics vary, but in the US and the UK, generally figures are given of around 95% of women participating in hair removal, with the lowest percentage, of 65%, in Germany. I would note, however, with reference to figures concerned with different national rates of hair removal, that such figures are often framed by ideas of nationality, race or ethnicity (as I will discuss further later in this chapter; see also Chapter 11 by Neil Cocks and Chapter 2 by Daniela Caselli).

2 Excepting pubic hair to some extent, in some cases. I am also including (women's) facial hair such as beards and moustaches as 'body hair' for my purposes here.

3 Some rare instances of female body hair (aside from the copious amounts of pornography, which will be discussed later) can be seen, for instance, in some of Frida Kahlo's paintings (see Chapter 11 for more discussion on this), and some of Della Grace or Trish Morrissey's photographs (see *She* magazine, January 1998, 40–3). See Laura Scuriatti's Chapter 8 in this volume for more discussion on this, the cover and article photos by Elise Dumontet for 'Plucking hell: why are women obsessed with body hair?', Polly Vernon, *Observer Woman*, 1 (15 January 2006), 38–9 (also available at: http://digital.guardian.co.uk/observer/2006/01/15/pages/wom.38.shtml), and two television documentaries on 'hairy women', including British Channel Five's 'Hairy women' (screened on 3 December 2002), and British Channel Four's 'Hairy Women: the secrets surrounding female body hair' (screened on 26 February 2003). See also the uproar (April 1999) around the film star Julia Roberts' appearance at a movie première with unshaven armpits (see Chapter 4 for further discussion on body hair in film and television).

4 The few articles that I have been able to find which are dedicated to discussing body hair as an issue (rather than its removal) are: Joan Ferrante, 'Biomedical versus cultural constructions of abnormality: the case of idiopathic hirsutism in the United States', *Culture, Medicine and Psychiatry*, 12 (1988), 219–38; Susan Basow, 'The hairless ideal: women and their body hair', *Psychology of Women Quarterly*, 15 (1991), 83–96; Amie Braman, 'Women and body hair: a cultural taboo', *The Lafayette*, 122: 17 (March 29, 1996), at: www.lafayctte. edu/~paper /spring96/march29/feature1.htm, pp. 1–2 (with thanks to Harriet Kline for finding this article. It is relevant to note that Braman was a student in Basow's department at Lafayette College); Marika Tiggeman and Sarah J. Kenyon, 'The hairlessness norm: the removal of body hair in women', *Sex Roles: a Journal of Research*, 39: 11–12, 873–85; Merran Toerien and Sue Wilkinson, 'Gender and body hair: constructing the feminine woman', *Women's International Forum*, 26: 4 (2003), 333–44, and Merran Toerien, Sue Wilkinson and Precilla Y. L. Choi, 'Body hair removal: the "mundane" production of normative femininity', *Sex Roles: A Journal of Research*, 52: 5–6 (March 2005), 399–406. It may be noted that Toerien *et al.*, several years on, are also still referring back to the articles by Ferrante, Basow, Braman, and Tiggeman and Kenyon as some of the few on body hair (which they define as I am doing here) from this perspective.

5 I leave aside here, for the moment, the case of the pornographic material on body hair as fetishism: here (as far as I can tell) body hair is not so much analysed or discussed as an issue overall, as simply presented or defended as a source of specifically sexual excitement for some. I will return to fetishism and body hair later in this chapter.

6 Terry Eagleton, *After Theory* (Harmondsworth: Penguin, 2002), p. 6.

7 Rosalind Coward, 'Slim and sexy: modern women's holy grail', in Sandra Kemp and Judith Squires (eds), *Feminisms* (Oxford: Oxford University Press, 1997), pp. 358–62, p. 360

8 Braman, 'Women and body hair', 2.

9 Ferrante, 'Biomedical versus cultural constructions of abnormality', 222–3.

10 Sigmund Freud, 'The taboo of virginity', in Angela Richards (ed.), *On Sexuality*, vol. 7, Penguin Freud Library (Harmondsworth: Penguin, 1977), pp. 265–83, p. 271.

11 Judith Butler, *Gender Trouble. Feminism and the Subversion of Identity* (London: Routledge, 1990), p. 2

12 Judith Butler, *Bodies that Matter: On the Discursive Limits of 'Sex'* (London: Routledge, 1993), p. 10.

13 Elizabeth Grosz, 'Psychoanalysis and the imaginary body', in Kemp and Squires (eds), *Feminisms*, pp. 299–308, p. 301, p. 303.

14 Michel Foucault, 'Questions of method', *Ideology and Consciousness*, 8 (1981), 3–14, 13.

15 Annette Kuhn, 'The body and cinema: some problems for feminism', in Kemp and Squires (eds), *Feminisms*, pp. 403–9, p. 409.

16 Susan Bordo, 'Normalisation and resistance in the era of the image', in Kemp and Squires (eds), *Feminisms*, pp. 451–5, p. 453, p. 455.

17 Ferrante, 'Biomedical versus cultural constructions of abnormality', 221.

18 Again, other areas may be seen as also included in such considerations, but I would argue that these are either defined as less 'serious' – in the case of make-up, or tattooing, for instance – or may be seen as in many ways subsumed within the concern with body shape and weight, as is the case with much (if not all) cosmetic surgery.

19 Susan Bordo, 'Normalisation and resistance in the era of the image', p. 451.

20 Susie Orbach, *Fat is a Feminist Issue* (London: Random House, 1988 (orig. pub. 1978)).

21 Orbach, *Fat is a Feminist Issue*, pp. 20–1.

22 Orbach, *Fat is a Feminist Issue*, p. 22.

23 Orbach, *Fat is a Feminist Issue*, p. 23.

24 Grosz, 'Psychoanalysis and the imaginary body', p. 307.

25 Peter Gay, *The Bourgeois Experience: Victoria to Freud*, vol. 1 of *Education of the Senses* (Oxford and New York: Oxford University Press, 1984), p. 194; quoting from *Punch*, 21 (1851), 20, 22, 35, 141, 155, 157.

26 I am here adopting Gayatri Spivak's distinction between 'self-confirming' others and 'absolute' others (Gayatri Chakravorty Spivak, 'Can the subaltern speak?', *Marxism and the Interpretation of Culture*, Cary Nelson and Lawrence Grossberg (eds), (Urbana: University of Illinois Press, 1988), pp. 271–313).

27 For a discussion of this, see for instance: Michael Boroughs, 'Body depilation in males: a new body image concern', *International Journal of Men's Health*, 1 (2002), 247–57.

28 In this sense, I am following here Sigmund Freud's reading of femininity as produced by penis envy, and masculinity by the castration complex (see, for instance: Sigmund Freud, 'On narcissism: an introduction', in Angela Richards and Albert Dickson (eds), *On Metapsychology: The Theory of Psychoanalysis*, The Penguin Freud Library, vol. 11, James Strachey (trans. and gen. ed.) (Harmondsworth: Penguin, 1984 (orig. pub. 1914)), pp. 59–99.

29 Sigmund Freud, 'Fetishism', in Angela Richards (ed.), *On Sexuality*, vol. 7, Penguin Freud Library (Harmondsworth: Penguin, 1977), pp. 351–7, p. 354.

30 Donna Haraway, *Simians, Cyborgs, and Women: the Reinvention of Nature* (London: Routledge, 1991), p. 8.

31 Sigmund Freud, 'Fetishism', pp. 356–7.

32 Robin McKie, 'Beauty is skin deep – and also fur free', *Observer*, Sunday, 8 June 2003, available at: http://observer.guardian.co.uk/uk_news/story/0,6903,972905,00.html.

33 For more extensive arguments against evolutionary psychology's claims, see: Hilary Rose and Steven Rose (eds), *Alas Poor Darwin. Arguments Against Evolutionary Psychology* (London: Jonathan Cape, 2000). Bodmer's claims, as cited by McKie, include the assumption that sexual selection is indeed the province of the male – that is, that the male is the sexual selector – but that assumption is precisely part of what I wish to both draw attention to, and critique, here.

34 Charles Darwin, *The Descent of Man, and Selection in Relation to Sex*, introduction by James Moore and Adrian Desmond (Harmondsworth: Penguin, 2004, orig. pub. 1879), pp. 669–70. Here I thank my colleague, Dr John Holmes, for helping me to formulate my thinking on Darwin's ideas in relation to body hair.

35 I would note that the idea of the 'ornament' is also included by Darwin in relation to men, for instance also specifically in relation to men's beards (Darwin, *The Descent of Man*, p. 666), but my focus here is on the implications specifically for body hair and femininity.

36 Darwin, *The Descent of Man*, p. 670.

37 For Darwin, the very issue of who selects sexually, men or women, remains a difficulty, and he changes position on this several times in *The Descent of Man*. As he writes, for instance: 'in utterly barbarous tribes the women have more power in choosing, rejecting, and tempting their lovers, or of afterwards changing their husbands, than might have been expected' (p. 666).

2 'The wives of geniuses I have sat with'[1]: body hair, genius and modernity

Daniela Caselli

The current absence of a debate around the cultural meanings of body hair within the many existing feminist discussions around the post-capitalist and post-colonial female body would be surprising if it did not reflect how body hair, 'superfluous' and 'unwanted', is hardly visible. It cannot be shown; it can only be exposed.[2]

Much feminist criticism has been based on the idea of exposing the silent patriarchal structures of oppression, which can be shown as operating according to certain rules.[3] Feminism has derived part of its strength from its ability to denounce something which was then shown to be happening; this position becomes untenable when discussing a topic which is by definition disgusting, ridiculous or at best trivial – rather than pressing and dramatic.[4] The derisory marginality of body hair as a subject of cultural analysis leads feminism to acknowledge that, in order to have critical functions, it cannot merely state the existence of its object, but needs to argue for the conditions of its existence. This is a long-standing problem encountered by any feminist trying to communicate with those persons who deny the very need for feminism; it has been faced in different historical times: from Wollstonecraft's *A Vindication of the Rights of Woman* (1792) to the debate on suffrage and that on post-feminism. However, while in these examples the urgency to fight against gender inequalities is a fundamental instrument to justify the very existence of feminism, body hair remains something which is not only marginal (almost invisible), but also ridiculous and disgusting, as Karín Lesnik-Oberstein also argues in Chapter 1. Precisely because of these unappealing characteristics, body hair can have an important function within feminism, as it demonstrates that certain conditions need to be in place before it can become an acceptable topic for debate, even for feminists. It is difficult to discuss body hair precisely because it is either claimed to be a self-evident form of patriarchal control (and then can be quickly dropped) or dismissed as irrelevant. Those who try to expose this become exposed in turn; in order to discuss such a topic, one must be prepared to give up the reassuring pat of academic approval, at least until body hair has gained some theoretical currency.[5] That many feminists in history experienced a similar response is well documented; this work belongs and owes much to such a feminist tradition.

Body hair as a not-yet-legitimised topic for discussion can also be helpful to rethink some of the problems cyclically encountered by feminism, as the terms in which the marginal debate around body hair was conducted in the 1970s can illustrate.[6] Such a debate had a very strong pragmatic aim; its project was to encourage women to stop removing body hair, and it was based on an idea of going back to nature and to the natural body, free to enjoy its sexuality (famously, *The Joy of Sex* discourages shaving).[7] Remarkably, though, that particular political practice has never been able to reach its goal of simply showing body hair and claiming back its natural existence. On the contrary, it has remained a radical expression, a controversial performance, a reaction to a cultural norm, and an exposure akin to a freak show. A female body with hair does not overcome cultural normativity; rather, it situates itself in a different position in relation to it. This is theoretically relevant for more than one reason: only if we think of body hair as a construction will we be able to see it, discuss it and analyse it.

Constructivist approaches have had a rather sad fate of late, being reduced, as both Judith Butler and Eve Kosofsky Sedgwick have often lamented, to an idea of a socially imposed (and thus dispensable and disposable) structure over something real or already there.[8] But there would be no need for constructivism if this were the case; a plethora of political arguments in favour of social change have historically played that role. One can see how the early debate in feminism regarding body hair follows this logic in claiming that body hair is natural and that if we fight against social constructions and go back to nature we will have moved on in feminist terms. I would like instead to reflect, with Kosofsky Sedgwick, on 'the basis [. . .] for our optimism about the malleability of culture by any one group or programme.'[9] Body hair and the circumscribed place that it occupies within feminism demonstrates that it is problematic to assert that body hair is real or natural, while its lack or removal is constructed, social or artificial. Although this claim may well have a pragmatic aim, it remains unsatisfactory because visible body hair remains linked to ideas of threatening femininity (as in: 'she must be a lesbian'), national otherness (as in – if in the UK: 'she must be German'), gender masquerade (as in Salvador Dali's moustachioed Mona Lisa), disgust, and – at best – excess.[10] Whatever the position of the individual woman or group of women with regard to body hair, it is still framed by these meanings. Many feminists will, of course, argue in favour of a political relevance of one position over another, but I am more concerned here with the structure of the argument and its consequences. This chapter will focus on the various meanings of body hair, without taking for granted a dichotomy between natural and artificial – instead looking at its various formations. It is my contention that to analyse these meanings, rather than using them as a starting point, does not constitute a defeatist approach. On the contrary, such an approach can lay the foundations for understanding a cultural phenomenon which is characterised as irrelevant (and, as such, is of course very significant).

Female body hair is not a stereotype to be overcome for the general female good; rather, meanings circulate around body hair which define the conditions for the existence of masculinity and femininity. Body hair can thus be helpful to expose the machinery of gender, not in order to transcend it (and reach an allegedly neutral space) but to estrange its alleged naturalness. This is why women cannot simply show their body hair, but are forced to expose it. This is also why the very idea of showing is rhetorically not very helpful for feminism; rather, one must recognise that it is important to argue in favour of the conditions of body hair's visibility, rather than stating its visibility and naturalness as a starting point.

In my work, then, I will not assert that body hair is something real or natural, there to be shown; I will instead focus on how body hair is at times exposed in a number of literary and cultural texts which focus on femininity as threatening, analysing its different meanings and the conditions of its visibility. If body-hair detection is usually aimed at eradication, I will detect body hair in order to interrogate the functions of that which is defined as marginal, ridiculous, and invisible. The discussion will pursue the link between body hair, modernity, and the notion of feminine 'genius', focusing on texts which mention body hair – often only momentarily. I am not claiming to construct a narrative of historical development; rather, I have selected a number of texts on the basis of their references to body hair on women; their different claims to modernity; and the common link between hairiness, 'uncommon' intelligence, and femininity. In no way exhaustive, my readings will analyse the meanings of these passages, but also question what constitutes repetition or similarity among these texts. Hopefully, this will be a starting point for a feminist analysis of body hair as negotiating central meanings in relation to femininity and masculinity, which will be capable of expansion to other literary and cultural areas, notably those of race and ethnicity, to which I will be only partially referring here.

Body hair can be occasionally detected in contemporary popular culture. In Sydney Pollack's film *Tootsie* (1982), during the climactic scene of the kiss between Julie Nichols (played by Jessica Lange) and Michael Dorsey/Dorothy Michaels (played by Dustin Hoffman), the former can feel the latter's moustache. She (who assumes Michael to be a woman) suggests removing it, even though she liberally adds that some men do like that kind of thing. Dorothy/Michael replies that she doesn't like that kind of men. In 1998, some of Trish Morrissey's photographs in which women were asked not to bleach or shave their facial hair in order to be photographed, were exhibited at the National Portrait Gallery and have appeared in a number of magazines.[11] The October 1997 issue of Benetton's *Colors* magazine, under the direction of controversial Oliviero Toscani, was devoted to hair, although much of it was on head hair rather than body hair.[12] In 1999, Julia Roberts made her 'infamous' appearance at the *Notting Hill* première with unshaven armpits. In 1998, 'London's *Evening Standard* reported on rumours that someone in the American film industry wants Emma Thompson's hairy look in the film *The Winterguest* airbrushed out'[13] and, in 2000, Monica Tyson was photographed wearing shorts and clinging to Mike Tyson's tattooed biceps, her legs visibly unshaven.[14] A few recurrent elements can already be traced at this point: the fetishisation of body hair, so that while Dorothy Michaels/Michael Dorsey doesn't seem to feel attracted to that sort of men, Monica boasts one of them on her arm. The ridiculing of body hair; its being impermissible; its link with disgust; and the taming of its controversial potential through the association with head hair, are all visible in these contexts.[15]

This is gossip: mildly titillating perhaps, but in the end irrelevant. Interestingly, discussions on body hair in different cultural contexts also share some of the connotations of gossip: marginal, redundant, moderately interesting and yet unnecessary, at times threatening, as some examples will demonstrate. John Berger, in his *Ways of Seeing*, analyses Bronzino's *Allegory of Time and Love* and discusses femininity as the being-looked-at-ness:

> Her [Venus's] body is arranged in the way it is, to display it to the man looking at the picture. This picture is made to appeal to *his* sexuality. It has nothing to do with her sexuality. (Here and in the European tradition generally, the convention of not painting the hair on a woman's body helps towards the same end. Hair is associated with sexual power, with passion. The woman's sexual passion needs to be minimized so that the spectator may feel that he has the monopoly of such passion.) Women are there to feed an appetite, not to have any of their own.[16]

This is a rather extraordinary statement, and yet only mentioned parenthetically. Brackets, with their ancillary function, relegate 'the convention of not painting the hair on a woman's body' in the margin of a more wide-ranging discussion precisely by stating it as the obvious. Neither supported by evidence, nor developed further, such an apparently self-evident claim begs the question of how exactly body hair, femininity and 'sexual power' interact.

In this context, feminine sexual power cannot mean the power deriving from attractiveness, from the being-looked-at-ness, as this has been just defined as something that 'has nothing to do with her sexuality' and all to do with 'his'. 'Sexual power' and, perhaps even more puzzlingly, 'passion', seem instead to be related to the idea of power as control, thus linked to masculinity. However, often feminine 'sexual power' also means predatory sexuality, something which indeed is neither under-represented nor defined as unrepresentable in the history of Western painting or art in general.

The parenthetical position of this intriguing comment can be taken as an example of the marginal position of body hair in discourse; at once ridiculous and obvious, too well-known and irrelevant, body hair links power and masculinity in ways which are less obvious than Berger's assertion seems to indicate.

Expanding on Berger's parenthetical comment and working on this marginality, I would like to map out the main points of my discussion of literary texts by looking first at a 2001 newspaper article, in which Peter Conrad interviews the Italian opera-singer Cecilia Bartoli for the *Observer*.[17] He opens his article by writing:

> I am still not entirely sure that I met Cecilia Bartoli. When I turned up at the Royal Opera House, where she makes her debut tomorrow in Haydn's *L'anima del filosofo*, I was introduced to a short, squat girl – plumply pasta-fed, dark-complexioned and scruffily dressed – who bore no resemblance to the siren in the Rolex advertisement, or even to the zanily energetic virtuoso who had so often delighted me on stage.

It is with a mixture of disappointment, revulsion and incredulity that the siren of the advertisement is set against this how-very-Italian 'short, squat girl'. Bartoli's dark complexion and her scruffy clothes are there to introduce immediately an idea of masculinity, which is spelled out as follows:

> Is Bartoli, I wondered, actually a male castrato trapped in a woman's body? Two books about her by American female fans read like Sapphic mash notes. She disposed of the query with another shower of lyrical laughter. But when I asked her if there was any opera she dreamt of singing even though it might not be physically possible, she answered at once: 'Verdi's *Otello* – though I am not sure whether I would be Otello or Iago!' Desdemona is clearly not an option.

The classic crude equation between women defined as masculine and lesbianism seems to spin out of control in this example of patriarchal logic at work. Bartoli is not a woman, she has the appearance of a woman (tainted by the masculinity of her dark complexion, however), but is in fact a vessel (that most feminine of metaphors). She is a body, which contains, not a man but a castrato, and, indeed, a *male* castrato, as if the Italian term might fail to make sufficiently clear its link with this rather desperate-sounding masculinity. The female body is a trap; Bartoli's femininity can only be appearance and her masculinity can only be there as lack. The artificial female body is a disguise, which is insufficient if compared to either the whole masculine body or the ideal feminine one. Clichés about Bartoli's nationality pepper Conrad's account and are closely related to his desire for clear definitions of masculinity and femininity. Indeed, just in case we were tempted to follow what for Conrad is the American Sapphic example and identify Bartoli as somebody a bit too powerful for a heterosexual woman, we are immediately reassured:

> Beneath Bartoli's vivacity, there lurks a grim Latin fatalism, which is what she sympathises with in *La Cenerentola* [. . .] She can tolerate comedy, as long as the characters are stoically suffering. 'Ah, Cenerentola – she is a fantastic woman. She takes life day by day, which is why she manages to be happy. Not like the ugly sisters, who are always saying: 'I want a man, I want to be rich' or asking, 'Am I beautiful?' Bartoli has a man: the wine-making musicologist Claudio Osele [. . .] She is surely rich [. . .] and when cleaned up and coiffed for the stage, she is beautiful. But she is also a Roman, who grew up surrounded by the wreckage of glory. Hence the manic glee of her singing: its willed optimism, like Genio's admonitions to Orfeo, is a command to seize the day. 'It is very mysterious,' she said to me about her gift. 'You either have it or not. It is a kind of aura. But why me? And for how long will I have it? I don't think I want to know.' She then wrapped herself in her anonymous rehearsal clothes, picked up her backpack, and slouched off unrecognisably into the street. But that aura, her spirit-guide, accompanied her. Covent Garden's translators call Genio a Sybil, which unfortunately evokes the quibbling heroine of *Private Lives*. Why not admit that Genio means Genius? For that is what Cecilia Bartoli possesses.

If she, like her Cenerentola, might appear not to be too bothered about men, she nonetheless 'has a man'; she is also rich and, at least 'when cleaned up and coiffed for the stage', she is also 'beautiful'. Her grim Latin fatalism, just like her 'manic glee', end up being assigned, as with her dark complexion and short stature, to her Italianness and Romanness, apparently universally recognisable as such from Conrad's brush-strokes. More than in the clichés about the seductive and threatening Italianness that pervades British culture in all its forms, I am interested in the ways in which this is linked to masculinity.[18] Indeed, it is her masculinity, her wanting to play Otello, Iago and, indeed, Genio[19] (who in her interpretation sounds to Conrad as 'astral, disembodied, lecturing Orfeo in an aria whose coloratura is literally unearthly'), which links her to that most masculine of concepts, that of genius.[20] If Bartoli was, earlier on, a vessel containing a castrato, she is now 'the psychopompous who accompanies Orfeo to the underworld, a phantom referred to as Genio'. And how is this genius visible? Apparently by 'that aura' of genius, which redeems her from her 'anonymous rehearsal clothes' in which she wraps herself 'slouch[ing] off unrecognisably into the street.' Interestingly, however, if this sentence suggests that the aura of genius wrapping Bartoli rescues her from her scruffiness, she is singled out as a genius precisely because of her scruffiness, her dangerously Sapphic-inducing claims to power, and her alleged need to be 'cleaned up and coiffed' to look beautiful (that is to say, appropriately feminine).

Bartoli's 'scruffiness', 'dark-complexion' and need to be 'cleaned up and coiffed for stage' create for Conrad the disappointing and yet intriguing discrepancy between a short, squat and plump pasta-fed 'girl' and the siren of the Rolex advertisement. I wonder if I too am hallucinating auras when I read these elements as pointing in the direction of body hair. Bartoli is a castrato in disguise because her darkness and scruffiness cannot completely conceal a surfacing masculinity, which is instead wiped away in the Rolex advertisement, in which Bartoli's eyebrows are styled and brushed.[21] That very masculinity enables the critic to bestow upon her the title of genius: something that she 'possesses'; something that 'accompanies' her like Genio accompanies Orfeo; something that she performs on stage (where she is a disembodied presence); and, finally and almost reluctantly, something that she 'is', due to her multiple lack (lack of femininity and lack of masculine wholeness).

Conrad's interview maps out the links among body hair, power and masculinity to which Berger refers in relation to art history. A similar link can be found in Wilkie Collins' *The Woman in White* (1859–60), a novel which flags its modernity in more than one passage.[22] Many critics have commented on the stunning introduction of the character of Marian Halcombe, and on the obvious opposition between the dark, resolute and intelligent Marian and the fair and weak Laura Fairlie, described in Marian's words as: 'I am dark and ugly and she is fair and pretty'.[23] Also, many have commented on the link between femininity and normativity, not only in relation to Collins, but also to the sensation novel in general and, in particular, to Mary Elizabeth Braddon's novel *Lady Audley's Secret*.[24] In this context I am especially interested in analysing how in *The Woman in White* the normative, and apparently very fragile, threshold between femininity and masculinity is defined by body hair:

> My first glance round me, as the man opened the door, disclosed a well-furnished breakfast table, standing in the middle of a long room, with many windows in it. I looked from the table to the window farthest from me and I saw a lady standing at it, with her back turned towards me. The instant my eyes rested on her, I was struck by the rare beauty of her form, and the unaffected grace of her attitude. Her figure was tall, yet not too tall; comely and well-developed, yet not fat; her head set on her shoulders with an easy, pliant firmness; her waist, perfection in the eyes of a man, for it occupied its natural place, it filled out its natural circle, it was visibly and delightfully undeformed by stays. She had not heard my entrance into the room; and I allowed myself the luxury of admiring her for a few moments, before I moved one of the chairs near me, as the least embarrassing means of attracting her attention. She turned towards me immediately. The easy elegance of every movement of her limbs and body as soon as she began to advance from the far end of the room set me in a flutter of expectation to see her

face clearly. She left the window – and I said to myself, The lady is dark. She moved forward a few steps – and I said to myself, The lady is young. She approached nearer – and I said to myself (with a sense of surprise words fail me to express), The lady is ugly!

[. . .] The lady's complexion was almost swarthy, and the dark down on her upper lip was almost a moustache. She had a large, firm, masculine mouth and jaw; prominent, piercing, resolute brown eyes; and thick, coal-black hair, growing unusually low down on her forehead. Her expression – bright, frank and intelligent – appeared, while she was silent, to be altogether wanting in those feminine attractions of gentleness and pliability, without which the beauty of the handsomest woman alive is beauty incomplete.[25]

The gaze of the observer, Mr Walter Hartright, discloses certain objects, rests on others and moves from one to the other; it is at times in a position of complete activity (as when his glance 'discloses' the breakfast table), at others of passivity (as when his eyes 'rest' on Marian or when he is immediately 'struck by the rare beauty of her form'). The link between male gaze and feminine beauty is very explicit in this passage, as demonstrated by the description of her waist, 'perfection *in the eyes of a man*, for it occupied its *natural* place, it filled out its *natural* circle.' The repetition of the word 'natural' also makes clear how 'the eyes of a man' turn what they are seeing as beauty into naturalness that derives from its coincidence with the masculine norm; as Jenny Bourne Taylor puts it, 'Hartright sees others in accordance with their conformity to established conventions'.[26] The criteria for feminine beauty are based on a circular logic; a masculine point of view can only see beauty as that which corresponds to predefined male categories. Such a coincidence produces nature. Marian possesses in fact an 'unaffected' grace, her beautiful figure is 'undeformed by stays' and all her qualities are defined as the opposite of excess and artificiality. Indeed, if they are in danger of appearing excessive, they are quickly redefined as the norm: she is 'tall, yet not too tall' and 'comely and well-developed, yet not fat'. In line with the double role of the viewer as passively charmed and actively constructing the object of his desire, Marian is the object on which the silent voyeur's gaze luxuriously lingers; her partial invisibility and her easy elegance stir the viewer. Yet, the symmetry of this male dream is shattered by Marian's face, which, rather than crowning Nature's deed, belies it, turning it into an 'anomaly'. The repetitive structure which creates the progressive apprehension of Marian's facial traits begins with the assertion of her ominous darkness, tempers it with her promising youth, and culminates with the disclosure of her ugliness. Ugliness of a particular kind; it is linked to her darkness, and yet that well-known swarthy complexion which characterises a whole genealogy of villains only partially affects Marian; indeed, Marian's complexion is *almost* swarthy. Moreover, her ugliness is explicitly linked to her facial hair; she *almost* has a moustache and her head hair grows unusually low down her

forehead. That 'almost' allows the narrator to put to paper what would otherwise be, by his own account, inexpressible, while also mediating
Marian's role as the unconventional heroine of the novel, constantly
moving between masculinity and femininity. However, while her movements back and forth between masculine and feminine spheres are often
signalled throughout the text by her darkness, Marian's facial hair will
never be mentioned again. Literally inexpressible, body hair has a 'repellent' potential in the text:

> To see such a face as this set on shoulders that a sculptor would have longed to
> model – to be charmed by the modest graces of action through which the sym-
> metrical limbs betrayed their beauty when they moved, and then to be almost
> repelled by the masculine form and masculine look of the features in which the
> perfectly shaped figure ended – was to feel a sensation oddly akin to the help-
> less discomfort familiar to us all in sleep, when we recognise yet cannot recon-
> cile the anomalies and contradiction of a dream.[27]

Marian's dark and hairy face needs reassuring adverbs in order to be
mentioned at all. The viewer is once again *almost* repelled; the discomfort
felt is *oddly akin* to the one felt in dreams. On the one hand, Marian's facial
hair, which contributes to the production of her ugliness in the eyes of Mr
Hartright, is not quite completely what it is said to be, otherwise it would
not be possible to mention it. We could say that she has a moustache, yet
not too much of moustache. On the other hand, it is the very combination
of her normatively feminine figure and her masculine face which
creates an effect of repulsion, and yet not quite completely repulsion.
Interestingly, the rhetoric conjures up a docile readership through the reference to 'the helpless discomfort familiar to us all in sleep', recognisable
to all of 'us'. The familiarity is produced by the mention of a common
response; the discrepancy between Marian's figure and face creates a familiar and yet irreconcilable contradiction. Her dark hair has destroyed her
role as muse and object of desire; has irreparably broken what had been
defined as the masculine, that is to say natural, correspondence to a model
(longed for by the sculptor); and has pushed her into the inexpressible, the
irreconcilable, the familiar and yet helpless oddity of dreams. Marian's
masculinity does not simply appear in this text; it erupts with the power
of a dream. This, I would suggest, happens only in the passage that mentions her facial hair. While, as we will see later, masculinity and femininity are always mutually implicated in this text, the disturbing and
threatening quality of the anomaly that is Marian is due to the presence of
facial hair.

Masculinity is explicitly present in this passage through the repetition
of the very adjective 'masculine' three times; in addition to this, her mouth
and jaw are 'large, firm, masculine', her eyes are 'prominent, piercing, resolute', her expression is 'bright, frank and intelligent'. Nobody could ask

more from a hero, but when applied to a heroine these qualities turn into a defect. Once again, femininity is defined as exclusively dependent on the masculine gaze; female beauty is defined in terms of 'feminine attractions of gentleness and pliability', implying of course not only a subject to be attracted by the object, but also a recipient for the gentleness and a forger of such pliability (as the character of Count Fosco will never stop reminding us). Without these relative qualities 'the beauty of the handsomest woman alive is beauty incomplete'. A woman can be handsome but she can only be beautiful in the eyes of the man who has established the norm. Very clearly then, a lack of firmness, frankness and intelligence are the established characteristics which produce femininity. Marian herself will almost immediately denounce this through an attack against her sex which is also an unveiling (which will later be developed into a critique) of the basic structures of patriarchy, able to establish competition among the oppressed:

> How can you expect four women to dine together alone every day, and not to quarrel? We are such fools, we can't entertain each other at table. You see, I don't think much of my own sex, Mr. Hartright – which will you have, tea or coffee? – no woman does think much of her own sex, although few of them confess it as freely as I do.[28]

Although lack characterises femininity, Marian's masculine traits can in turn only be defined as lack. Through her excessive, anomalous darkness and facial hair, Marian is wanting and incomplete precisely because lacking her appropriately feminine lack.[29] Yet, as this passage indicates, Marian critiques the defects of her sex while supplementing them with the duties of the perfect hostess, who is indeed more than capable of entertaining (although in ways which Mr Hartright will perceive as rather unconventional) and of looking after her guests' needs.

Susan Sontag, in her 2000 preface to Annie Leibovitz's *Women*, uses the description of Marian Halcombe quoted above to critique femininity as attractiveness and to question the aim of a book of photographs devoted to 'the depiction of a minority (for this is what women are, by every criterion except the numerical)'.[30] Interestingly exploring the link between femininity, attractiveness, and the male gaze, Sontag uses the excerpt from *The Woman in White* to argue that intelligence 'was in fact considered disabling, and likely to be inscribed in [a woman's] appearance'. The 'fate' of Marian Halcombe is, according to Sontag, that of being the 'most admirable character in Collins' novel, awarded every virtue except the capacity to inspire desire. Moved only by generous, noble sentiments, she has a near angelic, that is feminine, temperament – except for the troubling matter of her uncommon intelligence, her frankness, her want of "pliability."'[31] In Sontag's interpretation, in the case of Marian 'face trumps body – as intelligence, to the detriment of female sexual attractiveness, trumps beauty'.[32] Sontag's interpretation reflects the current tendency to transform nineteenth-century explorations of sexuality into a narrative of oppression or repression.[33] She reads the text as mirroring a not better defined 'past', which is especially puzzling in relation to a novel which, as I briefly mentioned earlier, makes a point of its being 'modern'.[34] Hartright, indeed, does define Marian, at the close of the novel, as 'the good angel of our lives'; however, if this definition may appear, as it does to Sontag, to cast her into the role of the good spinster, Hartright (whose role in the story is at best dubiously heroic)[35] is also forced to let her end their story, acknowledging her role as heroine of the novel. The heroic status of Marian operates on other levels too; she is heroic when she climbs the roof of the veranda 'for Laura's sake', in order to overhear the famous conversation between Count Fosco and Sir Percival. However, she is also depicted as heroic in her own reporting of Count Fosco's account of her fearlessness, beauty and intelligence. If there ever is a heroic register in the text, it is to be found not in Count Fosco's overflowing letters or flourished professions of admiration to Marian, but in Marian's reporting the Count's words about her.

Sontag's assertion that Marian is not given 'the capacity to inspire desire' is inaccurate; Marian is the object of Count Fosco's desire, who 'at sixty' worships her 'with the volcanic ardour of eighteen.'[36] Following Sontag's reading, one may be tempted to argue that it is precisely because Marian is unable to boast feminine attractions, that the only character attracted to her is the villain of the story. Marian, then, could be read, in line with Sontag's interpretation, as exceeding the proper limits of feminine appropriateness, and thus condemned by the narrative to solitude and spinsterhood, perhaps vindicating her very special kind of beauty. Indeed, Sontag does this when she claims that 'for a long time the beauty of a woman seemed incompatible, or at least oddly matched, with intelligence and assertiveness'.[37] Yet, I would contend that the text does something a little more interesting with the character of Marian. The remarkable amount of sexual tension built around Marian and Count Fosco is destined not to be consumed; the Count's desire is in fact initially described in her diaries as a source of excitement (always mixed with fear), but, in the end, Marian, like Dorothy Michaels/Michael Dorsey in *Tootsie*, does not like *that* kind of man; she only loves Laura. This, I would argue, is not to be read as the punishment deserved by Marian's impermissible masculinity, but linked instead to what Sontag rightly identifies as her welcome 'lack of pliability'. Indeed, Count Fosco is, above all, a tamer, a powerful forger of female docility; his once frivolous wife is transformed in his hands into the tamest of pets. Fosco reiterates his attraction towards Marian's strength, intelligence and independence in terms that underline the competitive aspect of his desire. His ability to tame his wife's hyperfeminine extravagances is a warning of what he would do if he could put his hands on

Marian's 'unfeminine' strength and intelligence. The most dangerous among the Count's plots is that of seducing Marian; her escaping that kind of man, the fetishist of rebellion and excess, is her means of vindicating her behaviour as *not* excessive. Rather than a repressed spinster, she is a character who, in ways that recall Jane Eyre, is neither ready to play the roles demanded from the heterosexual imperative, nor to claim this refusal as rebellious and extravagant. Instead, her claims to strength and independence are vindicated as legitimate; necessarily, however, such claims remain linked to masculine power and genealogy. The text leaves to Marian the theatrical and anthropologically charged gesture of lifting little Walter in the air, proclaiming him *'the Heir of Limmeridge'*.[38]

Following a very common move in much feminist literature, Sontag is forced to transform her reading of the text into a proof of the progress made since by women; commenting on 'the anomalies and contradictions of a dream' used to describe the narrator's discomfort in seeing Marian, she writes: 'The contradiction in the order of sexual stereotypes may seem dreamlike to a well-adjusted inhabitant of an era in which action, enterprise, artistic creativity, and intellectual innovation are understood to be masculine, fraternal orders [. . .] To be sure, no novelist today would find it implausible to award good looks to a woman who is cerebral and self-assertive. But in real life it's still common to begrudge a woman who has both beauty and intellectual brilliance.'[39]

While I am not arguing that no progress has been made for women in the last century, I am reluctant to share Sontag's optimism about novelists, not only in the light of the innumerable literary examples which contradict her assertions, but also on a theoretical level. Indeed, Sontag's optimism is based on the idea that sexual roles are stereotyped; to defy the stereotype means to progress. Why, then, does Sontag's sophisticated discussion not once mention Marian's moustache? Marian's facial hair remains, just as for Hartright, the inexpressible, that which marks the limit of our enlightened feminist liberation. Rather than reading the text as a nineteenth-century representation of sexual stereotypes, it is more productive to look at how this text uses body hair as the inexpressible in order to question the construction of the sexed body. It is indicative that in the London West End production of the musical 'freely adapted' from the novel, Marian – as Matthew Sweet puts it – 'has been shorn of her moustache.' Interviewed before the 2003 opening, lyricist David Zippel, who collaborated with Andrew Lloyd Webber and playwright Charlotte Jones in the writing of the musical, justifies their choice by arguing that 'in the book it's only one line' and makes 'the case that the theatre audience would find a heroine with facial hair something of a distraction. [. . .] He may be right' – adds Sweet in his review – 'Marian's mannish features are mentioned in the opening chapters, and we are free to forget them thereon – but it does seem a pity to jettison one of the story's most

Collinsian oddnesses.'[40] This can lead one to note, with Sweet, that 'modern popular taste is much more conservative than its 19th-century equivalent', although the fact that all the main contemporary reviews mention Marian's 'ugliness' but not her facial hair does not necessarily indicate that facial hair used to be perceived as either acceptable or unconventional.[41] Most importantly, I would like to ponder on the significance of that 'one line' whose potential to cause such a 'distraction' needs to be quickly neutralised through an enforced forgetfulness. Once again, the determination to characterise body hair as marginal, superfluous and meaningless points to the absolute need to contain its potential for disrupting gendered categories. While Zippel worries about facial hair 'distracting' an audience that he sets up to entertain with the help of Jones and Lloyd Webber, Sweet wants to defend it as a characteristic 'oddness', thus reincorporating it into a narrative of eccentricity which, I would argue, the novel resists. Sweet's suggestion to 'glue something suitably hairy to her [Maria Friedman playing Marian] top lip' in order to see the audience's reaction, further demonstrates how body hair (even when 'defended') needs to remain safely circumscribed by the opposition between the natural and the artificial. If in Sweet's proposal the performance of facial hair on stage amounts to exposing its artificial and reassuring detachability, the arguably more radical alternative of having an actress exposing her own facial hair would equally indicate that staging body hair's 'naturalness' means skirting dangerously close to the freak show.

Sontag's silence and the musical's airbrushing of Marian's facial hair illustrate 'the relationship by which social taboos institute and maintain the boundaries of the body as such.'[42] Body hair is that important margin which can help us to understand the limits of a feminist position which claims to have overcome the stereotype and reached an enlightened state, able to make us either denounce injustice or celebrate justice.

Body hair can also be helpful in looking at how the dialectic between lack and excess, femininity and masculinity, is a complex one, which continues throughout *The Woman in White*. Mr Fairlie's character has 'something singularly and unpleasantly delicate in its association with a man, and, at the same time, something which could by no possibility have looked natural and appropriate if it had been transferred to the personal appearance of a woman.'[43] Even Laura, by definition the object of desire in Hartright's narrative, has 'something wanting',[44] which links her to her double, the woman in white. In line with what has been said by critics about both Collins' *The Woman in White* and Braddon's *Lady Audley's Secret*, we could state that these passages demonstrate how norms and measurements, against which each character is set, work as a critique of those same unattainable and conventional norms.[45] Such norms cannot be overcome because they are not 'stereotypes' but rather the conditions that allow gender to exist as such at all. Indeed, the long description of the artificiality of the concept of nature supports this position by defining 'our capacity of appreciating the beauties of the earth we live on' as, 'in truth, one of the civilised accomplishments which we all learn as an Art.'[46] If Nature is Art, we cannot overcome Art to go back to Nature.

This text, then, operates a thorough critique of the interaction between masculinity and femininity as allegedly natural categories, and constructs Marian as constantly oscillating between the two. For instance, Marian laments what George Eliot would have called ladies' silliness,[47] but she also attacks the male gender, and perhaps nowhere as harshly as in the passage in which men are accused of breaking domestic love.[48] Marian declares her masculine desire for exercise, as when she longs for a wild gallop to kill the time that separates her from the return of her beloved Laura from Italy.[49] She also displays her sound female common sense when she declares herself more interested in not soiling her petticoats than in visiting the empty wings of Sir Percival Glyde's estate built at the time of 'that highly overrated woman', Queen Elizabeth,[50] thus earning the governess's approval.[51] As a concluding example, Marian's vindication of her womanhood when forced by circumstances to do the housework ('What a woman's hands *are* fit for', she said, 'early and late, these hands of mine shall do')[52] recalls Sojourner Truth's classic feminist invective against the politically dubious nature of the concept of frail femininity, rather than being an acquiescent acceptance of her role as housewife or 'angel' of the story.[53]

In *The Woman in White*, the single mention of Marian's facial hair, which, as noted above, is defined as the inexpressible, marks the eruption of masculinity in the heroine, signalling her potential danger. Rather than pathologising her, Marian's hairiness indicates a critique of femininity and masculinity. This will, however, not provide us with a 'happy ending' able to satisfy a need for the glorification of the hairy woman; no lover will admire Marian's moustache. She would not like that kind of man.

In the cases of the extraordinarily gifted Cecilia Bartoli and Marian Halcombe, facial hair has marked the limit between attraction and revulsion; as Pepys wrote in his diary in 1668 after visiting a hairy or bearded woman in Holborn: 'it was a strange spectacle for me, I must confess, and I liked it very much.'[54]

Another 'genius' who can be discussed in relation to body hair is Sylvia Plath, who in her letter of October 16, 1962 writes to her mother 'I am a writer . . . I am a genius of a writer; I have it in me'.[55] She has discussed body hair at least twice, once in *The Bell Jar* and once in the poem 'In Plaster'.[56] In *The Bell Jar* (1963) body hair is mentioned when Esther is in hospital after having attempted suicide:

'You have a visitor.'
'I don't want a visitor.'
The nurse bustled out and whispered to somebody in the hall. Then she came back. 'He'd very much like to see you.'

I looked down at the yellow legs sticking out of the unfamiliar white silk pyjamas they had dressed me in. The skin shook flabbily when I moved, as if there wasn't a muscle in it, and it was covered with a short, thick stubble of black hair.

'Who is it?'

'Somebody you know.'

'What's his name?'

'George Bakewell.'

'I don't know any George Bakewell.'

'He says he knows you.'

Then the nurse went out, and a very familiar boy came in and said, 'Mind if I sit on the edge of your bed?'

He was wearing a white coat, and I could see a stethoscope poking out of his pocket. I thought it must be somebody I knew dressed up as a doctor.

I had meant to cover my legs if anybody came in, but now I saw it was too late, so I let them stick out, just as they were, disgusting and ugly.

'That's me,' I thought. 'That's what I am.'

'You remember me, don't you, Esther?'

I squinted at the boy's face through the crack of my good eye. The other eye hadn't opened yet, but the eye doctor said it would be all right in a few days.[57]

The last stanza of 'In Plaster' (dated 18 March 1961) reads:

I used to think we might make a go of it together –
After all, it was a kind of marriage, being so close.
Now I see it must be one or the other of us.
She may be a saint, and I may be ugly and hairy,
But she'll soon find out that that doesn't matter a bit.
I'm collecting my strength; one day I shall manage without her,
And she'll perish with emptiness then, and begin to miss me.[58]

I would like to begin my discussion of these two excerpts using a quotation from David Holbrook, a critic whose chauvinism has provoked stunned dismay in many Plath scholars.[59] He asserts:

At a National Poetry Festival Germaine Greer claimed that Sylvia Plath was the most 'arrogantly feminine' poetess who ever wrote. A phenomenological analysis suggests that, while knowing outwardly that she was a woman, Sylvia Plath could scarcely find herself with anything that was feminine at all. She is, perhaps, the most masculine poetess who ever wrote, yet, since masculinity requires the inclusion of the anima, she is not that either: she is sadly pseudo-male, like many of her cultists.[60]

Holbrook's 1976 assertions take us back to Peter Conrad's more recent ideas about Sapphic Americana and feminine vessels containing masculine genius, instructively working against any simple historicisation of feminist progress. Although I am not interested in critiquing Holbrook's references to phenomenology and psychology, I find it significant that the idea of the pseudo-male (defined as sad by Holbrook, qualified by a giggle in Conrad) is a source of embarrassment in both. It marks that boundary between masculinity and femininity, which *The Woman in White* produces through Marian's unspeakably disturbing moustache. Holbrook's misogynist assertion further draws attention to the presence of the double, which many critics have observed in Plath's texts. Although Holbrook's discussion focuses on Plath the person, rather than on the texts (continuing a pernicious long-term practice critiqued by Jacqueline Rose),[61] I would like to argue that the idea of a shell containing something disgusting, unrecognisable and masculine, is indeed present in many of her works and acquires interesting connotations when associated with body hair.

The Bell Jar constantly creates a contrast between external images and internal feelings,[62] confounds 'external' and 'internal' reality,[63] and questions ideas of truth. The narrator openly contradicts herself and presents an 'I', which is not only divided, but also radically untrustworthy.[64] Critics have often discussed *The Bell Jar* as a novel analysing the dilemma of women in the United States in the 1950s, marking the beginning of the 'have it all' dilemma. Against such a reading, which tends to celebrate the novel as a rebellion against (once again) stereotypes, I would like to read the text as questioning what constitutes femininity as such and if, indeed, identity can be even conceived outside of the system that defines femininity as hierarchically inferior to masculinity. The outcome, I would further like to suggest, is different from the celebratory one suggested by many of Plath's readers. For instance, the attempt to return to purity through taking a hot bath able to make her feel 'pure and sweet as a new baby' after the night out with Doreen, is self-defeating.[65] To escape the horrors represented by Doreen's attractive sexuality, vulgarity and feminine artificiality, Esther temporarily occupies the position of the angel, the new-born baby, confirming the idea of femininity as innocence and purity associated with the rather irritating Betsy, who cannot work as a role model either.[66] The rite of purification is not without dangers: by forgetting these horrors, Esther might be ready to repeat them, a preoccupation that pervades the text and characterises its resistance against the forgetfulness induced by electroshock and advised by her mother.[67]

The text, paralleling the rite of forgetfulness, claims that the sane position from which the narrator retrospectively speaks about her past 'madness' is that of cliché. The narrator tells us at the beginning that she has a baby; motherhood, however, is a condition defined in the course of the narrative as able to induce madness because of its conventionality. This double-bind short-circuits the relationship between sanity and madness, which is, as has been often argued by critics, closely linked to femininity and to genius.[68] The cliché is also a linguistic one: as Jacqueline Rose has suggested, the language produces itself as that of *The New Yorker*. On the one hand, the position of the narrator is that of the outsider: in ways that are reminiscent of Holden Caulfield, Esther is the critical eye exposing the norm. On the other hand, though, the text also advertises itself as normative, popular, cliché; it is the already said. We have references to popular culture,[69] repetitions, phrases that produce familiarity,[70] and intertextuality.[71] Everything in this text is something else, from the 'nice blond girl who looked like June Allyson but was really somebody else',[72] to Dr Nolan who 'was a cross between Myrna Loy and my mother',[73] to the two Mrs Tomolillos.[74] By creating a formulaic style and by giving a baby to the 'sane' narrator, the text implies that to give up the cliché of a painfully contradictory self means to inhabit another cliché of feminine identity.

Rather than being a novel which condemns sexual stereotypes, *The Bell Jar* spins out an endless series of them, fills pages and pages with them, and does not leave space for much else. By doing so, it questions the very idea of stereotype, which crumbles under the sheer weight of repetitions. Gender roles are not something which can be overcome, but are the categories which enable the existence of the gendered self, while also producing its oppression. This text, then, does not condemn gender norms from the outside, but places itself within the categories which enable gender differences to operate as such; this, of course, does not prevent the text from elaborating a critique of them. One example may clarify this argument – Esther has often been read as strongly opposing Mrs Willard's infamous maxims: ' "What a man wants is a mate and what a woman wants is infinite security," and, "What a man is is an arrow into the future and what a woman is is the place the arrows shoots off from" '.[75] The image that Esther sets up against Mrs Willard's dicta is, however, also very conventional: 'The last thing I wanted was infinite security and to be the place an arrow shoots off from. I wanted change and excitement and to shoot off in all directions myself, like the colored arrows from a Fourth of July rocket.'[76] Esther uses a conventional image, which defines national identity, in order to fight against a conventional image, which defines femininity. The narrator, then, can step out of a structure that defines identity through gender only by remaining within a structure that defines identity through nationality. Such ideas also come into play when Esther's identity is threatened; looking at herself in the mirror just before the nervous breakdown, she describes herself as 'Chinese' and, having smeared her face with blood, she later sees herself as a 'sick Indian'. The self has become foreign to itself, and it characterises this radical difference through conventional and heavily connoted images of racial otherness.

Body hair has a similar function in this text, linking estrangement and disgust. The white silk pyjamas, in which purity, luxury and feminine attractiveness meet, create the background against which the 'yellow' legs stick out. The pyjamas' unfamiliarity reflects that of the legs, which are not immediately recognised as belonging to the speaker. The 'yellow' colour, the lack of muscular tone, and, above all, the 'short, thick stubble of black hair', make these legs something separate from the speaker. Unfamiliarity joins lack of control: the narrator has been dressed by somebody else and cannot recognise her paradoxically familiar and yet deceiving interlocutor. Within this context of uncertainty and unfamiliarity, the only plan declared by the narrator is that of covering the source of disgust – her hairy legs – from anybody's sight; the plan fails, the legs are exposed, displaying her ugly and disgusting self: ' "That's me," I thought. "That's what I am." '

The narrator first acknowledges the unfamiliar hairy legs and then identifies them with a self now regarded as ugly and disgusting. The 'short, thick stubble of black hair' covering her legs inspires a disgust and a wish for excorporation; it is either not part of the body ('the legs' rather than 'my legs') or, once it is incorporated, it infects the whole self. Disgust (by definition, something to be expelled) affects the whole self, which wishes to eject parts of itself.

Illness and the body are also prominent in the poem 'In Plaster', a text which presents many of the issues about identity discussed in relation to *The Bell Jar*. Femininity as a vessel to be filled – an image used by both David Holbrook and Peter Conrad – is a central figure in 'In Plaster'. The 'I' exclaims, 'I shall never get out of this! There are two of me now:/This new absolutely white person and the old yellow one,/And the white person is certainly the superior one.' The 'white person' who is 'certainly the superior one', not needing food, one of the 'real saints', with no personality, lying in bed with the 'I' 'like a dead body' this *alter ego* 'was shaped just the way I was'. The mournful associations between this 'she' of plaster and femininity become even more explicit in the course of the poem, which elaborates a relationship between the two sufficiently close to be 'a kind of marriage'. The 'I' hits her, then realises that 'what she wanted was for me to love her'. So the 'I' gives her a soul, observes her grateful attitude, blooms 'out of her as a rose/Blooms out of a vase of not very valuable porcelain', patronises her, criticises her for her 'slave mentality'. She is tidy, calm, patient and able to humour weaknesses 'like the best of nurses'. Clearly, the white 'she' and the yellow 'I' have a relationship, which is explicitly based on feminine and masculine roles. Troubles begin when the 'I' says 'In time, our relationship grew more intense'; 'she wanted to leave me, she thought she was superior', 'she was resentful' and 'she began to hope I'd die'. The sense of entrapment expressed in the opening line comes back even more forcefully, when the white she is said to think that 'she could cover my mouth and eyes, cover me entirely,/And wear my painted face the way a mummy-case/Wears the face of a pharaoh, though it's made of mud and water.' The mutual dependency is complete: 'I wasn't in any position to get rid of her. She'd supported me for so long I was quite limp/[. . .] Living with her was like living with my own coffin:/Yet I still depended on her, though I did it regretfully'.

The 'two of me, now' seem to share their gender (they look alike, one could pass herself for the other) and yet one is superior because of her whiteness; the other because of her masculine position of authority. To claim, in line with Holbrook or Conrad, that femininity is simply a vessel containing a stronger male authority limited and stifled by the suffocating female carapace certainly would do justice to the poem. The racially connoted struggle between power and submission, authority and lack of personality, voice and silence cannot be reduced to the opposition between masculinity and femininity because of the reference to hairiness. 'She may be a saint, and I may be ugly and hairy', says the 'I', focused on survival ('Now I see it must be one or the other of us'); the juxtaposition of saintliness as a form of beauty with the ugliness of hairiness works in two ways. One the one hand, it states again the superiority of masculinity, which can do without these things ('She'll soon discover that that doesn't matter a bit'); on the other hand, the hairiness of this 'I' (who has the shape of a she) is, like in *The Bell Jar*, linked to disgust and inferiority. In *The Bell Jar*, disgust is incorporated at the price of excorporating the body from the self: if the hairy parts of the body are disgusting and initially unrecognisable as mine, and yet I am the body, then the whole self is disgusting and somehow also the me. 'In Plaster' is a struggle between the two 'me' positions which allow mutual existence. The opposition of saintliness and hairiness is similar to that between exciting and yet repulsive sexuality and pure and yet lethargic babyishness in *The Bell Jar*. It is also linked to the opposition between the yellow and the white selves, parallel to *The Bell Jar*'s alien 'Chinese' face and the unrecognisable 'yellow' hairy legs. This deadly struggle between the 'two of me' will not produce a winner. However, it promises one; suspiciously, though, such promise is made by the only 'me' who speaks in the text. Rather than a way out, this is a poem claiming the desire for release while accounting for the loss this would imply; the goal of collecting one's strength is that of leaving the 'other me' to 'perish with emptiness' and to have her 'begin to miss me.' The *cupio dissolvi* of the 'I', which affects the white 'she', amounts to leaving this feminine shell without a content; this is claimed to be the condition of the I's survival. And yet, such a survival can only happen when she will 'begin to miss me', thus reinstating the need for her existence.

The disgusting and ugly hairiness briefly exposed by these two texts fits into a wider poetics, which negotiates masculinity and femininity within the self. Its aim is not to simply celebrate one or the other, but to explore what are defined as the cruel conditions of their mutual existence.

The last text which I would like to analyse in relation to body hair, modernity and extraordinary femininity is *The Lady Who Loved Insects*, a twelfth-century fragment translated from the Japanese into English by Arthur Waley in 1929.[77] I do not wish here to provide a historical reading of the text, but I would like to use it in my discussion on body hair because, although it displays a familiar link among femininity, hairiness and modernity, the interplay between seduction, attraction and hairiness is notably different from that encountered in the texts analysed above.

An unnamed third person narrator tells us that the lady who loves insects is the daughter of a Provincial Inspector and the next-door neighbour of the lady who loved butterflies. She 'would sit' for hours on end 'gazing' at her favourite creature, 'the common caterpillar', 'a furry black form that nestled in the palm of her hand'. 'She was a strange girl, and used to say "Why do people make such a fuss about butterflies and never give a thought to the creatures out of which butterflies grow?"' This strange girl of whom 'people on the whole were frightened [. . .] and kept away', had for companions only 'a number of rather rough little boys', and a propensity for radical questions, since she 'hated anything that was not natural'.[78] 'Consequently', the narrator continues, 'she would not pluck a single hair from her eyebrows nor would she blacken her teeth, saying it was a dirty and disagreeable custom. So morning, noon, and night she tended her insects, bending over them with a strange, white-gleaming smile'.[79] She would dismiss the 'silly and vulgar prejudice' affecting those among her visitors who showed the 'slightest distaste for her pets', and, 'as she said this she would stare at the visitor under her black, bushy eyebrows in a way that made him feel very uncomfortable'.[80] The lady refuses the association between hairiness and disgust endorsed by her parents, who tell her that ' "people as a rule only make pets of charming and pretty things. If it gets about that you keep hairy caterpillars you will be thought a disgusting girl and nobody will want to know you." "I don't mind what they think", she answered, "I want to enquire into everything that exists and find out how it began." '[81] The ambitious young scientist, who makes her parents feel 'that she was much cleverer than they', soon becomes a local 'oddity' among the young people of the district, while her habit of calling her servants by insect-names is thought 'queer and stupid.'[82] Such 'modern' refusal of customs inspires a 'young man of good family' to give her a fright by sending her a fake snake with a note saying 'Creeping and crawling I shall sneak my way to your side, for my persistence is tireless as my body is long', to which the lady replies in *katakana*, on 'a stout, sensible-looking sheet of paper': 'If indeed we are fated to meet, not here will it be, but in Paradise, thou crafty image of a snake.'[83] At this point 'a certain Captain of Horse saw this letter and being much struck with it [he] determined to obtain an interview with the writer.'[84] Seeing her going out of the house (and being reproached for this breach of custom by one of her maids) in order to look at some caterpillars, the Captain observes her:

> She had pulled her mantel over her head, but her hair hung loose beneath it, and very lovely hair it was too, but rather untidy-looking, and the Captain thought it must be a long time since she had combed it. Her thick, very dark eyebrows gave her face a rather forbidding air. Her other features were by no means bad. But when she smiled her white teeth gleamed and flashed in a

manner that rather disgusted him, for there was something wild and barbaric about it.

'What a sad case!' thought the Captain. 'If only she took an ordinary amount of trouble with herself she really would not be bad-looking.' Even as she was he did not find her altogether unattractive; for there was about her a strange kind of vehemence, a liveliness of expression, a brilliance of complexion and colouring that could not fail to make some impression on him. [. . .]

For a moment he saw her in full length. She was rather tall. Her hair floated out behind as she moved. It was very thick, but the ends were somewhat wispy, no doubt through lack of trimming. But with a little more looking after it would have made (he thought) a fine crop of hair. Certainly she was no great beauty, but if she dressed up and behaved like other people she would, he was sure, be capable of cutting quite a decent figure in Society. What a pity it was! Where had she picked up the distressing opinions that forced her to make such a melancholy spectacle of herself?[85]

As Peter Conrad says of Bartoli, 'when cleaned up and coiffed for the stage' she is beautiful.

This excerpt in translation can be connected to a number of points discussed earlier in the course of this chapter. The lady is tall, yet not ugly. Part of her attractiveness lies in her extraordinary vitality and energy, which the Captain finds hard to define because it is so distant from his (disappointed) expectations. The observer, able to see her at full length, in a position reminiscent of that of Walter Hartright, laments how her hair, usually a source of feminine attraction, is neither combed nor trimmed; the lady is unable to be beautiful because she is natural, her features are 'by no means bad', although 'naturally' she is 'not a great beauty'. The judging male gaze appropriates the object of desire transforming it in a possession by asserting its potential value on the market of society. The whiteness of her teeth and the darkness of her bushy eyebrows produce the by-now familiar combination of fascination and disgust encountered in the course of this chapter. Untidy, wild, barbaric, forbidding, tall, dark and brilliant, the lady who loves insects is, like Marian Halcombe, an oddity and an anomaly in the eyes of the male spectator. Unlike Marian, however, who jokes about her ugliness, the lady who loved insects has chosen not 'to work on femininity', to modify a diary entry by Sylvia Plath, because she loves 'everything that is natural'. Her bushy eyebrows and gleaming teeth urge the Captain to resort to a rather different idea of naturalness, which is produced by the quotations in the market of feminine beauty. It is indeed a 'pity' that the lady does not take 'an ordinary amount of trouble with herself' in order to increase her value on the market. Such a squandering of resources is immediately pathologised: she is 'a sad case', and since she cannot have chosen to 'make such a melancholy spectacle of herself' she must have 'picked up' these 'distressing opinions' from somewhere. Paradoxically, such 'melancholy spectacle' seems to be far from discouraging for the narrator/spectator who displays his fascination for the taming potential conveyed by the unconventional lady's body.

The natural artificiality of feminine beauty is clearly exposed by the Captain, echoing the complex interaction of the two observed in *The Woman in White*. However, this is also a story of seduction. Rather than expressing the ardour of an eighteen-year-old like Count Fosco does with Marian, the Captain writes a note to the lady: 'Forgive me that at your wicker gate so long I stand. But from the caterpillar's bushy brows I cannot take my eyes',[86] to which she replies 'By this you may know the strangeness of my mood. Had you not *kawamushi* called me, I would not have replied.'[87] The Captain answers 'In all the world, I fear, exists no man so delicate that to the hair-tips of a caterpillar's brow he could attune his life' and then goes back 'laughing to his home'.

'What happened next will be found in the second chapter!' the last line of this fragment tells us, leaving us without a conclusion. Remarkably, the Captain judges her a 'melancholy spectacle' and takes away her agency when attributing it to alien distressing opinions, which must have influenced her. Yet he also acknowledges the Lady's hairiness as part of herself. The finale of this fragment is promising insofar as the Lady's bushy eyebrows have been given visibility as an essential part of whom she is, and the Captain has accepted that a radical act of submission is needed in order to touch 'the hair-tips of a caterpillar's brow'. On the other hand, the potential for this caterpillar to turn into butterfly, paralleling the appropriately feminine interest of the young lady next door, is also present in the story. The mixture of disgust and attraction, the Pygmalionesque need to clean her up and coif her expressed earlier, and the laughter that closes the fragment, cast a shadow on the promise of a happy ending. Or, rather, they indicate how the very idea of a happy ending depends on the masculine agent, who can choose to stoop in order to conquer. Instead, even though the lady's hairiness is the result of a choice, it remains a spectacle, as the long narrative devoted to her partial exposure in the garden demonstrates. Hairiness is part of a claim to modernity insofar as it defies conventions and declares femininity as artificial; however, its opposite, that is 'natural femininity', remains unnatural and needs to be tamed, even though the taming process might involve being 'delicate' like the Captain rather than forceful like Count Fosco.

A few remarks are needed at this point about another woman of 'genius': Ada, the protagonist of *Ada, or Ardour* by Vladimir Nabokov.[88] This genius of an entomologist, also loves insects (or 'leps', as she calls them) and has a propensity for being 'untidy and forgetful in matters of grooming.'[89] Her head hair is an endless source of desire for Van, who describes her paleness as such that 'one's gaze, stroking her white shins and forearms, could follow upon them the regular slants of fine dark hairs, the silks of her girlhood.'[90] Ada's passion for insects can at times surpass that for her cousin Van (in fact her brother) himself, as when her interest for an 'accursed insect' (in Van's words) or rather for 'the newly described, fantastically rare *van*essian' (in Ada's reproachful notes to Van's account)[91] interrupts the scene of Van's departure from the Eden of Ardis Hall. Ada is linked to nature in the 'dactylic trimeter that was to remain Van Veen's only contribution to Anglo-American poetry' that addresses her as 'Ada, our ardors and arbors';[92] her name is pronounced by her mother, Marina, 'in the Russian way, with two deep, dark "a"s, making it sound rather like "ardor"'.[93] 'Je raffole de tout ce qui rampe (I'm crazy about everything that crawls)',[94] Ada says in words which could have been used by the Lady Who Loved Insects. What Van calls 'that downy tenderness, that despair of desire'[95] is also discussed by Demon (Van's and, without her knowledge, Ada's father), who establishes a link between nature, passion and taboos when he claims: 'If I could write [. . .] I would describe, in too many words no doubt, how passionately, how incandescently, how incestuously – *c'est le mot* – art and science meet in an insect, in a thrush, in a thistle of that ducal bosquet.'[96]

Both the Lady Who Loved Insects and Ada apparently are untidy children of nature. In *Ada*, 'Osberg's little gitana' asks 'what is the precise minimum of hairs on a body that allows one to call it "hairy"?'[97] The text makes very clear that 'a pinpoint glint of pubic floss, gold-powdered'[98] can be pleasurable, just like Lucette's armpits are, showing 'a slight stipple of bright floss'[99] later to become 'the russet feathering of her armpits',[100] which Van – in line with *The Joy of Sex*'s precept of using armpit hair as a resource – doesn't want shaved.[101] However, Van also makes clear, in a bout of jealousy towards Ada, that 'A brunette, even a sloppy brunette, should shave her groin before exposing it'.[102] Ada's 'regular slants of fine dark hairs' could be 'the silks of her girlhood', a source of pleasure for the male gaze, which needs to be brought back to the idea of femininity as a mixture of childishness and artificiality. When her sexuality comes into play in relation to another man, she needs to become a 'well-bred girl', stop looking at other men and 'shave her groin'.[103]

In *The Woman in White* and in the texts by Plath, body hair is unnatural, repulsive and disgusting. It is, however, also an important component of attraction and seduction, focusing the male urge to restore the artificiality of normality. In *The Lady Who Loved Insects* and in *Ada, or Ardor*, body hair is more explicitly a source of passion. Yet, the impermissible quality of body hair remains in place; this passion is eccentric, just like that for caterpillars rather than butterflies in the Japanese fragment. The Captain wishes to bring the melancholic and forbidding-looking lady back to society, while Van and Ada's passion can exist only at the price of breaking a taboo.

Women 'of genius' must negotiate the difficult implications of masculinity and femininity brought up by body hair. After all, the moustachioed

Alice B. Toklas, the paradoxical narrator in Gertrude Stein's *The Autobiography of Alice B. Toklas* ironically tells us that she ought to have written a book about the 'the wives of geniuses I have sat with.'[104]

Notes

1 Gertrude Stein, *The Autobiography of Alice B. Toklas* (Harmondsworth: Penguin, 1966), p. 18.

2 For an account of the few existing debates on the issue, see Chapter 1 of this volume, by Karín Lesnik-Oberstein. A notable exception to such a lack of academic debates is the special issue of *Eighteenth-Century Studies*, 38:1, (Fall 2004).

3 See Antony Easthope's discussion of visibility and ideology in *What a Man's Gotta Do: the Masculine Myth in Popular Culture* (Boston: Unwin Hyman, 1990).

4 On the role of body hair as an example of triviality in Terry Eagleton's discussion of critical theory, see Chapter 3 of this volume, by Louise Tondeur.

5 'After all, it is incredible that the subject [body hair] is still taboo. We freely discuss anal sex, female sexual dysfunction, pedophilia and boob jobs. But body hair in the wrong place is still off limits. Isn't it time to come clean? Isn't it time to ditch the depilation, storm the shelves of chemists, burn the bleach and spike the tweezers? Of course it is. But hey, sister, you first.' Mimi Spencer, 'Why can't we just let our hair down?', *Guardian* (23 January 2003), available at: www.guardian.co.uk/gender/story/0,,880432,00.html (accessed on 13 January 2006). See also for very similar arguments to those of Spencer – with the addition of the journalist's confession of her own inability to remain unshaved – 'Plucking hell: why are women obsessed with body hair?', Polly Vernon, *Observer Woman*, 1 (January 2006), pp. 38–9. Also available at: http://observer.guardian.co.uk/woman/story/0,,1684090,00.html (accessed on 16 January 2006).

6 See Germaine Greer's brief discussions of the role of body hair in her *The Female Eunuch* (London: Paladin, 1971) and *The Whole Woman* (London: Doubleday, 1999). Journalist Mimi Spencer has also argued that 'depilation is the battle that feminism lost.' Mimi Spencer, 'Why can't we just let our hair down?'.

7 Alex Comfort, *The Joy of Sex: Fully Revised and Completely Updated for the 21st Century* (New York: Octopus Publishing Group, 2002 [1972]).

8 Judith Butler, *Bodies That Matter: On the Discursive Limits of 'Sex'* (London: Routledge, 1993).

9 Eve Kosofsky Sedgwick, *Epistemology of the Closet* (Hemel Hempstead: Harvester Wheatsheaf, 1991), p. 41.

10 Mimi Spencer's 'Why can't we just let our hair down?' openly criticises – through Dr Susan Basow of Lafayette College – the association made by American college students between hairiness and old-fashioned feminism and lesbianism. Nevertheless, it too falls back – albeit somewhat ironically – on to exoticism when trying to create forms of visibility for body hair: 'Remember the German rock star Nena – noted for her "99 Red Balloons" and

her rude gush of underarm undergrowth? The hair – luxuriant and ape-like, as I recall – carried a hint of the erotic, a sort of Euro-exotica that gave her the appeal of an up-for-it she-wolf. At the time, boys loved it. Give us more Nenas, more of Julia Roberts's armpit fur, more European tennis champs. Put it on the cover of *Vogue*.' Moreover, although 'the lesbian' seems to appear rather often on our cinema and TV screens, the homophobia governing even the apparently most harmless production is evident. One example would be *Kissing Jessica Stein* (2001), directed by Charles Herman-Wurmfeld, in which normality and excess are happily redistributed along the axis of heterosexuality and homosexuality by the ending.

11 *She* (January 1998), 40–3; *Guardian*, 'Weekend section' (17 October 1998), 22–30, on the John Kobal photographic portrait award 1998.

12 *Colors* (September–October 1997).

13 *Diva* (February 1998), 7.

14 Dea Birkett, 'Look, look at that!', *Guardian* (31 January 2000).

15 See Chapter 1 of this volume.

16 John Berger, *Ways of Seeing* (London: BBC and Penguin, 1972), pp. 54–5.

17 Peter Conrad, 'Dangerous diva with a backpack', *Observer Review* (14 October 2001), 6.

18 For an analysis of notions of 'foreignness' in conjunction to body hair, see Neil Cocks's Chapter 11 in this volume.

19 'She sings not only Euridice, but also the psychopompous who accompanies Orfeo to the underworld, a phantom referred to as Genio. [. . .] Her Genio sounds astral, disembodied, lecturing Orfeo in an aria whose coloratura is literally unearthly.' Conrad, 'Dangerous diva with a backpack', 6.

20 See Christine Battersby, *Gender and Genius: Towards a Feminist Aesthetics* (London: Virago, 1989). Julia Kristeva argues after Hannah Arendt that the notion of genius is the ultimate justification of the *homo faber*, since the fabrication of such a notion reifies what is posited as his need to transcend both craft and object. Julia Kristeva, *Le Genie feminine: la vie, la folie, les mots* (Paris: Gallimard, 2003 [1999]), vol. 1, p. 166.

21 '*Mamillius*: You'll kiss me hard, and speak to me as if I were a baby still (*To Second Lady*) I love you better. *Second Lady*: And why so, my lord? *Mamillius*: Not for because your brows are blacker – yet black brows they say / Become some women best, so that there be not / Too much hair there, but in a semicircle, / Or a half-moon made with a pen. *Second Lady*: Who taught you this? *Mamillius*: I learned it out of women's faces. Pray now, / What colour are your eyebrows? / *First Lady*: Blue, my lord. / *Mamillius*: Nay, that's a mock. I've seen a lady's nose / That has been blue, but not her eyebrows.' Shakespeare, *The Winter's Tale*, Act II, scene 1, 6–16, in *The Oxford Shakespeare. The Complete Works*, ed. Stanley Wells and Gary Taylor (Oxford: Oxford University Press, 1999), pp. 1107–8.

22 Wilkie Collins, *The Woman in White* (Harmondsworth: Penguin, 1994 [1859–60]). See, for instance, a passage describing Marian's relief when inspecting a wing of Sir Percival Glyde's mansion: 'It is an inexpressible relief to find that the nineteenth century has invaded this strange future home of mine, and has swept the dirty "good old times" out of the way of our daily life.' p. 180.

23 Collins, *The Woman in White*, p. 26. See Kenneth Robinson, *Wilkie Collins: A Biography* (London: Davis-Poynter, 1974 [1951]), p. 138. Philip O'Neill, *Wilkie Collins: Women, Property and Propriety* (Basingstoke: Macmillan, 1988), pp. 118–19. For a lucid discussion of femininity, masculinity and narration, see Jenny Bourne Taylor, *In the Secret Theatre of Home: Wilkie Collins, Sensation Narrative, and Nineteenth-Century Psychology* (London: Routledge, 1988), pp. 115–18.

24 Lyn Pickett, *The 'Improper' Feminine: the Women's Sensation Novel and the New Woman Writing* (London: Routledge, 1992); O'Neill, *Wilkie Collins*, p. 119; Nicholas Rance, *Wilkie Collins and the Other Sensation Novelists: Walking the Moral Hospital* (Basingstoke: Macmillan, 1991).

25 Collins, *The Woman in White*, pp. 24–5.

26 Bourne Taylor, *In the Secret Theatre of Home*, p. 117.

27 Collins, *The Woman in White*, p. 25.

28 Collins, *The Woman in White*, pp. 25–6.

29 Richard Collins analyses the role of Marian's moustache in his 'Marian's moustache: bearded ladies, hermaphrodites, and intersexual collage in *The Woman in White*', in Maria K. Bachman and Don Richard Cox (eds), *Reality's Dark Light: the Sensational Wilkie Collins* (Knoxville: The University of Tennessee Press, 2003), pp. 131–72. Richard Collins assumes femininity and masculinity as being recognisably separate entities: this leads him to define Marian as a hermaphrodite or 'intersex' in combining aspects of both. I do not read *The Woman in White* as producing gender in this way: instead I read it here as unstable and mutually implicated. He also sees the text as being both in tune with contemporary medical and popular narratives of bearded ladies and able to 'subvert Victorian notions of gender' (p. 137). For my different position with regard to a historical interpretation of the meanings of Marian's moustache, see my discussion below.

30 Annie Leibovitz, *Women*, with a preface by Susan Sontag (London: Jonathan Cape, 2000), p. 19.

31 Sontag, 'Preface', in Leibowitz, *Women*, pp. 27–8.

32 Sontag, 'Preface', in Leibowitz, *Women*, p. 28.

33 For a witty analysis of the role of Victorian times in the twentieth century, see Matthew Sweet, *Inventing the Victorians* (London: Faber and Faber, 2002).

34 This is a distinctive feature of nineteenth-century literature, as Isobel Armstrong has demonstrated in *Victorian Poetry: Poetry, Poetics and Politics* (London: Routledge, 1993).

35 Matthew Sweet has made this point in his review of the London West End production of *Woman in White* 'Master of vice', *Independent* (22 August 2004); a fuller discussion of the complexities of narration in the novel can be found in Jenny Bourne Taylor, *In the Secret Theatre of Home*, pp. 108–13.

36 Collins, *The Woman in White*, p. 544. According to Robinson 'Courage and a lively and intelligent mind compensate for the beauty which her [Marian's] creator was bold enough to deny her. [. . .] We believe in her absolutely, and it is small wonder that Wilkie was inundated with letters from bachelors begging him to divulge her real name and address in order that they might seek her hand in marriage.' Robinson, *Wilkie Collins*, p. 138.

37 Sontag, 'Preface', in Leibowitz, *Women*, pp. 29–30.

38 Collins, *The Woman in White*, p. 596.

39 Sontag, 'Preface', in Leibowitz, *Women*, pp. 28–9.

40 Sweet, 'Master of vice'.

41 See the reviews of *The Woman in White* collected by Norman Page in his *Wilkie Collins: The Critical Heritage* (London and New York: Routledge and Kegan Paul, 1974).

42 Judith Butler, *Gender Trouble* (London and New York: Routledge, 1999 [1990]), p. 167.

43 Collins, *The Woman in White*, p. 31.

44 Collins, *The Woman in White*, p. 41.

45 O'Neill, *Wilkie Collins*, pp. 116–17.

46 Collins, *The Woman in White*, p. 43.

47 Collins, *The Woman in White*, p. 27. George Eliot, 'Silly novels by lady novelists' (1856), *Selected Critical Writings* (Oxford: Oxford University Press, 1992), pp. 296–321.

48 Collins, *The Woman in White*, p. 159.

49 Collins, *The Woman in White*, p. 174.

50 Collins, *The Woman in White*, p. 197.

51 Collins, *The Woman in White*, p. 180.

52 Collins, *The Woman in White*, p. 390.

53 Sojourner Truth, *Ain't I a Woman?* (1851), speech delivered at the Women's Convention, Akron, Ohio. www.edchange.org/multicultural/speeches/truth_ a_woman.html.

54 C. J. S. Thomson, *The History and Lore of Freaks* (London: Senate, 1996 [1930]), p. 193.

55 Sylvia Plath, *Letters Home. Correspondence 1950–1963*, selected and edited with a commentary by Aurelia Schober Plath (New York: Harper and Row, 1975), p. 468.

56 I would like to thank Penny Summerfield for having pointed out this reference.

57 Sylvia Plath, *The Bell Jar* (1963) (London: Faber and Faber, 1999), p. 182.

58 Sylvia Plath, *Collected Poems* (London: Faber and Faber, 1961), pp. 158–60, p. 160.

59 See, for instance, Susan Bassnett, *Sylvia Plath* (Basingstoke: Macmillan, 1987), p. 2.

60 David Holbrook, *Sylvia Plath: Poetry and Existence* (London: Athlone, 1976), quoted in Bassnett, *Sylvia Plath*, p. 2.

61 The classical critical attitude towards Plath is to 'treat the texts as the person and then disagree so strongly as to what these texts reveal' (Jacqueline Rose, *The Haunting of Sylvia Plath* (London: Virago, 1991), p. 4).

62 'I was supposed to be having the time of my life. [. . .] Only I wasn't steering anything, not even myself.' Plath, *The Bell Jar*, p. 2.

63 For instance, the text constantly establishes a relationship between the historical event of the Rosenbergs's electrocution and electroshock. Plath, *The Bell Jar*, p. 1 and pp. 151–2.

64 '"I can't sleep . . ." They interrupted me. "But the nurse said you slept last night" [. . .] "I can't read." I raised my voice. "I can't eat." It occurred

to me I'd been eating ravenously ever since I came to.' Plath, *The Bell Jar*, p. 186.

65   Plath, *The Bell Jar*, p. 22.

66   Doreen sports 'full-length nylon and lace jobs', while Betsy (nicknamed 'Pollyanna cowgirl') wears 'starched cotton nighties'; both the sexually aggressive 'white negress' and the future farmer's wife use their head hair as a form of seduction, dyed blonde in the first, in a ponytail in the second. Head hair is mentioned a large number of times in Plath's *Journals*, always in relation to feminine attractiveness. The 28 January 1959 entry reads: 'Must get my hair cut next week. Symbolic: get over instinct to be dowdy lip-biting little girl. Get bathrobe and slippers and nightgown & work on femininity.' Sylvia Plath, *The Journals of Sylvia Plath, 1950–1962*, ed. Karen Kikil (London: Faber and Faber, 2001), p. 467. Al Alvarez describes Plath as a genius and uses the example of her unwashed head hair as an indication of her disintegrating mental stability: 'her hair, which she usually wore in a tight, schoolmistressy bun, was loose. It hung straight to her waist like a tent, giving her pale face and gaunt figure a curiously desolate, rapt air, like a priestess emptied out by the rites of her cult. When she walked in front of me down the hall passage and up the stairs to her apartment [. . .] her hair gave off a strong smell, sharp as an animal's.' Al Alvarez, *The Savage God. A Study of Suicide* (London: Weidenfeld and Nicolson, 1971), pp. 30–1.

67   This rite of purification is explicitly linked to the immersion in the Lethe in the poem 'Getting There'.

68   See Shoshana Felman, *Writing and Madness* (Ithaca, NY: Cornell University Press, 1985) and *What Does a Woman Want? Reading and Sexual Difference* (London and Baltimore: Johns Hopkins University Press, 1993). See also Battersby, *Gender and Genius*, pp. 103–47.

69   *Readers' Digest*, *Christian Science Monitor*, *New Yorker* and *Vogue* all appear in the text. The novel also presents characters and situations as *déjà vu* and as belonging to a specific cultural climate (produced in a particular way by this specific text), such as, for instance, 'young men with all-American bone structures.' Plath, *The Bell Jar*, p. 2.

70   Such as those created by phrases such as '*one of these* full-length nylon and lace jobs.' Plath, *The Bell Jar*, p. 5; emphasis mine.

71   See, for instance, the following fabricated intertextual reference: 'I had read one of Mrs Guinea's books in the town library – the college library didn't stock them for some reason – and it was crammed from beginning to end with suspenseful questions: "Would Evelyn discern that Gladys knew Roger in her past? wondered Hector feverishly" and "How could Donald marry her when he knew of the child Elsie, hidden away with Mrs Rollmop on the secluded country farm? Griselda demanded of her bleak, moonlit pillow." ' Plath, *The Bell Jar*, p. 43.

72   'The movie was very poor. It starred a nice blond girl who looked like June Allyson but was really somebody else, and a sexy black-haired girl who looked like Elizabeth Taylor but was also somebody else, and two big, broad-shouldered bone-heads with names like Rick and Gil. It was a football romance, and it was in technicolour. I hate technicolour. Everybody in a technicolour movie seems to feel obliged to wear a lurid new costume in each

new scene and to stand around like a clothes-horse with a lot of very green trees or very yellow wheat or very blue ocean rolling away for miles and miles in every direction.' Plath, *The Bell Jar*, p. 44.

73 Plath, *The Bell Jar*, p. 196.

74 Plath, *The Bell Jar*, p. 69 and p. 187.

75 Plath, *The Bell Jar*, p. 75.

76 Plath, *The Bell Jar*, p. 88.

77 *The Lady Who Loved Insects*, translated from the Japanese by Arthur Waley, dry-points by Hermine David (London: The Blackamore Press, 1929); the fragment has also been reprinted in the volume edited by Ivan Morris: *Madly Singing in the Mountain. An Appreciation and Anthology of Arthur Waley* (London: Allen and Unwin, 1972), pp. 248–55. The latter is the edition which I will use here.

78 Waley, *Madly Singing in the Mountain*, p. 248.

79 Waley, *Madly Singing in the Mountain*, p. 248.

80 Waley, *Madly Singing in the Mountain*, pp. 248–9.

81 Waley, *Madly Singing in the Mountain*, p. 249.

82 Waley, *Madly Singing in the Mountain*, p. 250.

83 Waley, *Madly Singing in the Mountain*, pp. 250–1.

84 Waley, *Madly Singing in the Mountain*, p. 252.

85 Waley, *Madly Singing in the Mountain*, p. 254.

86 Waley, *Madly Singing in the Mountain*, p. 254.

87 An explicatory note tells us that '*kawamushi*' means 'hairy caterpillar'.

88 Vladimir Nabokov, *Ada, or Ardor* (Harmondsworth: Penguin, 2000 [1969]), p. 172.

89 Nabokov, *Ada, or Ardor*, p. 171.

90 Nabokov, *Ada, or Ardor*, p. 51.

91 Nabokov, *Ada, or Ardor*, p. 127; emphasis mine.

92 Nabokov, *Ada, or Ardor*, p. 63.

93 Nabokov, *Ada, or Ardor*, p. 37.

94 Nabokov, *Ada, or Ardor*, p. 49.

95 Nabokov, *Ada, or Ardor*, p. 81.

96 Nabokov, *Ada, or Ardor*, p. 343.

97 Nabokov, *Ada, or Ardor*, p. 283.

98 Nabokov, *Ada, or Ardor*, p. 455.

99 Nabokov, *Ada, or Ardor*, p. 166.

100 Nabokov, *Ada, or Ardor*, p. 377.

101 Nabokov, *Ada, or Ardor*, p. 372.

102 Nabokov, *Ada, or Ardor*, p. 181.

103 In James Joyce's *Ulysses*, described by Brian Boyde as the only work of genius of the twentieth century able to stand up to Nabokov's *Ada* (see his 'Afterword' in the edition of *Ada* mentioned above, pp. 479–95, p. 479) body hair negotiates the metamorphosis of Bella into Bello. James Joyce, *Ulysses* (Harmondsworth: Penguin, 1986), volume II, chapter 1.

104 Gertrude Stein, *The Autobiography of Alice B. Toklas*, p. 18. The book is famously dependent on the paradox of the Cretan liar: Alice B. Toklas, the narrator, declares on the last page that the book has been written by Gertrude Stein. In relation to further issues mentioned in this chapter, it is of interest

to note that at the website www.gayheroes.com/gertrude.htm (accessed 23 November 2005), the following anecdote is included about 'Gertrude Stein and Alice B. Toklas . . . the most famous lesbian couple ever, well, until maybe [American actresses] Ellen [de Generes] and Anne [Heche]': 'With her short cropped hair, Gertrude definitely challenged the gender stereotypes of her time, and Alice B., with a bit of hair on her lip, raised a few eyebrows herself. Once after they had visited Gertrude's 3-year-old nephew, he said, "I liked the man alright, but why did the woman have a moustache?" '.

3 A history of pubic hair, or reviewers' responses to Terry Eagleton's *After Theory*

Louise Tondeur

Reviewers' responses to Terry Eagleton's *After Theory* have, in part, been concerned with a comment made in the introduction: 'Not all students are blind to the Western narcissism involved in working on the history of pubic hair while half the world's population lacks adequate sanitation and survives on less than two dollars a day.'[1] In the first half of this essay, I want to engage with the reviewers' responses to this quotation. In the main, the reviews that I am concerned with appeared in the *Tablet*, the *Independent*, the *Guardian* and the *Graduate Journal of Social Science*.

Something which each of the reviews seems to take for granted is that the history of pubic hair is indeed something being studied by academic researchers. But, as I will go on to argue in response to the *Guardian* review, I read Eagleton as using wit and exaggeration as a means to shift perception *rather than to give evidence*. In such a reading, Eagleton is not primarily diagnosing that pubic hair specifically is being studied by a number of post-graduate students, rather, it seems to me that the reviews assume that this is, naturally and self-evidently, the point of his comment. In doing so, I will go on to argue here, these reviewers are as much revealing something of their own assumptions about hair, gender and politics, as an understanding of Eagleton's arguments in *After Theory*.

There are fifteen theses on the British Library databases (either at MA, MPhil. or PhD level) which include pubic hair in either the abstract or the title. The *Tablet*'s description of the study of pubic hair as 'a particularly poignant example' of an 'inconsequential' area of study, suggesting a typicality to the study of pubic hair, therefore does not hold up to the evidence. The British Library databases list hundreds of thousands of theses, going back to 1716. But only fifteen of those have involved pubic hair. This suggests the reverse of the *Tablet*'s sentiments in the extreme. There is, in this sense, no typicality to the study of pubic hair. It is, in fact, extremely rare to find detailed scholarly work which has pubic hair as one of its main focuses. What is more, all of these theses, bar one,[2] are in the area of science, criminology, health, psychology or education. What all these theses have in common is that they are overwhelmingly pragmatic. They all have a practical application, especially in terms of sociology or health education (or 'sanitation' – to use Eagleton's term). Ironically, all the academic study listed by the British Library databases which has pubic hair as a main focus is framed around the works' practical application in terms of engaging with social problems. Add 'history' to the database search terms and the results are zero: just as no-one searches around for a 'stray mongrel to clutch'[3] on the escalators in the London Underground, there is, as far as I am aware, no substantial academic work on the history of pubic hair. To read Eagleton as implying that either of these is simply necessarily the case is, to me, overlooking the implications of his rhetorical style. Therefore, in the second half of this essay, I want to go on to look at whether it would be possible to write a history of pubic hair at all, and to imagine, if it should prove possible, what the key texts might be.

A google.com search for 'terry eagleton' 'pubic hair' brings up about seventy-six results,[4] and from this search it appears that several reviews of *After Theory*, published both online and in printed media, use the pubic hair quotation in order to express a sentiment similar to that which appeared in the *Tablet*:

> To think oneself out of the current state of affairs requires thinking politically, something which most theorists have ceased to do. Eagleton memorably calls this 'the gradual darkening of the dissident mind' and devotes many excellent pages in the first third of the book to documenting it. His pet hate is West-centred narcissism, a vice that he presents in its most stark form in the inconsequential topics cultural theorists now choose to study. Researching the history of pubic hair while half the world's population lacks adequate sanitation is a particularly poignant example.[5]

The review continues a page later:

> We research pubic hair because it is better not to think about our situation at all. Or if this slack-jawed indifference bothers us, we will ensure that what we think is inert; passive and neutral with respect to our situation. Then we can interpret the world as much as we like without risk of thinking ourselves back into our predicament. But we will also have given up hope of thinking ourselves out of it. For we will have renounced the ambition to change the world.

The *Tablet* review reads as if the central argument of the introduction to *After Theory* somehow hangs together around the apparent blindness to world politics induced by the study of pubic hair (or rather the study of irrelevant/irreverent topics). But I want to suggest that the success or failure of the introduction to *After Theory* does not reside in its ability to persuade on the issue of whether the study of pubic hair equates to a belief in it being 'better not to think about our situation at all'. It is the *Tablet* review itself which generates this reading, one which therefore becomes self-referential: the success or failure of the review resides in its ability to persuade on this issue. Furthermore, judgement formulated as success or failure rests on a binary paradigm. A closer look reveals other binary paradigms: irrelevant/irreverent topics of study versus worthy areas of study, pubic hair versus changing the world. These are not without political implications. In the *Tablet* review, the Eagleton quote, detached from *After Theory*, stands ready to be manipulated into one side of a political argument, one which undermines the Marxist formulations which inspired Eagleton's comment in the first place.

A more extreme example of this phenomenon of the manipulation of a quotation occurs with a phrase taken from the interview with Eagleton which was published in the *Independent*. Many of the other google.com search results appear because they use the quotation: 'they prefer to focus their energy on the history of pubic hair',[6] often in isolation. Here is the passage in which the phrase appears:

> Students today, he asserts, are engaging neither with history nor with post-structuralism. 'What is sexy instead is sex', he announces, in the first chapter, on 'The Politics of Amnesia': 'Quietly spoken middle-class students huddle diligently in libraries, at work on sensationalist subjects like vampirism and eye-gouging,[7] cyborgs and porno movies.' Cast adrift in the stormy currents of postmodernism, they prefer to focus their energy on 'the history of pubic hair' or the evolution of Friends.[8]

It is interesting to note the effects of hypertext when considering the decontextualised use of the phrase from the *Independent* interview. The use of google is not an unbiased or a transparent process. What appears to have happened, I would suggest, is that when many of the online writers who refer to this Eagleton quotation came to compiling their web contributions, they too used a search engine and found the *Independent* quotation, whether on the *Independent*'s pages or on another web page. This process divorces the phrase not only from *After Theory* but also from the *Independent* interview. Hypertext allows the phrase to hang in cyberspace, apparently with no backwards reference. It can then be reused, transformed, into a new mode of reference, and takes the same tone as the *Tablet* review: a liberal conservative notion of what is and what is not a worthy topic of study. More than that, the second half of the Eagleton quotation has its power removed: 'half the world's population lacks adequate sanitation and survives on less than two dollars a day' is hidden by a rather safe and comfortable moralistic narrative on irrelevant/irreverent subjects of study. In other words, this transformation enacts precisely what Eagleton could be said to be warning us against: irrelevant/irreverent study becomes the focus, inaction on poverty and social justice is hidden.

These reviewers of *After Theory* are involved in a covert reformulation or manipulation of the Eagleton quotation, which led me to wonder whether it would be possible to engage in an *overt* reformulation or manipulation of the quotation. My own reformulations arose from my reading of another review. John Mullan's piece on *After Theory* from the *Guardian* does not mention pubic hair, but does quote from the passage in which the pubic hair quote appears:

> He senses that the campus campaign against traditional lit. crit. has been won. Nowadays 'quietly-spoken, middle-class students huddle diligently in libraries, at work on sensationalist subjects like vampirism and eye-gouging, cyborgs and porno movies'. Hooray! But no, the postmodernism that has made deviancy the norm has disengaged us from political conflicts. There is no hypocritical respectability to rail or rebel against. He rather misses the 'old-fashioned bourgeois values' that underpinned 'liberal humanist' approaches to reading and teaching. At least the battle lines were clear.[9]

Mullan reads Eagleton's style as humorous, as I do, but, as part of that, he reads the pubic hair as an 'aside': 'He is jokey, roguish, strictly jaundiced. He is still in love with the supposedly comic similes and illustrations that were such an odd part of his style in his memoir *The Gatekeeper*.'[10] This humorous prose style is one which Eagleton used to great effect in *Literary Theory*:

> there is no kind of writing which cannot, given sufficient ingenuity, be read as estranging. Consider a prosaic, quite unambiguous statement like the one sometimes seen in the London underground system: 'Dogs must be carried on the escalator.' This is not perhaps quite as unambiguous as it seems at first sight: does it mean that you must carry a dog on the escalator? Are you likely to be banned from the escalator unless you can find some stray mongrel to clutch in your arms on the way up?[11]

As a comparison of the Mullan with the other responses to *After Theory* suggests, Eagleton's introduction does much more than argue that it is irresponsible to study pubic hair. This idiomatic prose style, which I referred to in my introduction, is an Eagleton trait and one which he repeats throughout *After Theory*. In this formulation, it does not matter what silly, trivial, irreverent area of study is substituted for '*working on the history of pubic hair*'. As Mullan reads also, where in Eagleton, there is a movement from the general to the specific and back again, the specific example does not sum up appropriately the general, but instead can be read as a key to reading material *differently*. Eagleton produces the unusual, witty and exaggerated as a means to shift perception, rather than primarily to give evidence. What *After Theory* does is to situate the rise of Marxist theory and its acolytes and then use this positioning to discuss contemporary thinking. In this reading, pubic hair, along with '*Friends*', vampirism, eye-gouging, cyborgs and porno movies,[12] is part of a list of a certain construction of the apolitical, which is then discussed at length, rather than in and of itself 'a particularly poignant example'[13] of academic immorality, as the *Tablet* seems to suggest.

At the same time, 'history of' proposes that there was a time when pubic hair was different, that some kind of transformation has taken place, either to the hair itself or to the context of the hair. The idea that you can tell its history also suggests, however, that something about pubic hair remains stable over time, in order to create a link through the many 'pubic hair stories' and to maintain a kind of through-line of meaning. But reading Eagleton as being ironic or witty about such 'a history' suggests instead that pubic hair is *always* stable, it doesn't change, and it doesn't require comment. All of which leads me to ask: once I read pubic hair as suggesting sexuality, gender, health, prostitution, all of which are, I would suggest, extremely pertinent topics when thinking about social justice, does its 'history' somehow become more important and less 'jokey'?

As a way of following through the method of reformulating and manipulating the quotation employed by the *Tablet* and the online reviewers who pick up on the line from the *Independent*, here are my own reformulations of the quotation. They arise out of my previous reading of the *Guardian* review and the use of the word 'history' in Eagleton, a reading in which I self-consciously position myself as a *hair researcher*. To elaborate, Jane Austen and Herrick, two of the examples Eagleton uses later in his chapter, could both be inserted in his quote instead of 'pubic hair', while retaining the sense of the reading. Trivial and traditional subjects of study would then no longer be so clearly oppositional. Now, any kind of study which does not seek to address world poverty (or politics in general in Eagleton's introduction) could be symptomatic of Western narcissism. In this reading, pubic hair, '*Friends*', vampirism, eye-gouging, cyborgs and porno movies are no different in and of themselves from Jane Austen and Herrick, unless they engage with politics – and rigorous scholarship which involves more, as Eagleton puts it, than sitting in front of the television – [14] they are narcissistic, or what the *Tablet* calls 'inconsequential topics.'[15]

In Eagleton's argument there seems to be something about the rigorous nature of the scholarship which is in itself either political or apolitical, which reaffirms Austen and Herrick as warranting rigorous study because pubic hair, '*Friends*', vampirism, eye-gouging, cyborgs and porno movies themselves engender an apolitical or slapdash, TV-focused, methodology. 'Not all students are blind to the Western narcissism involved in [studying Jane Austen or Herrick] while half the world's population lacks adequate sanitation and survives on less than two dollars a day.'[16] Why does this formulation feel, I would suggest, much more uncomfortable? Because it implicates more people? It no longer necessarily supports the notion that some subjects are self-evidently worthy of study while others are not.

But consider the meaning of 'narcissism' for a moment. It is not quite the same as the *Tablet*'s 'inconsequential'. In Eagleton's aside, I read it more as 'looking only at oneself' and not at 'the world's population' outside oneself. Eagleton's idiom is effective for me because of the image that it creates: gazing at my own pubic hair is the ultimate form of looking only at myself, because it would require me to adopt a position through which I would prevent myself from seeing anything else around me. But I would like to rework this image for a moment: as a woman, examining my own pubic hair symbolically requires me to return to the place of my own birth and to go back into myself.

Think about the hundreds of examples of Sheela Na Gig carvings which have been found throughout the UK.[17] In them, a grotesque figure, almost always with no hair, as if she is a baby and an old woman at the same time, holds open her own vulva. For pagan scholars, Sheela Na Gig celebrates the circle of a woman's life: we emerge from our mother's vulvas, as adults we can give birth ourselves. She is therefore a powerful reminder of the narcissism involved in gazing at my own pubic hair. Courbet's *The Origin of the World*, from 1866, also illustrates this point, but from another angle. His painting asks us to gaze on a woman's naked body and to focus on her pubic hair in particular, whereas the *title* is outward looking. Both the Sheela Na Gig figures and the Courbet seem to say: this is where 'the world's population' comes from. Both Courbet's title and Sheela Na Gig's wide-eyed outward gaze break an insular circularity of 'narcissism'. Take this kind of 'narcissism' into consideration and marry it to Eagleton's call to thought and action on poor health and poverty, and a recent United Nations report into Women and Health makes interesting reading:

> Every minute of every day, a woman dies because of complications during pregnancy and childbirth. The majority of these deaths are preventable . . . The number of HIV infections among women continues to rise and is rapidly reaching and surpassing the number of infections among men . . . Although more women than ever before know of modern contraceptive methods, a huge gap persists between availability and usage. Cultural taboos and women's lack of knowledge about their bodies, as well as lack of autonomy to determine the size of their families, are major obstacles, particularly among rural women and teenagers.[18]

The idea that educating a woman in health issues, pertaining to nutrition and sexual health in particular, means educating a whole family, is a pragmatic approach which UNICEF and other agencies have been putting into practice in recent years.[19] I would like to offer yet another reading of the Eagleton quotation, as asking something more in line with the following: as a theorist, narcissistically 'reading myself' (to rewrite Hélène Cixous for a moment[20]) am I more shocked by my own essentialist rendering of women in the above paragraphs, or by the UN's assertion that while I was reading it several woman died of preventable 'complications during pregnancy and childbirth'?

This allows me to rewrite the Eagleton quotation once more. I might insert other broader phrases into this much-quoted extract from Eagleton's introduction while retaining the sense of the reading. In the first, optimistically, female narcissism becomes a methodology: 'Not all students are blind to the [need to employ a female] narcissism [by developing a greater understanding of female sexual health] while [every minute of every day, a woman dies because of complications during pregnancy and childbirth.]'. Or I could rewrite it – using phrases which might serve pessimistically to read *any* academic study as narcissistic by removing it from the quotation altogether – so that it would look like this: 'Not [everyone is] blind to the Western narcissism involved in [working in a hairdressers, running a shoe shop, shopping in Tesco, drinking coffee, having a bath, flushing a toilet] while half the world's population lacks adequate sanitation and survives on less than two dollars a day.'

What becomes poignant, to use Maximillian de Gaynesford's word, is that these reformulations makes the quotation appear *more* radically political than the original, which seemed to suggest that blame for Western narcissism lies with certain post-graduate students of cultural theory. If we rephrase it like this, and thereby perhaps unleash more of its meaning, or political power, blame for Western narcissism lies with everyone in the Western world.

David Beer's review, which appeared in the *Graduate Journal of Social Science*, interprets Eagleton's pubic hair reference in an ostensibly less literal and less moralistic manner. Beer problematises what he sees as Eagleton's central argument, that he means us to 'shift our focus to larger questions and dispense with our analysis of pubic hair, pornography, or sit-coms.'[21] For Beer, pubic hair is an example of 'the minutia [*sic*] of everyday life' and we are being encouraged to focus our attention on larger 'metaphysical questions'[22] instead:

> The central argument of Eagleton's text is that cultural theorists should move toward a focus upon the bigger transcendental questions required by the transforming cultural environment. Or, rather, Eagleton's text is a challenge to cultural theorists to transfer their attention to questions of truth, morality, fundamentalism and death, in order to ensure the relevance and survival of cultural theory. For Eagleton, this can only be achieved by an overcoming of the fear caused by the sustained avoidance of these universal issues in favour of the minutia [*sic*] of everyday life. As a result of this focal shift cultural theory will re-separate itself from everyday life and will then be in a position better suited to its critique.[23]

This sets up another apparently oppositional binary paradigm: 'the minutia [*sic*] of everyday life' versus 'metaphysical questions.' I read the operation of this oppositional as pernicious in its political implications and it is one which recurs in writing about hair, so much so that if I am to continue to take Cixous's advice and 'write [my]self'[24] self-consciously into a position as a *hair researcher*, *hair critic* or even a *hair theorist*, I might be allowed to name the operation of this particular binary paradigm a *hair trope*. To illustrate this point, I want to start by looking briefly at two ideas contained within in the phrase itself.

First of all, the Eagleton pubic hair quotation is reminiscent of another one, the debate around which is discussed by Eve Kosofsky Sedgwick. It was the *title* of her paper 'Jane Austen and the masturbating girl' which, Kosofsky Sedgwick relates, caused the reaction described at the beginning of the essay of the same name in *Tendencies*: 'The phrase itself is already evidence. Rodger Kimball in his treatise on educational "corruption," *Tenured Radicals*, cites the title "Jane Austen and the Masturbating Girl" from an MLA convention program quite as if he were Perry Mason, the six words a smoking gun.'[25] That it is the title at stake, and not the paper itself, is pertinent here. The Eagleton sentence was read as a quotation ready for manipulation in the ways in which I have demonstrated and so too, apparently, was the title 'Jane Austen and the masturbating girl'. It was used, with misogynist and homophobic force, to symbolise all that was wrong with 'radicals' in academia in general but feminist theory in particular.

As in the Eagleton, Jane Austen becomes the torch-bearer for traditional literary criticism and hence (so called) traditional or family values. Here masturbation takes the place of pubic hair as what is wrong with academia – what is trivial, irrelevant/irreverent, frivolous, unnecessary. Furthermore, both masturbation and pubic hair are seen to operate in another similar way: both are read as corrupting, immoral, undermining family values. Reading them as trivial, or frivolous, seeks to deny their apparent potentially corrupting or subversive power. What a comparison of the *After Theory* reviews to the Sedgwick makes clear is that both masturbation and pubic hair are about sexuality itself, in its most dangerous and threatening manifestations.

The notions embedded in the Terry Eagleton quotation are reminiscent too of another thinker, in that the most (in)famous essay on pubic hair is Freud's *The Medusa's Head*. It is interesting to note, then, that narcissism is also a famous Freudian concept. That sexuality is directly linked by Freud to health and well-being is almost too obvious to point out, but it makes the reviewers' use of the Eagleton quotation all the more ironic. Not only is the Eagleton phrase held in balance, in a kind of parallelism, by two references to Freud – narcissism and pubic hair – but through two allusions to mythology: Narcissus and the Medusa.

Cixous engages with Freud's essay in *The Laugh of the Medusa*, through an investigation of female sexuality as well as a call to women to write. In it, she compares women's writing to masturbation (which it might be possible to read as 'looking only at myself' or female narcissism). Once more, pubic hair and masturbation are read as powerful and disruptive manifestations of sexuality. And, once more, trivialising them becomes only a method of disempowerment. This raises a number of questions for me: are the accusations of narcissism also a method of disempowerment?

Gananath Obeyesekere's *The Medusa's Hair*[26] is another well-known response to Freud's *Medusa's Head*, this time by an anthropologist, and not 'Western' in its focus. Do psychoanalysis and anthropology form the respectable aspect of pubic hair study? If pubic hair is a respectable area of study for psychoanalysis and anthropology, but the cultural theorist and literary critic are to be reproached (according to the *Tablet* review) for reading manifestations of this work as appropriate and serious texts to be studied and discussed, then what power struggles are involved in the demarcation of subject-specific areas of study?

If we read Cixous's *The Laugh of the Medusa* as a response to Freud's *Medusa's Head*, we could go as far as to call the Medusa of the title a figure whose snakes operate as a phantasy of female pubic hair. The laugh of the Medusa might then become, for this reading, *The Laugh of [Pubic Hair]*. Therefore, when I 'write [my]self'[27] as a *hair theorist* and call 'the minutia [sic] of everyday life' versus 'metaphysical questions' paradigm a *hair trope*, I am reminded of the Cixous for more than one reason. But perhaps most pertinent to Beer's reading of the Eagleton quotation is Cixous's engagement with silliness. Because if pubic hair is involved in the every-day–trivial–silly versus metaphysical–central–important paradigm, it is also involved in another overlapping one, which we might also describe as a *hair trope*. Hair is either silly or monstrous:[28]

> Who, surprised and horrified by the fantastic tumult of her drives . . . hasn't accused herself of being a monster? Who, feeling a funny desire stirring inside her (to sing, to write, to dare to speak, in short, to bring out something new), hasn't thought she was sick? Well, her shameful sickness is that she resists death, that she makes trouble. And why don't you write? Write! Writing is for you, you are for you; your body is yours, take it. I know why you haven't written . . . Because writing is at once too high, too great for you, it's reserved for the great, that is for great men; and it's silly . . . you wrote, irresistibly, as when we would masturbate in secret, not to go further, but to attenuate the tension a bit, just enough to take the edge off. And then as soon as we come, we go and make ourselves feel guilty – so as to be forgiven; or to forget, to bury it until the next time.[29]

I am reminded of Robert Coover's 1992 article in the *New York Times*, in which he discusses 'the tyranny of the line'.[30] Here are the political implications: in this model, pubic hair, the everyday silliness, women, are all on the bottom half of the line. As Cixous reminds us, if something is being called silly, there is likely to be a political motivation, an attempt at subjection and the removal of power involved in the process. Pubic hair is silly, masturbation is silly, women's writing is silly, because to call them anything else would be to allow them to unleash their power.

Everyday, normalising, mundane, trivial consumption forms part of a system which supports the global market-place. I pick up a bottle of shampoo from the shelf in Tesco and a whole chain of marketing events trails off into the distance behind it.[31] Picking up a home-preparation bikini-line waxing-kit sets off a similar chain: the so-called triviality of pubic hair works very well when it comes to selling products to women. As books like Joanna Blythman's *Shopped*,[32] Judi Bevan's *Trolley Wars*[33] and Felicity Lawrence's *Not on the Label*[34] have demonstrated, the super-markets' supreme power comes from convincing us that we have a duty to visit them once a week, turning them into modern churches, where religion is replaced by consumption. This is surely a very pertinent issue for the Marxist theorist. If one wishes to discuss capitalism, what better place to go?

Here is Robert Coover's tyrannical line again: thought on one side, the normalising of buying and selling on the other; the special on one side, the mundane on the other. In Beer's reading of Eagleton, the everyday or the mundane may be disallowed, yet the everyday pull of the (super-) market is tremendous. So labels such as the everyday or the mundane are part of a politically motivated process of normalisation and the making invisible of that process. This is a serious business, because according to *Ten Top Natural Beauty Products* by Ysanne Spevack:

> The global beauty industry . . . is worth about £110 billion ($160 billion). To give this huge sum of money perspective, we spend more on beauty in the west than we do on education. Which sounds stupid, but is possibly perplexingly clever as both attractive men and women have been found in studies to earn more than their less attractive counterparts.[35]

Pubic hair is part of this multibillion-dollar beauty industry, which saw no reason to stop at head hair and male facial hair, so that it now embraces head hair, facial hair, leg hair, underarm hair and pubic hair. In other words, money can be made from pubic hair too. When it comes to a history of the market, pubic hair is an example of market forces in hyperdrive.

Far from being a rather trivial frivolous, girly subject, beauty, and therefore hair, is one of the key players in the global market-place. If one wishes to discuss capitalism, *one cannot help but talk about beauty*: depilation, waxing, shaving and pubic hair are all part of the package. A history of pubic hair would therefore be, in part, a history of the rise of the product, a history of marketing as it applies to bodily transformation, and I could therefore again reformulate the *After Theory* quotation, taking into account what Ysanne Spevack says: 'Not all students are blind to the Western narcissism involved in [spending $160 billion on hair and beauty products] while half the world's population lacks adequate sanitation and survives on less than two dollars a day.'[36]

This is one of the places where research into a history of pubic hair might start, right back with the key ideas that *After Theory* elaborates. As a self-conscious (narcissistic?) rebellion against the texts which suggest pubic hair not only as *typifying* apolitical research, but also as the ultimate frivolity, marginalia or topic unworthy of study, I wanted to find out what approaches would be necessary if a researcher were to write a history of pubic hair. The rest of this essay will engage with how this might work.

I have already suggested that one starting place could be the reformulation of Eagleton's quotation using the Ysanne Spevack text. Therefore we might argue that a cultural history of pubic hair should more accurately be described as a cultural history of both the modification and manifestation of pubic hair. The modification of any hair on the body is only another form of body modification in general, which includes the wearing of clothes. The first thing which becomes obvious when working out a possible research methodology for a 'history of pubic hair' is, then, the history of clothes and fashion.

Body modification is compulsory for me. If I did not modify my body, through wearing clothes, hair alteration and washing for instance, I would either be arrested, or admitted to a psychiatric hospital (lack of personal grooming, which includes body-hair removal for women, has been used in the diagnosis of mental illness, as Karín Lesnik-Oberstein reminds us in Chapter 1 of this volume). One of the main functions of body modification is the demarcation of gender and of fertility. As well as reading pubic hair modification as part of the interplay of market forces, we might go further by seeing it as only one particular part of this process of demarcation. There are several investigations into the meanings of body modification available, which provide a ready-made methodology for the pubic hair historian, for instance, the work of Julian Robinson, in particular *The Quest for Human Beauty*[37] and *Body Packaging*,[38] in which he discusses seventeenth- and eighteenth-century pubic decoration and fashions.

What other starting points are available to the pubic hair historian? I said that there have been no substantial academic works on the history of pubic hair, but there is research within art history on the history of nakedness in painting and sculpture. Anne Hollander's *Seeing Through Clothes* has already begun to formulate a methodology for interpreting pubic hair in art: 'Florentine painters developed an image based on the Classical absolutely hairless female body: and so abstract was this formal vision that it could subdue the female nipple, as well as the pubic fleece, and even cause the hair of the head to form linear arrangements as neutral in texture as the lines and shapes of the body.'[39] What is interesting here, is the linkage of pubic hair to clothing. The female subject is here seen as *more 'naked'* with pubic hair, and as 'nude' rather than naked without it:

> the hair-by-hair rendering of the female pubic fleece makes a definite contrast with the thick golden braids or smooth, rippling fall of the coiffure. Pornography has always conventionally stressed this very contrast. In naked pornographic figures it helps to emphasize the difference between being clothed and being unclothed . . . by indicating clearly that female head hair . . .

is a potential element of *clothing*, whereas . . . body hair makes common nakedness more secret, slightly more bestial and ignominious, and thus more provocative. The less they match, the dirtier the image. Eighteenth-century pornographic art often showed the fuzzy pubic region under lifted skirts, looking quite different in substance from the powdered wig above. If the pubic hair is missing altogether and the woman is officially clothed only in her coiffure . . . she is therefore *nude*, as if accompanied by drapery, rather than *naked*, as if accompanied by clothes.[40]

Another important work which discusses what, after reading Hollander, we might call an eighteenth-century hair aesthetic is Johannes Endres' 'Diderot, Hogarth and the aesthetics of depilation' which appeared in the *Eighteenth Century Studies Journal*'s special issue on hair.[41] His essay opens with the following assertion: 'From a cultural–historical perspective, the interpretation of body hair has only just begun. As a threadlike, many-celled type of skin, hair seems to demand consideration in terms of categories emerging from everyday life and its practical organisation in relation to custom and fashion, beauty, and cosmetics.'[42]

I would like to add one more work to the list of possible starting points for the pubic hair historian. Jonathan Gil Harris's essay on Shakespeare's hair begins like this: 'Renaissance historicism has witnessed something of a sea change in recent years. If the new historicism of the 1980s was preoccupied primarily with the fashioning of early modern subjects, the growing tendency at the millennium, evidenced in the recent turn to "material culture," is to engage with objects.'[43] The 'object' Harris goes on to discuss is a lock of hair, likely to be a fake, which was said to be from the head of William Shakespeare. This lock of hair, Harris argues, creates a desire in the viewer which can never be sated, as if the hair promised to allow us to journey through time and to touch Shakespeare himself. The way in which an artefact can create, and at the same time refuse to sate, such a desire, is important in a discussion of pubic hair in any art form, lest we go searching for 'pubic hair clues' which create and refuse to satisfy, a similar longing to know.

Given this reading of Harris, might the pubic hair historian risk invoking 'the tyranny of the line'[44] by attempting to create a chronology of pubic hair? If she is brave enough, she might start with Martin Kilmer's essay 'Genital phobia and depilation'[45] which discusses Aristophanes' *Lysistrata and the Assembly Women*.[46] Lysistrata, for instance, links the plucking of women's pubic hair to the desire for peace:

We pluck and trim our entrances,
Like good little spiders the flies come strolling in
Caught! They're begging for it, hard
And what do we do? We just don't want to know.
They'll be falling over themselves to give us peace.[47]

Considering the political motif in the Eagleton quotation, it is notable that a women's peace movement, which arose out of protest against contemporary warfare, is called The Lysistrata Project.[48]

Lyndal Roper's *Oedipus and the Devil: Witchcraft, Sexuality and Religion in Early Modern Europe* might then provide a next step. Roper talks about the way in which parts of the body were used as magical objects. For instance, in considering the 'distinct magical capacities'[49] of men and women's bodies, Roper discusses a male sorcerer and notes '[O]nly under torture was he prevailed upon to admit that [the] hair was pubic hair he had taken from the "secret parts" of a girl in Switzerland.'[50] Witchcraft uses correspondences rather than a rational notion of cause and effect. A detachable part of the body, pubic hair for instance, will correspond to the person from whom it comes, rather like the lock of Shakespeare's hair does in the Harris essay of the same name, and can therefore be used for magical purposes.

I have found one website which claims to tell the history of pubic depilation,[51] and, while it skips uncritically from the Ancient Egyptians, to the Ancient Greeks, to Bassano de Zra on the Turks, to Catherine de Medici, and thence to the 1960s, it should provoke some pertinent questions. Martin Kilmer on Aristophanes (as a foundation for a chronology) might be complemented by this web-based 'history' precisely because of such questions. Lyndal Roper on hair as a form of magical correspondence, read alongside the Harris, might provide a way of problematising the very notion of a chronology and of foundations.

To continue the theme of depilation, Anne Hollander mentions John Baptista Porta's *Ninth Book of Natural Magick or How to Adorn Women and Make Them Beautiful*, from the sixteenth century. The book includes a chapter called 'To make hairs part smooth' which includes a recipe for 'a common depilatory'. Porta's recipe is evidence that women of this time already had a discourse available to them with which to discuss and practice the removal of body hair. Porta refers to 'the Ancients' in this chapter, which suggests he was aware of a tradition of depilation: 'The Ancients used these as Saferna, and as Varro reports and teaches in his book of Husbandry. If, says he, you would make anyone smooth from hair, cast a pale Frog into water, and boil it to a third part, and with that anoint the body.'[52] As Michael D. Parkins suggests in his paper, 'Pharmacological Practices of Ancient Egypt',[53] we may also see evidence of a knowledge of an œuvre of depilation materials in the *Papyrus Ebers*. For instance: 'It [the hair] is to be removed as follows: Carapace of a turtle, it shall be cooked, it shall be crushed, it shall be added to fat from the leg of a hippo. One shall anoint therewith, very very very frequently.'[54]

In *Seeing Through Clothes*, Anne Hollander also mentions, in passing, the work of Watteau. Donald Posner's book *The Lady at Her Toilet*,[55] discusses Watteau's painting of c. 1715, *The Morning Toilet*, in the context of other erotic images of the eighteenth century. He suggests that Watteau was influenced by popular images of pubic depilation, such as the anonymous engraving *The Intimate Toilet*,[56] which clearly shows a woman with a razor and a bowl, shaving her pubic region. Toilet scenes are a fruitful source for the pubic hair historian. They abound, particularly in what Posner refers to as popular or pornographic images. Other images of the 'intimate toilet' or what is sometimes called 'the toilet of Venus' can be found in Eduard Fuchs' *Geschichte der Erotischen Kunst*[57] and *Illustrierte Sittengeschichte*.[58]

There are a number of web-based sources of information on this topic, one of which I have already mentioned. Two others are particularly useful: They are Jerry Saltz's article 'Pudenda agenda'[59] and *Hot Pink*.[60] *Hot Pink* is an e-book, available for download from the publishers, which operates as an instruction manual in pubic depilatory practices today. For instance, the *Hot Pink* entry on merkins reads:

> You may have heard of merkins, also known as pubic wigs, which were originally used by gentry to cover baldness or blemishes that resulted from treatments for and symptoms of venereal diseases and lice . . . the Oxford English Dictionary dates the first use of the word in this sense as 1617 . . . Other definitions: In the early 1700s, it also referred to the vulva itself

Given that there are contemporary artists working with pubic hair as a material, such as Jackie Sumell and Margaret Morgan, for instance,[61] and considering the number of pubic hairstyles referenced in the *Hot Pink* book, the pubic hair historian may wish to continue to formulate her or his methodology by rethinking Slavoj Zizek:

> to reach an even more intimate domain – do we not encounter the same semiotic triangle in the three main hairstyles of the feminine sex organ's pubic hair? Wildly grown, unkempt pubic hair indexes the hippie attitude of natural spontaneity; yuppies prefer the disciplinary procedure of a French garden (one shaves the hair on both sides close to the legs, so that all that remains is a narrow band in the middle with a clear-cut shave line); in the punk attitude, the vagina is wholly shaven and furnished with rings . . . Is this not yet another version of the Levi-Straussian semiotic triangle of 'raw' wild hair, well-kept 'baked' hair and shaved 'boiled' hair?[62]

She might then go on to consider the recent trend in publications which claim to tell the history of women's genitalia or the orgasm,[63] as they too could be said to provide an existing methodology with which to work.

To conclude, I would like to return to my own versions of the Eagleton quotation that I started with:[64] 'Not all students are blind to the [need to employ a female] narcissism [by developing a greater understanding of female sexual health] while [every minute of every day, a woman dies because of complications during pregnancy and childbirth.]'; 'Not [everyone is] blind to the Western narcissism involved in [working in a hairdressers, running a shoe shop, shopping in Tesco, drinking coffee, having a bath, flushing a toilet] while half the world's population lacks adequate sanitation and survives on less than two dollars a day.'; 'Not all students are blind to the Western narcissism involved in [spending $160 billion on hair and beauty products] while half the world's population lacks adequate sanitation and survives on less than two dollars a day.';[65] 'Not all students are blind to the Western narcissism involved in [studying Jane Austen or Herrick or anything which has no practical social application] while half the world's population lacks adequate sanitation and survives on less than two dollars a day.' What if the pubic hair historian, having established their research methodologies, were to return to *After Theory* and consider their 'history of pubic hair' in the light of these reformulations? Wouldn't it then hold the possibility of becoming highly political, Marxist, radical, even? Isn't that the desire present in Terry Eagleton's *After Theory* after all?

Notes

1   Terry Eagleton, *After Theory* (New York: Basic Books and London: Allen Lane, 2003), p. 6. My bracketed insertions and italics.

2   The one exception is a piece of creative writing, in which pubic hair is mentioned but does not appear to be the main focus.

3   Terry Eagleton, *Literary Theory: An Introduction* (Oxford: Blackwell, 1983), pp. 6–7.

4   Search carried out several times from 20 March 2005 to 28 March 2005.

5   Maximillian de Gaynesford, 'Lead book review: a diehard Marxist at the crossroads: *After Theory*', *Tablet*, 29 November 2003. Retrieved from the *Tablet* website at: www.thetablet.co.uk/cgi-bin/book_review.cgi/past-00158 (accessed on 5 March 2005).

6   de Gaynesford, 'Lead book review: a diehard Marxist at the crossroads'.

7   A similar critique could be engaged in with the other examples of the trivial or ephemeral Eagleton uses. 'Eye-gouging', for instance, occurs in two of the pillars of the literary canon: Shakespeare's *King Lear* and Sophocles's *Oedipus Rex*.

8   Christina Patterson, 'Terry Eagleton: culture and society. Christina Patterson talks to Terry Eagleton about love, sex, God and the global crisis', *Independent*, 27 September 2003. Retrieved from the *Independent*'s website at: http://enjoyment.independent.co.uk/books/interviews/article88642.ece (accessed on 5 March 2005).

9   John Mullan, 'What Terry did next. John Mullan enjoys *After Theory*, the latest "text" from the high priest of theory, Terry Eagleton', *Guardian*, Saturday 29 November 2003. Retrieved from the *Guardian*'s website at: http://books.guardian.co.uk/review/story/0,,1094735,00.html (accessed on 5 March 2005).

10   Mullan, 'What Terry did next'.

11   Eagleton, *Literary Theory*.

12 Eagleton, *After Theory* (my bracketed insertions and italics).
13 de Gaynesford, 'Lead book review : a diehard Marxist at the crossroads'.
14 In my reading, perhaps 'using a search engine' could replace the television in Eagleton's example of unrigorous scholarship.
15 de Gaynesford, 'Lead book review: a diehard Marxist at the crossroads'.
16 Eagleton, *After Theory* (my bracketed insertions and italics).
17 A map of Sheela Na Gig finds was retrieved from: www.sheelanagig.org (on 20 November 2005).
18 'Women and health.' Retrieved from: www.un.org/womenwatch/daw/followup/session/presskit/fs3.htm (accessed on 20 November 2005). Captioned: 'This fact sheet is based on "Review and Appraisal of the Implementation of the Beijing Platform for Action: Report of the Secretary-General. (E/CN.6/2000/PC/2). Published by the United Nations Department of Public Information DPI/2035/C. May 2000."'
19 This is an idea which is taken up by Rashmi Sharma in an article in the Indian *Tribune* in a 1998 special edition on women. Rashmi Sharma. 'Educating a woman means educating a family', *Tribune*, Chandigarh, India, 19 June 1998. Retrieved from the *Tribune*, Online Edition at: www.tribuneindia.com (accessed on 20 November 2005).
20 See, for instance: Hélène Cixous, 'The laugh of the Medusa', *Signs*, 1:4 (1975), 875–93. See also the reprint in Robyn R. Warhol and Diane Price Herndl (eds), *Feminisms: an Anthology of Literary Theory and Criticism* (New Brunswick, New Jersey: Rutgers University Press and Basingstoke: Macmillan, 1991), pp. 347–62.
21 David Beer, 'Before a return to metatheory: Eagleton's *After Theory*', *Graduate Journal of Social Science*, 1:2 (November 2004), retrieved from: www.gjss.org/documents/journal_issue_2/8.pdf (accessed on 5 March 2005).
22 Beer, 'Before a return to metatheory'.
23 Beer, 'Before a return to metatheory'.
24 Cixous, 'The laugh of the Medusa'.
25 Eve Kosofsky Sedgwick, 'Jane Austen and the masturbating girl', in Eve Kosofsky Sedgwick, *Tendencies* (Durham: Duke University Press 1993; London: Routledge 1994), pp. 109–29, p. 109.
26 Gananath Obeyesekere, *Medusa's Hair: an Essay on Personal Symbols and Religious Experience* (Chicago: University of Chicago Press, 1984).
27 Obeyesekere, *Medusa's Hair*.
28 For further discussion of hair as trivial or monstrous, see Chapter 1 of this volume.
29 Cixous, 'The laugh of the Medusa', pp. 347–62.
30 Robert Coover, 'The end of books', *New York Times* (21 June 1992). Retrieved from the *New York Times* website at: http://partners.nytimes.com/books/98/09/27/specials/coover-end.html (accessed on 21 October 2005).
31 As Caroline Cox demonstrates so well in *Good Hair Days* (London: Quartet Books, 1999), hair is a site of market forces at play.
32 Joanna Blythman, *Shopped: The Shocking Power of British Supermarkets* (London: Fourth Estate, 2004).
33 Judi Bevan, *Trolley Wars: the Battle of the Supermarkets* (London: Profile, 2005).

34 Felicity Lawrence, *Not on the Label: What Really Goes into the Food on Your Plate* (London: Penguin, 2004).

35 Ysanne Spevack, *Ten Top Natural Beauty Products*, retrieved from the Organic Food website at: www.organicfood.co.uk/lifestyle/bathingbeauties.html (accessed on 5 March 2005).

36 Eagleton quote reformulated to include Spevack, *Ten Top Natural Beauty Products*.

37 Julian Robinson, *The Quest for Human Beauty: An Illustrated History* (New York: W. W. Norton & Co., 1998).

38 Julian Robinson, *Body Packaging: A Guide to Human Sexual Display* (Los Angeles: Elysium Growth Press, 1988).

39 Anne Hollander, *Seeing Through Clothes* (Berkeley: University of California Press, 1993), p. 137.

40 Hollander, *Seeing Through Clothes*, pp. 137–8.

41 Johannes Endres, 'Diderot, Hogarth and the aesthetics of depilation', *Eighteenth Century Studies*, 38: 1 (2004), 17–38.

42 Endres, 'Diderot, Hogarth', 17.

43 Jonathan Gil Harris, 'Shakespeare's hair: staging the object of material culture', *Shakespeare Quarterly*, 52: 4 (Winter 2001), 479–91, 479.

44 Coover, 'The end of books'.

45 Martin F. Kilmer, 'Genital phobia and depilation', *Journal of Hellenic Studies*, 102 (1982), 104–12.

46 See: Aristophanes, *The Birds, Lysistrata and The Assembly Women and Wealth*, Oxford World's Classics, trans. Stephen Halliwell (Oxford: Oxford University Press, 1997).

47 Aristophanes, *Lysistrata*, in Aristophanes, *Plays*, vol. 1, Classical Greek Dramatists series, trans. Kenneth McLeish (London: Methuen, 1993), pp. 151–5, p. 202.

48 Information was retrieved from The Lysistrata Project website: www.lysistrataproject.org (accessed in May 2005).

49 Lyndal Roper, *Oedipus and the Devil: Witchcraft, Sexuality and Religion in Early Modern Europe* (London: Routledge, 1994), p. 188.

50 Roper, *Oedipus and the Devil*, p. 189.

51 'The history of depilation', retrieved from 'The world of the nudest nudist: the classical beauty of the smooth hairless body' website at: www.wnn.nu/UK/History/historyhair.html (accessed in May 2005). Captioned: 'Courtesy of "Helios", a former Dutch naturist magazine: the new trend: away with pubic hair!'.

52 John Baptista Porta (Giambattista della Porta 1537–1615), Chapter IV: 'To make hairs part smooth' in John Baptista Porta, *The Ninth Book of Natural Magick: How to Adorn Women, and Make them Beautiful*. Retrieved from: 'The works and life of John Baptista Porta' web pages at: http://homepages.tscnet.com/omard1/jportac9.html#bk9IV (accessed on 20 March 2005).

53 Michael D. Parkins, 'Pharmacological practices of Ancient Egypt', in W. A. Whitelaw (ed.), *The Proceedings of the 10th Annual History of Medicine Days*, March 2001. Retrieved from the University of Calgary website at: www.hom.ucalgary.ca/Dayspapers2001.pdf (accessed on 2 May 2004).

54 *Papyrus Ebers*, 476. Please note: this extract from the *Papyrus Ebers* was retrieved from: http://nefertiti.iwebland.com/index.html (accessed in May 2004), a website set up by Egyptologist André Dollinger. See: Anon., *The Papyrus Ebers, the Greatest Egyptian Medical Document*, trans. B. Ebbell (Copenhagen: Levin & Munksgaard and London: Oxford University Press, 1937).

55 Donald Posner, *Watteau: A Lady at Her Toilet* (London: A. Lane, 1973).

56 This eighteenth-century engraving appears in Posner, *Watteau: A Lady at Her Toilet*, p. 42.

57 Eduard Fuchs, *Geschichte der Erotischen Kunst* (Munich: Albert Langen, 1912).

58 Eduard Fuchs, *Illustrierte Sittengeschichte* (Munich: Albert Langen, 1909). I am indebted to Anne Hollander for referring me to Posner and Fuchs.

59 Jerry Saltz, 'Pudenda agenda', captioned 'Jerry Saltz is art critic for the *Village Voice*, where this review first appeared.' Retrieved from the Artnet website at: www.artnet.com/Magazine/features/saltz/saltz4–10–02.asp (accessed on 20 March 2005).

60 Deborah Driggs and Karen Risch, *Hot Pink: the Girls' Guide to Primping, Passion, and Pubic Fashion*, was downloaded from: www.hotpinkbook.com (in March 2005).

61 Margaret Morgan's 'Freud's beard' was retrieved from her website at: www.margaretmorgan.com/other/freud.html (accessed on 20 November 2005). Fiona Morgan's article on the artist Jackie Sumell 'Bush's pubic enemy No. 1: a feminist art student launches a hair-raising protest' was retrieved from the Salon web pages at: http://dir.salon.com/politics/feature/2001/03/28/bush/index.html (accessed on 5 March 2005).

62 Slavoj Zizek, *The Plague of Fantasies* (London: Verso, 1997), pp. 5–6.

63 For instance: Natalie Angier, *Woman: An Intimate Geography* (London: Virago Press, 1999); Natalie Angier, 'In the history of gynecology, a surprising chapter', *New York Times*, 23 February 1999, retrieved from the Ishi Press website at: www.ishipress.com/vibrator.htm (accessed in May 2005); Jelto Drenth, *The Origin of the World: Science and Fiction of the Vagina* (London: Reaktion Books, 2004); Carol Livoti and Elizabeth Topp, *Vaginas: an Owner's Manual* (London: Fusion Press, 2005); Rachel P. Maines, *The Technology of Orgasm: 'Hysteria', the Vibrator, and Women's Sexual Satisfaction* (Baltimore: Johns Hopkins University Press, 1998); Jonathan Margolis, *'O': The Intimate History of the Orgasm* (London: Arrow, 2004).

64 Several versions of the Eagleton quotation with my bracketed insertions and italics.

65 Eagleton quote reformulated to include Spevack, *Ten Top Natural Beauty Products*.

4 Hairs on the lens: female body hair on the screen[1]

Alice Macdonald

> Fain would I kiss my Julia's dainty leg,
> which is white and hair-less as an egge.
> (Robert Herrick, 1648, 'Her legs')

Flying to Chicago a few years ago, I realised, from the sound of predominantly female laughter, that the in-flight movie *What Women Want*[2] was being particularly well received by the women passengers. Early in this romantic comedy, marketing executive Nick Marshall (Mel Gibson) investigates women's consumer needs by experimenting with some feminine products himself, and the scene that was causing the most female glee involved him wrestling with the pain and paraphernalia of waxing his legs. The hilarity seemed, however, to be tempered with a knowingness – a rueful acknowledgement that the joke was as much on us, as women, as against Mel Gibson's character. For so deeply entrenched is the picture of smooth and hairless legs a part of Western femininity that it is likely that most of the women on that plane would have been in the habit of removing some or all of their body hair[3] by a variety of methods, however painful or tedious. Even some radical feminists find this convention hard to resist,[4] for the recurring images of shapely depilated legs that come at us from the visual media have so conditioned our minds' eye that even if we hold contradictory convictions,[5] the majority of Western women only feel acceptable to themselves and to society if their bodies are largely hair-free.

The cinema is particularly responsible for the confirmation and perpetuation of this convention of femininity. Indeed, the camera's sweeping gaze as it runs up the length of a starlet's smooth bared leg – from ankle to thigh – has become such a Hollywood cliché[6] that for male characters in drag roles, hair-free legs as much as the addition of buxom breasts are primary requisites for gender transformation. In *Some Like It Hot*[7] the first sight we get of Jack Lemmon and Tony Curtis, metamorphosed into Daphne and Geraldine, is a close-up of their hairless and stockinged legs as they struggle unsafely up the railway platform on their high heels. In *Tootsie*,[8] part of the elaborate preparations we see, as Michael Dorsey (Dustin Hoffman) transforms himself into Dorothy Michaels, includes shaving his legs in the bath. In such films, just as in *What Women Want*, the camera is not coy about showing body hair: we are even given a close-up of the painful plucking of Dorsey's eyebrows. But this is only because it is male body hair that is being removed and it is set in the redemptive space of comedy where the transvestite characters have already been safely established as heterosexual men. On the other hand, in action films like *GI Jane*,[9] *Alien*,[10] *Aliens*[11] and *Terminator 2*,[12] where the female protagonists' muscular bodies and 'masculine' determination could be interpreted by male culture as threateningly transgressive, the camera focuses on compensatory female signifiers such as breasts (Demi Moore in *GI Jane*); vulnerability (Sigourney Weaver in the final scene of *Alien*) or maternal status (Sigourney Weaver as Ripley in *Aliens* and Linda Hamilton as Sarah Connor in *Terminator 2*) and these 'musculinised'[13] stars also subscribe to the 'hairless ideal'. Even Private Vasquez in *Aliens*, the only other female crew member, whose pumped-up physique and close-cropped hair prompt a male colleague to ask if she has ever been mistaken for a man, reveals hairless armpits as she does pull-ups in front of the camera.

For the screen, the actual visualisation of female body hair is deemed too taboo to show. In *Bridget Jones's Diary*[14] we see Bridget (Renée Zellweger) using a pink razor to shave already smooth and shiny legs in the bath as she prepares for a 'hot date'. Similarly, in an episode of the American sitcom *Friends*, in which Phoebe (Lisa Kudrow) and her flatmate [room-mate] Monica (Courteney Cox) decide to wax their (presumably hairy) legs, we are never actually shown legs covered with hair. Instead, the wax is applied to already depilated skin, thus making a nonsense of the screams of pain when it is ripped off.

This effacement of female body hair and the resultant idealised image of the silky-smooth body of the Hollywood goddess, have become an aspirational ideal for many of the women in cinema audiences,[15] while the reverse – when female body hair is shown on a female character – is usually used to register something negative. Examples include the butch, sadistic Agatha Trunchbull (Pam Ferris), the moustachioed headmistress in the film version of Roald Dahl's *Matilda*,[16] or the batty Mrs Doyle (Pauline McLynn), who is the bewhiskered housekeeper in the British television series *Father Ted*.[17] For from folklore and myth comes a tradition that links female body hair with evil and danger: with promiscuity and lust because hairiness is associated with the devil or an animal nature; with ugliness through its association with hirsute hags and witches; with deviant sexuality from the supposed lesbianism of witches; with insanity, with unkempt hair being a sign of mental instability; and with the threat of castration linked to the Medusa and the 'vagina dentata'.

Such cultural associations are useful to film-makers, who can exploit them and the spectators' abilities to 'read the body'. Visual aspects, such as hair and skin colour, are used to categorise people, so that in film a character's appearance is part of the developments of the narrative. Perhaps

because of its malleability, hair, both on the head and on the body, is a particularly useful vehicle for cultural signification for the film-maker. For, as
Kobena Mercer has pointed out, the human practice of working upon
hair – the cutting, grooming, dressing or concealing of it – 'socialize[s] hair,
making it the medium of significant "statements" about self and society'.[18]

In the following pages, I will explore how film makes use of the two
extremes of female body hair – the idealised hairless female form and the
vilified hairy one. I will begin by outlining the normalisation of female
depilation by looking at the cultural and symbolic meanings that are
attached to body hair, and then the artistic heritage from which the 'hairless ideal' has sprung and which film perpetuates. Next, I will examine
how female body hair is employed as a negative signifier in two screen texts
based on the novel *The Life and Loves of a She Devil*, written by the feminist author Fay Weldon. Finally, I will conclude by discussing the viabil-
ity of presenting female body hair on the screen in a positive way.

Hair dos and don'ts[19]: the cultural meanings of female body hair

Traditionally, men and women have chosen hairstyles that reflect the larger
cultural concepts of masculinity and femininity. Similarly, any physiological differences in the hair growth and distribution pattern between male
and female bodies have been exaggerated to make the contrast between the
sexes even more legible. Although some men adhere to a hairless norm –
men who display their bared bodies regularly like dancers, body-builders
and action-hero film stars – it is women as a whole who bear the brunt of
compulsory hairlessness. This cultural norm may be explained by the three
functions which the hairless female body seems to serve: '(a) it exaggerates
the differences between women and men, (b) it equates female attractiveness with youth'[20] and (c) it connotes the 'to-be-looked-at-ness' of a body.

In a television programme in which comedian Ruby Wax visited *The
Jerry Springer Show*, she was seen talking to a woman in the audience who
bore a strong growth of dark hair on her upper lip. While Ruby chatted to
this woman in a chummy fashion, she ended her conversation by turning
to the camera and referring to her companion as 'whatever you are' – a
cheap jibe which raised a laugh but which also expressed the gender
anxiety upon which patriarchal order relies. In societies where it is cus-
tomary to conceal genitals beneath clothing, it is through secondary sex
characteristics – hair distribution, tone of voice and body outline – that
gender is signified. Since physique and voice are more difficult to change,
it is not surprising that a more pliant resource like hair is used to exagger-
ate any perceived differences between the sexes. Neither is it surprising in
a male-dominated society that it is to the female that the onus of underlining this demarcation falls. Thus it is women who are required to keep their
bodies as hairless as a child's and therefore as different from a grown male's

as possible. Indeed many rituals involving depilation of body and/or head hair are part of female initiation rites which mark the girl child's passage into womanhood.

It is probably in the area of facial hair, however, that the social need to establish sexual difference is most insistent, and although most Western men are clean-shaven, the hairless norms apply most severely here to women, for whom an untended growth of facial hair is seen as seriously transgressive. For, even more than hair elsewhere on the body, the symbolic meanings attached to female facial hair are all strongly negative.

This cultural hostility to 'superfluous' female hair can perhaps be understood in terms of Mary Douglas's theory of pollution and Julia Kristeva's concept of abjection. Douglas argues that societies impose meaning on their world by ordering and organising things into classification systems, where it is only by exaggerating the difference between these classes that a semblance of order is created – a notion which fits nicely with the cultural imperative of the artificially 'hairless' female body which confirms, in opposition, the masculinity of the male as hairy. However, since cultures need things to stay in their appointed place, Douglas argues, this notion can also give rise to negative feelings when either things turn up in the wrong category or fail to fit a category tidily. Thus a woman with hair growing in an area socially deemed male – like the chin, or the upper lip – will be seen as failing to fit gender expectations and will be regarded as transgressing one of society's 'cherished classifications'. These women are treated with social disapproval, since the failure to remove the offending hair – the 'matter out of place' – will be seen as a sign that she wishes to destabilise society itself.

Douglas's pollution theory would not define the facial hair itself as necessarily 'dirty', but would see the refusal to remove it from the face as a deviant act, since 'dirt is essentially disorder'.[21] L. S. Kubie, on the other hand, using a psychoanalytical approach, would define hair as dirt – for he defines '"dirt" as being anything which either symbolically or in reality emerges from the body'[22] – hence *clean* shaven. Kubie's definition leads neatly on to Julia Kristeva and her theory of abjection. For Kristeva, the concept of the abject body refers to the pre-Oedipal infant's struggle to separate from the mother's nurturing body and thus create an independent identity. The infant's expulsion or 'abjection' of the maternal body creates a border between inside and outside itself, and is expressed in reactions of disgust to body excretions (matter expelled from the body's insides). Such fear and loathing arise because these expulsions expose the fragility of the constituted border which constantly threatens to dissolve and re-engulf the subject. Writing about body shape, Bordo makes a similar point, which applies equally to 'superfluous hair', when she describes how in contemporary horror movies and werewolf films like *The Howling*,[23] *A Teen-Age Werewolf in London*[24] and *Alien*,[25] the images of 'bodily eruption [. . .]

[in which] a new alien, libidinous, and uncontrollable self literally bursts through the seams of the victim's old flesh', function symbolically as 'metaphors for anxiety about internal processes out of control'.[26]

The flip-side of Kristeva's 'abject' is that bodily excretions are not treated universally and instinctively with revulsion. Tears, semen and breast milk, for example, are often revered and valued. Kristeva's theory offers an inviting explanation for the 'adult/learned' fear of the female/maternal body, and for this reason is especially useful to my argument. For the concept of the abject can be used to include the argument that hair – since it can be seen as growing from within bodies and appearing on the outside – can also be regarded as bodily excreta, which provides one account of the fears that it may evoke. For, viewed in this way, the appearance of hair on a body surface can both constitute the animal within, which constantly threatens to overwhelm the human, and, in gender terms, may trigger anxiety about sexual identity. A woman who grows body hair in places that culture tells her are for male hair only, like the chest or the chin, might fear that she must really be a man underneath.

The hairless female body also functions as a measure of feminine attractiveness, both through its association with youth and its connotations with display – its to-be-looked-at-ness; qualities that are especially exploited in film. The prepubescent aesthetic of the hairless body, along with that other feminine ideal: a slim body shape, associate women with youth and diminish women's adult sexual status. This is interesting, since a large proportion of ethnographic evidence about head hair equates control of hair – its cutting, shaving, braiding or binding – with restrained sexuality. This connection seems equally applicable to the 'desirable' female body from which body hair has been removed – an erotic mix of sensual display and sexual control.

The 'hairless ideal' also functions as a measure of obedience to norms of femininity. Naomi Wolf suggests that part of society's response to the Second Wave and the gains that feminism has achieved for Western women has resulted in a beauty backlash which has more to do with women being forced to conform to 'desirable' behaviour than a desirable appearance.[27] The pressure to obey is evident both in the aspirational role models that appear all around us in the media and on the screen, and from the reverse: in the lessons that we learn from films in which female characters with visible body hair are generally cast in the negative – investigated and narratively punished.

The artistic heritage of 'the hairless ideal'

The hairless ideal that we see on the screen today is a legacy of artistic and cultural traditions which stretch right back to the ancient worlds.[28] Portraits which show the heightened hairline of Elizabeth I and Leonardo's eyebrowless *Mona Lisa*, tweezers and razors from ancient Egypt, and painted red vases from ancient Greece which show fully and partially depilated women, suggest that they have complied with Ovid's injunction in 2 BC to women to ensure: 'that no rude goat find his way beneath your arms, and that your legs be not rough with bristling hair!'.[29] The smooth marble bodies of Greek sculpture – whether hairless because of artistic censure or because they reflected the social custom of depilation – have over the centuries structured the cultural imagination in such a way as to make the glabrous female body an entrenched and irresistible feminine aesthetic. In such sculptures, male nudes may present hairless chests like contemporary body-builders, but they do also display body hair – usually in the form of hyacinth-like pubic curls. Female nudes, however, show no hair in the axillary or pubic areas. The art historian Nanette Salomon uses a comparison of two fourth-century Greek sculptures – one of a male nude, *Hermes with the Infant Dionysus* and one of a female nude *Knidian Aphrodite* – to further illustrate the asymmetrical terms of male/female nudity, and to mark the point at which woman began to be sexually defined by her pubis. A heroic figure, Hermes stands with both arms outstretched: in one he holds the baby Dionysus, revealing his naked body parts in a manner that does not mark out his pubic hair and sexual organs any more particularly than his foot or his nose. Contrastingly, the *Aphrodite* is posed with her right hand placed protectively in front of her pubis, in a way that codes her sexually. As Salomon suggests:

> the hand that points also covers and that which covers also points. We are, in either case, directed to her pubis, which we are not permitted to see. Woman, thus fashioned is reduced to her sexuality.[30]

Of course what is especially significant here is that the hand that covers/points also draws attention to a pudenda that is hairless.

As this traditional pose – known as the Venus pudica – expanded throughout the Western artistic tradition, so the image of female sexual vulnerability and desirability became intensified when presented as a reclining figure. In Titian's *Venus of Urbino*, the unclothed female is presented lying recumbent on a rumpled couch, her hand again covering/pointing to her pubis. Although her armpit is concealed by tendrils of her head hair and her hand all but covers her pubis, the marble-like texture of her nude body – so reminiscent of ancient sculptures – suggests that her body is hairless and that the darkness that can be seen between her legs is shadow rather than body hair. The sexual significance of hair is, however, not lost to the image, but is instead displaced on to the fur of the sleeping dog that lies curled on the couch by her feet. This narrative addition brings to the painting both nuances of animal sexuality and the sensual and tactile qualities associated with soft hair or fur which can then be safely projected on to the idealised and hairless Venus.

This strategy of displacement is common in film when it is necessary to present the 'hairless ideal' without losing the sensuality of a female sexuality of a more animal and fetishistic nature. The fur and feathers which trim the scanty costumes of a Hollywood chorus line stand for an animal eroticism which can be seen as displaced from legs encased in opaque tights and armpits which are always hairless. Similarly, the fur-trimmed coat and the feathered costume worn by Marlene Dietrich in *Blonde Venus*[31] and *Shanghai Express*;[32] the fur-trimmed travelling outfit worn by Margaret Lockwood's leading character in *The Wicked Lady*;[33] and the fur stole which Rita Hayworth wore slung over her naked shoulder in *Gilda*,[34] all convey a sense of dangerous and available sexuality. In *Gilda*, the fur against Rita's bare skin is especially erotic – both because of its sensory quality and because it evokes the transgressive image of the prostitute naked beneath the fur coat.

Conversely, when body hair is represented on a naked woman, it is usually used to signify something derogatory. As Anthea Callen has pointed out, Edgar Degas, though more popularly remembered for his charming pastels of ballet dancers, does this in his much less sympathetic paintings of prostitutes. By depicting naked women, with their legs splayed wide open at a time when there was an absence of genitalia in high art, and by suggesting a notion of the 'simian' in their facial features, he seems to be drawing a deliberate connection between their body hair and their 'deviant' lifestyles, as well as linking sexual appetite and virility in women to a degenerative femininity.[35]

'Hair'em scare'em':[36] the semiotics of body hair in *The Life and Loves of a She-Devil*

The 1986 BBC television series entitled *The Life and Loves of a She-Devil*[37] and the 1989 Hollywood film, *She-Devil*,[38] based on Fay Weldon's novel, both make use of female body hair as a negative signifier, and as such offer an almost unique opportunity to analyse this taboo phenomenon in the context of mainstream popular entertainment outside the horror genre. Perhaps as a reflection of differing cultural attitudes, while the British adaptation uses a deliberate and well-developed semiotic strategy that associates the growing negative aspects of Ruth's nature with her facial hair, the American film seems rather more squeamish and deploys comedy to cope with the 'hirsutism', focusing more on her facial moles as the signs of her deviance. With this in mind, it is interesting to note that when *She-Devil* was released, despite having well-known actors such as Meryl Streep and Roseanne Barr to play the leads, it was generally panned by the American press, who instead recommended the repeat showing of the BBC's television 'mini-series' which had been broadcast previously.

Weldon's picaresque narrative follows the progress of Ruth, a 'devoted-yet-dowdy'[39] wife and mother who is transformed into a 'she devil' when she discovers that her husband, Bobbo, is having an affair with the successful romantic novelist, Mary Fisher. While Mary is petite, feminine and classically beautiful and lives in a fairytale tower by the sea, Ruth is 6ft 2 inches, 15 stone, with moles and facial hair, and lives in the suburbs in a house that seems too small for her bulk. The narrative is driven by Ruth's need for revenge and her covetous desire to acquire for herself all that is Mary's: love, looks, wealth, power, the High Tower and, of course, Bobbo. Her plan – which involves assuming a variety of disguises – is successful, for by the end Ruth has amassed a fortune, and has bought and restored the Tower, where she now lives with a lover as an emasculated Bobbo is forced to look on. Following drastic cosmetic surgery she now even looks like Mary.

She-Devil: a black comedy

Unlike the television version, the physical unattractiveness of Ruth (Roseanne Barr) in the film *She-Devil* is not initially registered by her facial hair but by a brown mole on her upper lip. Her large, womanly body is exaggerated by the multi-reflections in the fitting room's mirrors where she is first shown struggling to zip herself into a dress that is several sizes too small. The trying-on session is a mixture of comedy and pathos, eliciting sympathy and setting the tone of the narrative. It is not until Ruth has burned down the family home, left her children with their father and his mistress, and is working as a care-assistant in an old-people's home, that we see her with a growth of dark hair on her upper lip. While an earlier shot of Ruth using a 'ladies' (pink) razor' has established her need to shave, the appearance now of a 'moustache' suggests either that she has merely ceased to care, or that she is deliberately and confrontationally rejecting feminine norms of appearance. Certainly her severe white uniform – together with her hair, which is pulled back in an unbecoming style – and her lack of make-up, complete a deliberately unprepossessing picture.[40] However, it is an image of plainness and severity but not necessarily one of threat. For not only does Barr bring her comic maternal persona from the TV sitcom *Roseanne* to the part of Ruth, but it soon becomes clear that this hirsute guise is a device merely to register Ruth as 'other' – 'one of the women that society has thrown away', as she says, and whom the employment agency that she sets up will seek to help, rather than a sign that she wishes to disrupt society generally. Her appearance also links her to another 'other' – Nurse Hooper, whose shortness marks her out to be as much of a 'freak' as Ruth. Again, this duo is not represented as threatening, but as amusing and as reminiscent of comedians from early cinema, like the large Oliver Hardy and the small Stan Laurel. In the kitchen scene where they first become allies, the sight of Ruth cramming a cream éclair into her mouth and the exaggerated relish that Nurse Hooper displays evoke a music-hall turn, especially as Hooper's nurse's cap – perched idiotically on the top of her head – makes her look even more like the diminutive Stanley. Similarly when they set about painting a room: the trouble that they have positioning the ladder; their men's overalls and caps worn back to front; the Keystone Cops-type soundtrack and the increased film speed, is a quotation from the silent movies – especially obvious when one remembers that the fat Oliver Hardy was the one with the moustache. As well as negotiating Ruth's facial hair through comedy, the film also diminishes any anxiety by quickly returning Ruth to conventional feminine appearance. By the time that she and Hooper are distributing fliers for their new agency, they are both shown wearing smart business suits, wearing make-up and feminine hairstyles, and Ruth's upper lip is free from hair. By the end of the film her mole has gone too, thus reassuring us that *She-Devil* is merely a black comedy (with the emphasis on the comedy).

The Life and Loves of a She-Devil: 'a comic turn, turned serious'

On the other hand, the *mise-en-scène* of the television version deliberately appropriates and builds on anxieties around female body hair and uses techniques of *film noir*: disorientating editing, giving the impression that Ruth can be in two places at once, and the paranoid tone of her voice-over establish the She Devil as an extremely dangerous *femme fatale*.

The narrative is also disrupted by shifts in direction, so that having been encouraged to identify with and be sympathetic to Ruth in the opening scenes, by the end she is callous and evil: the final episodes can be seen as constituting a betrayal or trick in terms of the earlier characterisation. The change in direction has important ramifications for the semiotic meanings attached to Ruth's physical presentation, as it implies that her facial hair, which may originally have elicited pity, comes to allude to a range of 'sexual perversions': bestiality; lesbianism; transvestism; transsexuality and sado-masochism. Along with the editing style, the special effects, the chiaroscuric lighting and the sinister soundtrack – which associate Ruth with witches, devilry and the occult – this raises notions of extreme deviance, danger and the forbidden.

Facial hair as signifier of the 'freak'

Initially, however, Ruth is established as 'the good mother' and the downtrodden wife for whom we are encouraged to feel compassion. We first meet her and her rival at an office party, where her husband Bobbo (Denis Waterman) is entertaining clients. Mary Fisher (Patricia Hodge) arrives in her white Rolls Royce clad in a gleaming evening dress which clings to her feminine figure, displaying a fragile and glamorous beauty which evokes the 'perfect product' – the immaculately groomed stars of classical Hollywood cinema. It is not until Mary and Bobbo are locked in a lover-like conversation that we are introduced to Ruth (Julie T. Wallace), who, as Bobbo's conscientious wife, is offering drinks around. She towers over them – her height exaggerated because she is standing and they are sitting on a low settee. Dressed frumpily in a dull dress of muddy green, ill at ease in her heels which make her even taller, her agitation causes her to spill the tray of drinks over her husband's immaculate guest. Duly chastised by Bobbo, Ruth retreats to a table behind them, finding solace in a bowl of crisps. A close-up of her face reveals that she bears a mole and the suggestion of a moustache on her upper lip which, like her long and unbecoming hair, is dark. Mary, in contrast, is all lightness – white sparkly dress, white coat, white car – a visual purity which is reflected by her name and its virginal association. At the end of the party, as Mary leaves wrapped in an expensive full-length fluffy mink coat which matches her hair, she makes Ruth in her old brown squirrel jacket look dowdier than ever.

Despite devoting time to her appearance, Ruth fails to win Bobbo back. And, following a disastrous dinner party, he abandons her and the children and moves in with Mary, not before telling Ruth: 'I don't think you are a woman at all. I think that what you are is a she devil'.[41]

Body hair as signifier of the 'beast within'

One reason that the dinner party starts off so badly is Ruth's discovery of dog hairs in the soup. This introduces two important themes in Ruth's representation: an analogy between her and animals because of her hairiness, and the concept of pollution that Mary Douglas formulates. In this case, the 'matter out of place' – the dog's hairs in the soup tureen – allude to the 'masculine' hairs on Ruth's face which transgress the conventions of gender and female sexuality. Other animal references are attached to Ruth, both in the novel and the serial, where she is described variously as a dog and a 'guinea-pig'.[42] Mary's dogs sense an affinity with Ruth, an affinity which is suspect in its hints of bestiality: 'The Dobermans panted after her. She exuded some new scent: of triumph, freedom and fear, all mixed. They found it heady. Their noses ruffled up under her sage-green smock'.[43] Such animal attention is a device commonly used in horror films to hint that a human character is really a werewolf in disguise: for example, the policeman's pet dog in *American Werewolf in Paris*.[44] The relationships that Ruth has with the furry family pets – the cocker spaniel, the cat and the guinea-pig – are also significant because they replicate her relationship with Bobbo and Mary in a way that both alludes to the limited domestication of her life, as well as hinting at the animalism which her facial hair suggests. Ruth likens herself to the guinea-pig, which in the novel is called Richard, linking them both through their shared initials and through the allusion to a powerless animal with a lion's heart. She dislikes this pet, with its whiskery face, the most: 'Its shoulders were too hunched and its eyes too deep. It reminded her of herself',[45] and perhaps, because of its caged activity exercising all day on a treadmill, draws a parallel with herself: the constricting space of the house and the walled garden, and the circulating routines of housework and motherhood.

Ruth is not alone in being associated with animals. Just as both she and Mary are shown wearing contrasting fur coats in the opening scenes, so Mary too is likened to an animal later in the narrative – but one whose fur is admired and stroked. She is associated with the pedigree spaniel Hannah, and so is not marked as being negatively hairy but glossy and beautiful. For, as the novel tells us, Mary has 'smooth little legs' [and is] 'shiny-calved, shiny-thighed'.[46] In other words, she is the epitome of the 'hairless ideal', and her animal sensuality is displaced on to the fur coats that she wears and the pure-bred dog she is associated with.

Unreal hair/wigs as signifier of sexual deviance
Having dumped her homeless children with Bobbo and his mistress, the second episode opens with Ruth transformed into Raunchy Rita, a tarty bimbo with false eyelashes, heavy make-up and plunging neckline. It is in this episode that the connection between wigs and 'superficial hair' is made. Following an outburst of tears – the last occasion that we see Ruth display any sign of human weakness – she wrenches off a wig to reveal her own hair underneath. The long red wig, itself an acknowledgement to the star (Rita Hayworth) whose name she has borrowed, and the gesture, which replicates Jack Lemmon's action in the closing moments of *Some Like It Hot*, alludes to artifice and gender transgression. For the removal of the wig recalls the now-defunct legal requirement at the end of any drag act to remove all wigs, thus disclosing the sex of the players. Again, as in Mary Douglas's theory of pollution, the wigs can be seen as 'matter out of place', because although they represent a female head of hair, they are unreal, and even upon a female head they suggest the 'deviance' of transsexuality and transvestism. Indeed, in many of Ruth's feminine disguises – as Vista Rose in white trilby and caped overcoat, for example – Ruth's bulky body and solid features make her look like a man in drag, for instance like Robin Williams in *Mrs Doubtfire*.[47] For this reason, the series of wigs that Ruth wears should be viewed alongside her facial hair, because they express the same form of deviance, but are used at times when a dark and hairy upper lip would be inappropriate to her disguise.

Facial hair as signifier of sado-masochism – the 'vagina dentata'
When Ruth goes to work for the judge who will decide on her husband Bobbo's fate when he comes to court on a trumped-up charge of embezzlement, the camera focuses on her moustache and the dental work she is having done which leaves her with gaping holes in her gums, or teeth ground down to the bone. In a particularly suggestive scene in which she and the judge sit by a roaring log fire, there are intimations of burning in

hell as he pokes a large, fat, finger into her mouth with its fringe of facial hair and blooded teeth, thus evoking the threatening image of a vagina dentata. Indeed, the judge has a penchant for sado-masochistic sex and, by being his ever-willing victim, Ruth ensures that Bobbo gets a longer sentence.

Notions of 'transgressive' desire are also expressed in the image of pubic hair, shown on the plaster model that the surgeons are working from in the final stage of Ruth's surgical transformation at a Californian clinic.[48] During this scene, the surgeon asks Ruth if she would like him to tighten her vagina and draw back the clitoris to heighten her sexual response: a request which disgusts the attendant female nurse. The nurse's censure, the overt reference to sexual pleasure, and the display of prominent pubic/sexual hair suggest a correlation between deviance and female sexuality reminiscent of Degas's prostitutes.

By the final episode, the drastic and agonising surgical regime has completely transformed Ruth into Mary's look-alike. This is a disconcerting image, as Ruth at her most 'feminine' is also at her most 'grotesque'. Her cosmetic rebirth furthermore makes a feminist reading problematic, for although it may be read as suggesting that all femininity is socially constructed through Ruth's 'excessive' and 'created' femininity, it does so by tapping into cultural fears regarding 'unruly' women and female body hair in a way that both exceeds Weldon's possible intentions,[49] and contradicts it. For, by marking facial hair as deviance and therefore as something that ought to be removed, it conversely supports the principle of cosmetic modification at the same time that it seems to be critiquing it. Thus, a novel which was written by a feminist woman, about women, stated to be for women readers,[50] becomes instead a text which can be read as confirming patriarchal constructions of, and prejudices against, women.

The viability of representing female body hair as a positive signifier

However well intentioned, any image which wishes to challenge mainstream representations is open to different readings, and any representation of female body hair on the screen runs the danger of at best being marginalised or used as a 'freak show' attraction: 'that most Wonderful Phenomenon of Nature, women with whiskers'.[51] One example of this is the female character, Serefine, who is transformed into a werewolf in *American Werewolf in Paris*.[52] Even when, as with Weldon, the author is sympathetic to the position of women, the opportunity to represent female body hair positively can prove too difficult for mainstream media. Another example of this is in the case of the film *The Company of Wolves*,[53] which is based on a short story by Angela Carter. This is a retelling of the fairy-tale of 'Little Red Riding Hood', and offers an opportunity to present female body hair as positive in the character of the wolf girl. Despite having the feminist Carter as both the author of the original and the co-writer of the film script, the film succumbs to commercial pressure and avoids being controversial by focusing instead on the 'animatronics' which show a 'literal' transformation of the man, *not the girl*, into a wolf.

Such capitulation might indicate that the portrayal of female body hair is not viable in mainstream cinema. However, *The Company of Wolves*, like the television serial of *The Life and Loves of a She-Devil*, are products of the 1980s, and more recently a few images of female body hair have begun to appear in the media, although they are often exploited for eye-catching properties and a consequent ability to sell. Like the comic greetings card with the strap-line 'Bad Hair Day', which shows a cartoon woman with heavy axillary and pubic hair sprouting from her underwear, these images are often negotiated through comedy or are deliberately appropriated for a presumed ability to shock through their hints of the pathological. Examples include the cover picture of the photographer Della Grace, entitled 'The bearded lady',[54] which focused on her facial hair, or the advance publicity for the biopic of the artist Frida Kahlo.[55] Kahlo's facial hair registers her political resistance to conventional feminine norms, and Salma Hayek, who plays Kahlo in the film, said she had grown a moustache for it. As Hayek commented: '[the film's producer Miramax] was not crazy for me to have a moustache for the whole film. I shaved myself a couple of times so it would grow naturally. It's very small but it is there.'[56] Indeed, the moustache amounts to the slightest of dark shadows on Hayek's upper lip and is further diminished in importance by the exoticism of her Mexican dress and coiffure. Instead, the film relies on her dark and heavy eyebrows – a less-taboo area for female facial hair – to signify Kahlo's 'hirsutism'.[57]

In the Hollywood mainstream film *Captain Corelli's Mandolin*,[58] however, we can find an unusual instance of female body hair being used positively, in a way that inverts the 'hairless ideal'. Set on the 'unspoilt' island of Cephalonia during the Second World War, the prostitutes that accompany the Italian force that occupy the island are set in opposition to the main female protagonist, the local doctor's daughter Pelagia (Penelope Cruz). While the Italian women represent a decadent form of 'civilised' femininity with their high-heeled shoes, parasols, fashionable silky clothes and cut and crimped hair, Cruz portrays a softer 'natural' rustic beauty. She is dressed in simple cottons and linens, softened and faded by the sun and washing. Her face is free from cosmetics and her hair offers a semiotic narrative of its own, either flowing long and loose, or braided in a traditional fashion in a reflection of her desire or its restraint. In a beach scene, the prostitutes' bodies – their breasts bared or covered in the sheen of flesh-coloured brassières, their smooth, hairless legs exposed to the thigh as they loll on the sand – portray a tainted 'hairless ideal' when they are contrasted with Cruz, whose figure displays a positive atavistic strength and beauty which includes glimpses of underarm hair at times when she is at her most sexual – lying in bed pining for Corelli and during their lovemaking.

Perhaps it will take an increasing number of such glimpses of body hair on well-established cinema beauties like Penelope Cruz and Julia Roberts[59] to begin to offer women other options than the monopoly of the 'hairless ideal'. Screen images have great power to manipulate taste and fashion; just as cinema has been particularly responsible for confirming the hairless aesthetic, so conversely it has the potential to contribute to changing it. Perhaps, then, as women might adjust to the look of body hair on female stars, so we might become more accepting of body hair on ourselves.

Notes

1   This chapter is based on the MA dissertation: ' "*Hair-razing*" female body hair: threat, transgression and taboo', which I submitted in September 1999 at the Centre for the Study of Women and Gender, The University of Warwick. I am indebted to Dr Karín Lesnik-Oberstein, whose lecture and then unpublished chapter: 'The last taboo: women, body hair and feminism' provided the topic, and some material, for the dissertation.
2   *What Women Want*, Nancy Meyers, Icon Productions, Paramount Pictures, Wind Dancer, USA, 2000.
3   Throughout this chapter, the general terms 'body hair' or 'hair on the body' will refer to any hair on the body other than head hair on the scalp, and will include pubic and facial hair. Similarly, 'hairless or hair-free bodies' will refer to bodies where hair has been removed from anywhere (including the pubic area and the face) apart from the scalp. Of course I appreciate that while some women may regularly depilate their underarms and legs, they may not also be in the habit of removing hair from their pubic region.
4   When Susan Brownmiller (*Femininity*, New York: Linden Books, 1984) says: 'Why do I persist in not wearing skirts? Because I don't like this artificial gender distinction. Because I don't wish to start shaving my legs again' (quoted in Elizabeth Wilson, *Adorned in Dreams*, London: Virago, 1985, p. 234), she reveals not only that she has internalised the 'artificial gender distinction' between hairless (female) legs and hairy (male) legs, but she also betrays her dislike of her own unshaven legs.
5   Feminist opinion is divided on the subject of female body modification such as the removal of body hair. Elizabeth Wilson (*Adorned in Dreams*) sees nothing negative in human beings adorning and modifying their bodies to advantage. According to her, we do not live primarily by our instincts but in socially constructed cultures, and there is therefore no such thing as a 'natural' woman's body. She argues that the desire for self-beautification should not be regarded as an oppressive need to conform but as a liberational opportunity for expression and pleasure. On the other hand, other feminists, like Susan Bordo (see, for instance, her *Unbearable Weight*, Berkeley and Los Angeles: University of California Press, 1993) and Naomi Wolf (*The Beauty*

Myth, London: Chatto and Windus, 1990) see this attitude as a form of false consciousness. They associate any form of body modification – from fashionable clothes to cosmetic surgery – with subordination and oppressive patriarchal control. Although their polemic focuses primarily on female body weight and shape, their viewpoint can apply equally well to 'the hairless ideal'.

6   See the introductions of Lana Turner's character in *The Postman Always Rings Twice* (Tay Garnett, MGM, USA, 1946) and Rita Hayworth's in *Gilda* (Charles Vidor, Columbia Pictures, USA, 1946) and Joan Crawford in a beach scene in *Mildred Pierce* (Michael Curtiz, Warner Bros., USA, 1945).

7   *Some Like It Hot*, Billy Wilder, Paramount/Mirisch, USA, 1959.

8   *Tootsie*, Sydney Pollack, Columbia/Mirage/Punch, USA, 1982.

9   *GI Jane*, Ridley Scott, Trap-Two Zero Productions Inc., and Hollywood Pictures Co., USA/UK, 1997.

10   *Alien*, Ridley Scott, Brandywine Productions and Twentieth Century Fox Film Corporation, USA/UK, Ridley Scott, 1979.

11   *Aliens*, James Cameron, Brandywine Productions and Twentieth Century Fox, USA, 1986.

12   *Terminator 2*, James Cameron, Carolco Pictures, Pacific Western Productions, Lightstorm Entertainment, USA, 1991.

13   Referring to the physiques of such action heroines, Yvonne Tasker uses the term 'musculinity' to describe the visible masculinisation of their bodies through their developed muscles (*Spectacular Bodies*, London: Routledge, 1993, p. 149).

14   *Bridget Jones's Diary*, Sharon Maguire, Miramax Films, Universal Pictures, Studio Canal, Working Title, Great Britain, 2001.

15   In *Daddy's Girl* (London: Palgrave, 1997, p. 50), Valerie Walkerdine touches on this aspect when she explains how the cultural norms of femininity, presented in comics and Hollywood films, provide a means of survival for young working-class girls by offering aspirational models of dress, appearance and behaviour which are enabling for social mobility. Similarly, immigrant women learnt how to conform to American conventions by copying the female characters in early cinema (Elizabeth Ewen, *Signs*, 5:3, (Supplement, 1980), 545–66).

16   *Matilda*, Danny De Vito, Columbia Pictures, USA, 1996.

17   Declan Lowney, 1995–98.

18   Kobena Mercer, 'Black hair/style politics', *New Formations*, 3 (Winter, 1987), 33–54, 34.

19   Title appropriated from Jeannette Marie Mageo's article: 'Hairdos and don'ts: hair symbolism and sexual history in Samoa', *Man: The Journal of the Royal Anthropological Institute*, 29 (1994), 407–31, which gives a useful synopsis of the cultural meanings which have been applied to hair by anthropologists over the last forty years.

20   Susan A. Basow, 'The hairless ideal – women and their body hair', *Psychology of Women Quarterly*, 15 (1991), 83–96, 86.

21   Mary Douglas, *Purity and Danger* (London: Routledge, 1978 (orig. pub.1966)), p. 2.

22   L. S. Kubie, 'The fantasy of dirt', *Psychoanalytic Quarterly*, 6 (1937), 388–407, 391, cited in: Joan Ferrante, 'Biomedical versus cultural constructions of

abnormality: the case of idiopathic hirsutism in the United States', *Culture, Medicine and Psychiatry*, 12: 2 (June, 1988), 219–38, 235.

23 *The Howling*, Joe Dante, Arco Embassy Pictures, International Film Investors, USA, 1980.

24 *A Teenage Werewolf in London*, John Landis, Lycanthorpe films, PolyGram Filmed Entertainment, USA/UK, 1981.

25 *Alien*, Ridley Scott, 1979.

26 Bordo, *Unbearable Weight*, p. 189.

27 See: Naomi Wolf, *The Beauty Myth* (London: Chatto and Windus, 1990).

28 For further discussion of this, see also Carolyn Williams's Chapter 6 in this volume.

29 Ovid, *The Act of Love and Other Poems*, trans. J. H. Mozley (Cambridge, Massachusetts: Harvard University Press; London: Heinemann, 1979 (orig. pub. 1939)), p. 131.

30 Nanette Salomon, 'The Venus Pudica: uncovering art history's "hidden agendas" and pernicious pedigrees', in Griselda Pollock (ed.), *Generations and Geographies in the Visual Arts* (London and New York: Routledge, 1996), pp. 69–88, p. 73.

31 *Blonde Venus*, Josef von Sternberg, Paramount Pictures, USA, 1932.

32 *Shanghai Express*, Josef von Sternberg, Paramount Pictures, USA, 1932.

33 *The Wicked Lady*, Leslie Arliss, Gainsborough Studios, UK, 1945.

34 *Gilda*, Charles Vidor, 1946.

35 Anthea Callen, *The Spectacular Body* (New Haven and London: Yale University Press, 1995), p. 84.

36 Title appropriated from the title of an article by Brenda Hirsch, *Psychology Today* (September, 1984).

37 *The Life and Loves of a She-Devil* was published by Hodder and Stoughton (London) in 1983. All quotations are from the Sceptre Paperback edition (London, 1984). The four one-hour episodes of the television adaptation, written by Ted Whitehead, produced by Sally Head and directed by Philip Saville, were first transmitted on 8 October 1986 (9.25 p.m. to 10.25 p.m.) and were shown on consecutive weeks. The first episode shared first place in the viewing figures for the BBC with 6.2 million, while the third episode's 9.95 million achieved the highest viewing figures both for the series and for BBC2 (Liz Bird and Jo Elliot, '*The Life and Loves of a She-Devil* (Fay Weldon – Ted Whitehead)', in George W. Brandt (ed.), *British Television Drama in the 1980s* (Cambridge: Cambridge University Press, 1993), pp. 214–33, p. 222). The following year, when it was repeated on BBC1, the viewing figures rose even further. It also won the BAFTA award for Best Drama Serial for 1986.

38 The film adaptation was written by Barry Strugatz and Mark Burns and directed by Susan Seidelman (*She-Devil*, Susan Seidelman, Orion Pictures, USA, 1989).

39 Ellen Baskin, '*The Life and Loves of a She-Devil*': Serials on British Television 1950–1994 (Aldershot: Scolar Press, 1996), p. 222.

40 Reportedly, Barr became so sensitive about her appearance in this role that a tunnel of black material had to be constructed, between her trailer and the set, to protect her from the intrusive eyes and cameras of the paparazzi, as she

walked to and fro or waited between shots (Ed Begley Jr (Bob), quoted in *American Film* (December, 1989), 64).

41 Weldon, *The Life and Loves of a She-Devil*, p. 47.

42 Weldon, *The Life and Loves of a She-Devil*, p. 12, p. 43.

43 Weldon, *The Life and Loves of a She-Devil*, p. 81.

44 *An American Werewolf in Paris*, Anthony Waller, Stonewood Communications, Hollywood Pictures Co., UK, 1996.

45 Weldon, *The Life and Loves of a She-Devil*, p. 43.

46 Weldon, *The Life and Loves of a She-Devil*, p. 17.

47 *Mrs Doubtfire*, Chris Columbus, Twentieth Century Fox Corporation, Blue Wolf Productions, USA, 1993.

48 The representation of pubic hair in the context of a Californian clinic is also at odds with American conventions regarding femininity. As Susan Basow points out in her article 'The hairless ideal': 'A major component of "femininity" in the United States today is a hairless body (even pubic hair may be shaved)' (*Psychology of Women Quarterly*, 15 (1991), 83–96, 83).

49 Although there are several direct references to Ruth's hairiness in the novel – 'the hairs on her upper lip and chin caught the light at dinner' (p. 40); 'She had hairs sprouting from moles beneath her chin' (p. 59) – the camera's unflinching focus on Ruth's upper lip, as well as the deliberate directorial strategy to use her body hair as a negative signifier, place greater emphasis on her facial hair than Weldon may have intended in the novel.

50 Weldon has stated that she assumes her readers are all women (see Michelene Wandor, *On Gender and Writing*, London: Pandora, 1983, p. 163).

51 Richard D. Altick, *The Shows of London* (Cambridge, Massachusetts: Belknap Press of Harvard University Press, 1978, p. 36, p. 257), quoted in: James Schiffer, '*Macbeth* and the bearded women', in Dorothea Kehler and Susan Baker (eds), *In Another Country* (London and Metuchen, New Jersey: Scarecrow Press, 1991), pp. 205–17, p. 205.

52 *An American Werewolf in Paris*, Anthony Waller, Stonewood Communications, Hollywood Pictures Co., UK, 1996.

53 *The Company of Wolves*, Neil Jordan, Palace Productions, ITC Entertainment, UK, 1984.

54 Deborah Orr, 'Say Grace', *Guardian Weekend*, 22 July, 1995, 11–16, front cover page.

55 *Frida*, Julie Taymor, Miramax Films, USA/Canada/Mexico, 2002).

56 Hayek, as cited on World Entertainment News Network, viewed on 20 June 2001.

57 For an extensive discussion of the Frida Kahlo film, see Chapter 11.

58 *Captain Corelli's Mandolin*, John Madden, Free Range Films, Miramax Films, Studio Canal, Universal Pictures, Working Title, UK/USA, 2001.

59 Julia Roberts caught press attention when she revealed underarm hair as she arrived at the London première of *Notting Hill* in April 1999 (Roger Michell, Polygram Filmed Entertainment, Working Title Films, Bookshop Productions, Notting Hill Pictures, UK/USA, 1999).

5 'La justice, c'est la femme à barbe!': the bearded lady, displacement and recuperation in Apollinaire's *Les Mamelles de Tirésias*

Stephen Thomson

Je ne crois pas à la justice. Son sexe est trop ambigu. La justice, c'est la femme à barbe![1]

In Dali's joking aphorism, the virility of the concept of justice clashes with the grammatical gender of the word, '*la* justice'. Suffering the indignity of being left to dangle in between, it deserves Dali's incredulity: if justice cannot keep itself in order, why should I allow it to stand in judgement over me? Justice is not, for all that, entirely discarded. It persists in the notion of a normal, adjusted, fitting, right[2] division of sexual characters that the bearded lady contravenes. For, although she figures sexual ambiguity, in so doing she also keeps it at arm's length as freakish. Moreover, the familiar type, *the* bearded lady, potentially brings with her a whole context of fairground spectacle; the barker, the entrance fee, the crowded tent. This is a curiosity or sport[3] that one pays good money to see in a specific, defined space. With the high concept of justice firmly in its sights, Dali's aphorism can comfortably send out for such a 'low' figure without feeling in any way compromised by it. The iconic prominence of Dali's own whiskers and his possible standing as something of a bearded lady are, of course, out of the question.

In this chapter, I will explore the currency of this figure in late nineteenth- and early twentieth-century French literature. In particular, I will examine ways in which that currency is caught up in techniques of unexpected juxtaposition and displacement associated with avant-garde movements of the period, in particular Surrealism and Dada. The bearded lady is indeed routinely linked with a rather loose notion of the 'surreal': the publicity for recent HBO series *Carnivale* is a case in point.[4] Such an instance is doubtless reductive, ignoring the aims and procedures of Surrealism proper in favour of a conventionally 'weird' decor. But even once such a rebuttal is made, it remains true that the avant-garde is not entirely uninvolved with ladies with whiskers. René Clair and Francis

Picabia's film *Entr'acte* (1924) features prominently a bearded ballet dancer, though accounts vary as to whether this is a man dressed as a ballerina, or a ballerina with beard. Whatever the case may be, the beard works here to disengage the ceremonial of tutu and slippers from their proper context so as to liberate their latent potential for the ridiculous. Similarly, the addition (by Marcel Duchamp) of a set of whiskers to a reproduction Mona Lisa, bearing the legend 'LHOOQ' (pronounced 'elle a chaud au cul', or 'she has a hot ass'), is enough to turn the famously enigmatic smile rakishly back on itself. It is worth asking, however, to what extent we are dealing in these instances with *the* bearded lady – the same one, the one that originates in the fairground. Though both instances produce something like a bearded lady, they get there by different routes. Moreover, one might say Duchamp borrows not so much the beard itself as the techniques of vandalism, reminding us that scribbled facial hair is one of the most elementary forms of irreverence that can be inflicted on any public face. Here, it is quite possible to see the figure of a bearded lady as incidental, as one particular outcome of *procedures* of collage, recombination or displacement. But, by the same token, one might argue that the production of such a familiar figure poses questions for the putative subversiveness of such strategies, especially where, as in Surrealism, they claim to be automatic, and to open up new ways of seeing.

The first surrealist play

Curiously enough, Surrealism may be said to have started with a bearded lady, although for many this is a false start. In Guillaume Apollinaire's play *Les Mamelles de Tirésias* (1917),[5] a woman named Thérèse renounces childbirth, promptly grows a beard, loses her breasts and changes her name to Tirésias. Her husband, equivocally feminised as a result, is obliged to repopulate France on his own, and does so with prodigious success. In the end, the couple are reunited and at least partially restored to their gender identities. Filling out this slender plot is all manner of absurd business. Two agents coming to the town of Zanzibar for obscure motives repeatedly kill each other in a duel, only to come back to life and start again. There are also moments of more pointed satire: the husband makes one of the children from old newspapers and he grows up to be a journalist. By the end, Thérèse has reappeared disguised as a (female) fortune-teller, approving of the husband's efforts at repopulation, but ready to resume her own duties. This, Apollinaire alleges, is the serious message of the play: France must be repopulated after the ravages of the Great War, still ongoing at the time of the play's first performance, and at present the French are not putting in the required effort.[6] But the play expressly wants to avoid becoming a 'pièce à thèse', taking instead 'un ton moins sombre'.[7] Indeed, Apollinaire presents the play, probably not entirely truthfully, as a piece of juvenilia raked out and dusted down for the occasion. At the same time, he wants to claim it as some sort of theatrical breakthrough. His preface proposes a theatre that is modern, simple, fast, and striking by virtue of its reductions (shorthands, ellipses) and exaggerations: 'cet art sera moderne, simple, rapide avec les *raccourcis* ou les *grossissements* qui s'imposent si l'on veut frapper le spectateur'.[8] Broadly speaking, the intrigue is the pretext for a patently stylised backdrop and props done in broad strokes and bright colours, in which exaggerated figures make crude gestures and loud noises.[9] It is to describe this theatre, and the dubious relation of serious subject to light means, that the term 'surréaliste' is coined.[10] What Apollinaire proposes under that heading is not so much a radical questioning of objective reality as a return 'à la nature même, mais sans l'imiter à la manière des photographes': when man invented the wheel in imitation of walking, says Apollinaire, he was an unwitting surrealist.[11] The representation of breasts by rubber balloons and balls is very much a case in point, and Apollinaire's preface makes great play of this.

Surrealism and the body

But, most critics agree, Apollinaire's notion of Surrealism is not particularly closely related to that made famous by André Breton in his manifesto of 1924.[12] Indeed, Breton himself distances his Surrealism from that of Apollinaire. Even as he pays homage to his now-deceased predecessor in his choice of the word, Breton laments his refusal or inability to leave behind mediocre literary means, and his theoretical incapacity.[13] But, in the same breath, he also acknowledges a surrealist tendency ('un entraînement de ce genre') in the poet's work, and the nature and extent of this 'entraînement' remains to be explored. The opening coup of *Les Mamelles* – the sudden appearance of a beard, and metamorphosis of breasts into balloons – provide one possible link. In Breton's first manifesto, bodily dislocations have an important role. The germ of his surrealist breakthrough is an imperfectly remembered phrase that came to him as sleep descended: 'Il y a un homme coupé en deux par la fenêtre'. The image can be rationalised visually – the lower half of the body is simply hidden by the window. But by the time that the window makes its appearance in the phrase, there is already a man cut in two.[14] There is a close analogy, and a complicity, here between the cut of the body and the cut of the phrase. Indeed, the attraction of dream phrases for Breton always lay in their incompletion.[15] At the outset of his poetic career, this led him to prize writing techniques that worked to '*raccourcir* de façon saisissante', i.e. to shorten in a striking manner an already given subject matter.[16] But the man cut in two leads him to reject the instrumentalism implicit in this. Here, the element of *raccourci* is integral to the phrase as it presents itself in the dream, and not a technique carried out on it.[17] Hence 'Surrealism' itself is defined as an 'automatisme psychique',[18] and its exponents are mere recording instruments, 'modestes *appareils enregistreurs*'.[19]

This doubtless marks an important difference in ideas from the sort of *raccourci* proposed by Apollinaire, which is indeed a technique carried out on an existing situation that retains its own comedy and pathos.[20] But one should surely not be too hasty to simply credit the rather tricky notion of agency claimed by Breton. And such caution is all the more pressing wherever an allegedly automatic process produces material resembling that produced by avowedly technical means. Having partially dismissed Apollinaire, Breton names Gérard de Nerval as another forerunner, and cites his account of Charles Nodier's notion that he had been guillotined during the revolution, told so persistently and with such conviction that people started to ask how he had stuck his head back on.[21] Again, the element of dismemberment is ambiguous insofar as the parts seem to remain attached. Are Thérèse's breasts/balloons not 'surreal' in this sense when they fly away but remain attached by strings, regardless of how their composition is explained?

Avant-garde procedures that deal in cutting up and recombination propose varying degrees of chance and intervention. But the body and the displacement of its parts are something of a constant. The collage and photomontage of artists such as Max Ernst or Hannah Hoch, or the sculptures of Hans Bellmer, feature detached limbs and oddly assembled bodies. Body parts recombine in odd ways to form bodies that are surely not *viable*, but may be in some way *whole*, at least in the sense that they compose something. One target of such works seems to be the notion of the body as a natural composition, and to this extent they may often be read as disruptive of gender certainties. Such works nevertheless cannot but affirm themselves as *compositions* in the artistic sense, even despite the arbitrary or aleatory nature of their procedures. This problematic is to the fore in the surrealist game of the exquisite corps, where a piece of paper is passed round and folded, leaving only the ends of the last segment visible. The 'body' produced in the end by the unseen efforts of different hands can be as fantastical as you like, but as in the traditional game of Head, Body and Legs (in which a variety of heads, bodies and legs from diverse animals are added by successive players to produce unusual beasts), the template of an ideal body structure (head, torso, limbs) hangs over the whole affair. The strategy is by nature ambivalent: it foregrounds and ridicules composition (the coherence of body, sentence, narrative) by inserting discrepant parts, but nevertheless relies upon and maintains that compositional shell. It is perhaps not possible to decree, in general terms, definitely, whether procedures of this sort are disruptive or recuperated. For each essay one would have to ask: how far does this tend towards disruption, and how far towards conservation? In light of this discussion, I will now go on to examine the staging of the breasts and beards in *Les Mamelles*, which provide not only its defining theatrical moment, but also one of its strongest links to the practices of Dada and Surrealism.

Breasts and beard

In almost any synopsis of *Les Mamelles*, the breasts and the beard have equal billing as the signs of Thérèse's gender switch. But from that point onwards, they have quite different fates. Very little is said about the beard in either the preface and dedicatory poems and prologue, or the body of the play. As Maya Slater comments, this is in line with the method that the play sets itself: 'extraordinary events and juxtapositions are presented without comment – a woman suddenly grows a moustache, we are shown a chamber-pot and told it is a piano', and so forth. Slater nonetheless immediately goes on to offer an explanation of sorts by invoking the bearded lady, while leaving the breasts/balloons as they are: 'the blind seer Tiresias is portrayed as a bearded lady with balloons for breasts'.[22] I will discuss towards the end of this chapter what it means to identify Thérèse as 'a bearded lady'. In criticism in general, however, it is the breasts that attract attention, seemingly because they are more productively inexplicable. Likewise, it is the breasts that Apollinaire's preface makes a case of, while the beard is passed over in silence. Victor Basch is wrong, says Apollinaire, to see the play as symbolic: there is not a single symbol in it, everything is quite clear. But it is perhaps in 'les balles qui figurent les mamelles' that he sees a symbol. Likewise, M. Deffoux wants to see the rubber of which they are made as a reference to contraceptive devices. Against this, Apollinaire cites a law of 26 February 1917 forbidding the sale of teats *not* made of rubber.[23] So, in the very act of refuting the charge of symbolism, the breasts seem to recommend themselves precisely because of their symbolic possibilities. In particular, they allow a seamless slide from the topic of the play to a broader thematics of artistic fecundity. Criticism often makes a link between ideas of birth in the text and literary creation. So, for Denis Bordat and Bernard Veck, *Les Mamelles* shows 'l'inquiétude du poète sur la naissance, sa naissance, son identité, sa création'.[24] Apollinaire does nothing to discourage *this* sort of symbolism, seemingly because it emerges 'naturally' from the matter at hand. The dedicatory verse that admires actress Louise Marion, 'Gonflant d'esprit tout neuf vos multiples tetons', can be read as a sort of auto-commentary: the breasts do indeed seem endlessly capable of having a new spirit breathed into them. 'La féconde raison', the verse continues, 'a jailli de ma fable': fertile reason sprang from my fable. According to Apollinaire's friend Albert-Birot, the breasts were the seed that gave birth to the play: 'germe qui donna naissance à la pièce'.[25] Reading the letter of Albert-Birot's birth metaphor, the breasts are responsible for engendering the play in which they appear. The poor beard, unable to compete with this remarkable symbolic fertility, slips into the background.

The same pattern can be observed in discussions of the nature and handling of the props that figure breasts and beards. Peter Read's *La Revanche d'Eros*[26] discusses in some detail the material make-up of the breasts, and the unavailability of inflatable balloons in wartime.[27] The availability of beards, on the other hand, seems not to be in question. Read does, however, touch on the staging of the beard: Thérèse hides behind the kiosk for the short moment it takes to put on 'ses nouveaux appas masculins',[28] in a phrase that rather recalls Thérèse's reference to her breasts as 'appas féminins'.[29] Presumably, this detail is drawn from a memoir or notice of the premiere, but no source is cited. The stage directions only say: '*Elle caresse sa barbe et retrousse sa moustache qui ont brusquement poussé*', then, after a further speech, '*Tout en caquetant, elle va se mirer dans la glace placée sur le kiosque à journaux*'.[30] How the beard is to be put on is not explained. In any case, Read's attention has already been drawn to the mirror (*la glace*) in which Thérèse admires her new self, for, in Apollinaire, 'tout miroir est lourd de signification': it is charged with a critique of mimesis and the creation of a new reality.[31] Whether or not the beard is to be put on under cover of the kiosk, as a figure it is hidden behind a screen of other figures that lend themselves more readily to notions of artistic creation.

The feminine body

The masculine body and its parts seem not to add up in the same way as the feminine body, and do not offer themselves so readily as a critical metaphor. The feminine body, on the other hand, is called upon with remarkable frequency to stabilise the œuvre. Stabilising an œuvre at once valued for, and menaced by, the heterogeneity of its figures is, indeed, a central preoccupation of Apollinaire criticism. Philippe Renaud[32] suggests that 'Apollinaire' has been particularly prone to dismemberment by admirers and inheritors.[33] Each carries off their 'morceau du Vrai Apollinaire', and if one were to reassemble him from the parts, one would produce some unspeakable 'chimère',[34] a monster made of heterogeneous parts. The error of previous criticism was to think that an essential Apollinaire could be 'born' (*naîtrait*) out of contradictory anecdotal material, leaving 'Apollinaire' to live on in an artificial life.[35] The difficulty for Renaud is to honour the heterogeneity of the '*corpus*'[36] without producing a monster. The quest to find a structural identity for Apollinaire has subsequently often turned to the feminine body. In a particularly systematic instance of this approach, Jean-Bertrand Barrère divides the work up under thematic headings, with an extensive glossary of major symbols to help one navigate between themes.[37] The word 'cheveux' is listed as a mark of '*tendresse*',[38] but the less tender hair of 'barbe' does not rate an entry. This is, indeed, consistent with the broad trends revealed by Barrère's method: the most frequently cited words include '*amour, œil, main, nuit*' and, most often of all, *'femme'*.[39] Woman, says Barrère, is at the 'heart'[40] of Apollinaire's poetry, so much so that her 'essential attributes' act as a sort of template ordering the whole work of figuration: 'Les attributs essentiels de la féminité déterminent divers groupes d'images provoquées par une analogie le plus souvent formelle'.[41] The feminine body is thus taken as a reassuring ground for such famously wayward figures as artillery shells like breasts.[42] Leroy C. Breunig goes, if anything, even further in this direction: 'The peacetime imagery is replaced by trenches, barbed wire, cannon, and hand grenades, but the analogies are as volatile as before, a German shell, for example, becoming in turn a woman's breast, a rose, a heart, a star'. Indeed, the 'privations of trench life' turn 'no-man's land into a vast erogenous zone'.[43] The 'volatility' of such series seems to be made possible by their gravitation towards a body that orders them and holds them in place. That this body is feminine, sexually charged, and fertile, seems to go without saying. As David Berry remarks: 'Having turned stars into sexual symbols, the *natural* consequence for Apollinaire's imagination is to turn them into images of fertility.'[44]

All of these critics are concerned to find an order in the œuvre that the work itself, or 'Apollinaire', dictates, naturally. This produces an odd tension between an admiration for the heterogeneity of Apollinaire's figures, and an insistence that these are all held together by a conventional, natural notion of the feminine body. The only place for the beard in this universe would be as a sign of monstrosity. But it is not even remarked upon as such. Indeed, so sterile is the beard, that it receives very little attention at all. All of this is in accord with the letter of *Les Mamelles* to the extent that the beard therein is indeed a mark, indeed a result, of willed sterility. The husband's method of childbirth, involving another sort of fertility, will require further consideration later. For the moment, however, I want to pursue the linking of monstrosity (as the non-identity of heterogeneous parts) and sterility in other works by Apollinaire and his contemporaries.

L'enchanteur pourrissant

The concern with childbirth and monstrosity can be seen in Apollinaire's first published book, *L'Enchanteur pourrissant* (1909). The story starts with a girl who refuses to marry but is tricked into bed by a devil. The offspring, Merlin, is seduced in turn by Vivienne into teaching her his secrets, until one day she entombs him and leaves him to die, although his immortal soul continues to speak.[45] The druids and beasts, real and fabulous, that congregate round his tomb have complicated views on the proper means of reproduction. The lugubrious Chapalu, one of a kind seemingly because made of the wrong parts of too many different animals – head of a cat, feet of a dragon, body of a horse, tail of a lion – has come looking for Merlin because he would like to be made 'prolific', even though he is quite happy living alone.[46] The dictator Béhémoth, on the other hand, exempts himself from his game of seeing who dies first, *because* he is 'sans origine, unique, immobile'. According to his decree, the animals that are neither male nor female are exempt also because they are useful providers, but it is just to kill the hermaphrodites because it is a long time since they had any reason to exist. Even as the other animals massacre them, the hermaphrodites find this 'raisonnable'.[47] Meanwhile, Chapalu counts himself out of the game.[48] The sexed animals that are left couple according to their tastes and races, but these are 'copulations mortuaires' and they take place under the 'dictature inféconde' of Béhémoth. The only unproblematic fertilisation at this point seems to be that of the parasites effecting the decomposition of Merlin's body.[49] One should not be too hasty to deduce a consistent gender ideology from such knockabout, libertine stuff, especially as it is not clear that there is a dominant point of view. Nevertheless, it is striking that the two monads Béhémoth and Chapalu, despite differences in perception of their state, are expressly designated as male. Meanwhile, femininity, and in particular reproductive capacity, is viewed with suspicion. The abbot's complaint that the cries of women – and more particularly that of a mother – disturb his solitude, may be explained as an anti-clerical jibe.[50] But, later, the chorus of women declares that there is a smell of woman in the forest – all the males are rutting, they say, because an unreality has taken the form of reality – thus linking more emphatically femininity to some profound disturbance.[51] The first druid seems to express distaste for menstruation as he recounts chasing some priestesses from his abode: although virgins, they were 'wounded', and their blood corrupted the air.[52] Furthermore, Lorie, one of the (female) fairies still seeking the wizard, suggests the only way that the lady of the lake can have died is in childbirth.[53] Overall, then, a libertine affirmation of sexuality is offset by a distrust or distaste of the fluid and productive aspects of femininity. Although he laments his loneliness,[54] Chapalu never mentions the possibility of a mate; he only says that he wants to *be rendered* prolific. Is it possible that he might follow the obscure method of the god who procreated without testicles, the god that the first druid sees figured in the cold menhir?[55]

Le Coeur à gaz

Apollinaire's preoccupation with dismemberment and the reassembly of odd bodies is by no means unique. Neither is the link with sterility and the enigmatic nature of the fecundity of art. Tristan Tzara's play *Le Coeur à gaz*, was first shown in 1921, but is mainly known for the performance of 6 July 1923 that is generally taken to mark the end of Dada in Paris: Breton sent his claque round and the evening ended in uproar.[56] Like Apollinaire, Tzara pleads the lightness, or 'manque de sérieux', of his play.[57] The play features characters named after body parts who, in the first act especially, take a great interest in manners of describing and combining body parts. The word 'coeur' is constantly disintegrating into *cour* (court), *courir* (to run), *cor* (horn), and of course *cou* (neck), which is also the name of one of the principal figures, suspended above the stage, opposite NEZ (nose) who is above the spectators. At one stage, EAR seems to announce a thesis:

OREILLE (*entre*)

Son cou est étroit mais le pied large. Il peut facilement tambouriner avec les doigts des pieds sur son ventre ovale qui a déjà servi de balle à quelques matchs de rugby. *Il n'est pas être car il est composé de morceaux.*[58]

The (notional, not presented on stage) figure that can drum on its belly with its toes, and have the belly used as a rugby ball, would indeed find it difficult to compose a complete being. But this last idea also offers a tempting parallel with the nature of the play. It is likewise made of parts that resist coalescing into a body, and lines that fail to respond properly as dialogue, or to trace a narrative, i.e. escaping the condition of a coherent entity is part of the programme. Read in this way, however, the line makes almost too much sense for its own good, giving the play a coherent purpose in the very act of denying itself one. This is doubtless the dilemma of any discrepancy charged with a moral and aesthetic purpose. Moreover, what if apparent discrepancies prove to run on invisible rails to all-too-predictable (albeit a posteriori) destinations? Just before the all-too-thetic line cited above, OEIL ends an apostrophe to 'Clitemnestre' with a remarkable affirmation of sterility: 'Quand aurez-vous le plaisir de regarder la mâchoire inférieure du revolver se fermer dans mon poumon de craie. Sans espoir de famille.' That is to say, 'When will you have the pleasure of watching the lower jaw of the revolver fix itself in my chalk lung. Without hope of family.' [My translation] At the end of the page there is mention (by SOURCIL, or 'eyelash') of a 'ciel à barbe', or bearded heaven/sky. Even if the meeting of these tropes on the same page is in some sense fortuitous,[59] it nevertheless implies that force fields and attractions of ideas are at work. Viewed alongside *Les Mamelles* and *L'Enchanteur*, the coincidence of sterility, unviable bodies and inappropriate beards is striking. Indeed, the bearded lady herself puts in a brief appearance in a speech by OEIL: 'Le temps porte des moustaches, comme tout le monde, même les femmes et les Américains rasés.' This itself follows directly from a speech by SOURCIL that deals in ideas of monstrous birth: 'son ventre est plein de tant de monnaies étrangères', and 'Une fois par jour nous avortons de nos obscurités'.[60] Moreover, the play was performed under the banner of Tzara's journal *Le Coeur à barbe*, further underlining the beard's currency as a device for neutering lyricism.

Gender and creation

Tzara's play raises another interesting parallel with *Les Mamelles* in its attitudes to gendered creation. Tzara's foreword disclaims the genius of the author, and the play refers to writing poems by cutting them up with scissors, echoing his famous instructions on how to make a Dadaist poem by cutting up newspapers.[61] Here, production putatively freed from any progenitor is offered teasingly as an artistic utopia. This recalls the son made of shredded newspapers, ink and glue who grows into a journalist in *Les Mamelles*.[62] But, in this latter case, sterile, monadic, male production is not the model of the avant-garde, but of the lowest writing possible, namely journalism, and the husband comes to regret his creation.[63] In any case, the husband's enterprise is identified as just that, an enterprise. He denies maternal instinct, declaring his interest in the wealth brought by children.[64] And at the end of the play, when Thérèse posing as the Cartomancienne praises his fecundity, the point is again wealth, and she is now a proselyte of fecundity to all Zanzibar, and is herself ready in any case to take up again her role of wife.[65] This is the allegedly serious point of the play. Has the husband's fecundity, on the other hand, ever been serious?

The link between his supposed gender and his mode of childbirth is worth some further thought. It is sometimes inferred that there is a swap of genders resulting from Thérèse's transformation. But does the play really suggest the husband becomes a woman? The policeman does take him for one,[66] although his remark that he or she is agreeable to the touch, like a rubber ball, is open to a variety of readings. At this point, the husband finds it just that he is a woman, since his wife is a man.[67] When the policeman proposes, however, he protests, 'je ne suis qu'un homme'.[68] Similarly, when in the next scene the husband decides it is up to him to make children, the kiosk comments, 'Voyez l'impondérable ardeur/Naître du changement de sexe'.[69] But he himself refers to 'les joies de la *paternité*', thus not only refuting the idea of a sex change, but further affirming a constant gender identity impervious to any change in reproductive function.[70] Even where the husband's gender is most expressly in question, his physical identity is affirmed. Presto, tickling the husband, recites:

> Comment faut-il que tu les nommes
> Elles sont tout ce que nous sommes
> Et cependant ne sont pas hommes[71]

That is to say, such creatures are not men, and one does not know what to call them, but *they are all that we are*. Although grammatically feminised (*elles*), these beings are not characterised by a lack of male parts, neither do they positively possess feminine parts. The stage directions are in no doubt whatsoever, referring to him as 'LE MARI' throughout, and on one occasion, tellingly, 'LE MARI *habillé en femme*'.[72] Certainly, although becoming male for Thérèse is cast in terms of the loss and gain of secondary sexual characteristics, there is no suggestion that the husband undergoes a reciprocal process. When Thérèse refuses to retrieve her discarded breasts, she points out that both of them have got along very well without them: 'Nous nous en sommes passés l'un et l'autre/Continuons'.[73] At no point, then, has he gained any female part, and there is no suggestion that he has lost anything either; not even a beard. Thérèse has put him into her dress, and this is the sole transformation he undergoes.

Can one credit, then, Peter Read's claim that while Thérèse 'adopts' a masculine identity, the husband takes the opportunity to let the feminine side of his nature blossom?[74] This reading seems to be based on an assumption that characteristics circulate in the play in a symmetrical dialectic of gain and loss; that what one loses another gains. Then again, Read's dialectic is not quite symmetrical: it also figures masculinity as positive gain or addition, even where a part is lost. Thus, also according to Read, by *giving up* her breasts at the end, Thérèse *keeps* part of her virile identity: 'elle choisit de conserver une part de son identité virile'.[75] But there is never any question of her keeping the part that she actually gained, that is to say the beard. Neither is there any mention of any other male part she might have gained, despite references to the numerous lovers that she has taken in the meantime. Thus, it is the breasts that present the symbolic possibilities and attract all the attention, while the beard is conceptually inconspicuous, taken as read, and relatively impotent as a positive expression of masculinity. And yet it seems also to be taken as read that the beard would ultimately, if retained, have a more intractable role in negating femininity. The same is true, if not more so, when it comes to fecundity. Even in being given away, the breasts will help to nurture repopulation: as Thérèse throws a basket full of balls at the audience in the final gesture of the play, she says: 'Allez nourrir tous les enfants/De la repopulation'.[76] The beard, on the other hand, coincides entirely with Thérèse's sterility.

Burlesque propriety

All in all, then, despite the play's gestures towards confusing and subverting gender norms, certain proprieties are observed. Despite radical pretensions, gender roles are never essentially disturbed. As noted earlier, there is a possible danger in reading such a ridiculous play with an entirely straight face. Nonetheless, Apollinaire's 'ton moins sombre', like Tzara's 'manque de sérieux', exists in tension with a notion of art, and what is more, avant-garde art. This leaves the applicability of, and responsibility for, any given gesture equivocal and mobile. Despite a multitude of elements that could be traced to burlesque or pantomime traditions, Apollinaire denies any debt to the 'moyens dont on use dans les revues'. He would see no problem in this, as popular art is an excellent fund, but

he protests that his whole fable follows logically from its 'situation princi-
pale', a man who makes children, which is entirely new in literature in
general.[77] But gender confusion on the stage is not necessarily new, or revolutionary. In the first production of *Les Mamelles*, Yéta Daesslé (a woman)
played the journalist, the son and the kiosk, and the gendarme was played
by Juliette Norville, but none of this need suggest any break with burlesque, or indeed theatre proper. My primary concern here, however, is
not to deny Apollinaire the sort of groundbreaking status that he claims,
but to examine how proprieties subsist in the midst of an aesthetic devoted
to exaggerations, shorthands and displacements, whether these be carried
out in the name of popular theatre or of the avant-garde.

In an essay of 1896, Apollinaire's great predecessor, Alfred Jarry, famous
for bringing the brutal slapstick and verbal abuse of puppet theatre into
art, writes of 'the uselessness of theatre to the theatre'. His ridicule of the
conventions of cross-dressing (*travesti*) may seem oddly essentialist for
such a connoisseur of the grotesque. It is because woman is the being that
remains beardless, with a high-pitched voice, that she is allowed to play
adolescent boys. But this cannot make up for her femininity, and in particular her odiously functional breasts: 'Cela compense peu le ridicule du
profil et l'inesthétique de la marche, la ligne estompée à tous les muscles
par le tissu adipeux – odieux parce qu'il est utile, générateur du lait.'[78]
Jarry's target here is the pretention to *trompe-l'œil* of conventional theatre
also rejected by Apollinaire in his preface. How this is supposed to relate
to the wilfully burlesque or ridiculous, he does not say. But once more,
there is a marked attachment to a notion of propriety in the gendering of
representation, and an anxiety over femininity.

Another aptly ambiguous instance would be Apollinaire's pornographic novel *Les Onze Mille Verges*.[79] Here all manner of sexual practices
and combinations can be found, including brutal torture and paedophilia.
Such a work seems to pursue the combinatorial logic of coupling to its fur-
thest conclusions, and to challenge any notion of tone or point of view to
their very foundations. Curiously enough, it also has a positive, eroticised
place for feminine body hair. Buttocks are regularly downy (*duvetées*),[80]
and the bush (*toison*) may go right up to the navel without any suggestion
of anything untoward.[81] Indeed, thick hair seems to be favoured. What is
more, the pubic hair is frequently referred to as a beard; so, for instance,
Zulmé has 'une délicieuse barbe blonde bien frisée'.[82] Indeed, in one
remarkable scene, the 'colosse barbu' Cornaboeux and Alexine pull each
other by their beards as they couple.[83] This preoccupation is if anything
further underscored by frequent references to the pubic mound of young
girls as 'imberbe', or 'glabre'.[84] The novel has a marked interest in body
hair that examines every possibility, from the beauty spot that 'orna-
ments' a face,[85] to the armpits.[86] The bearded lady is there after a fashion
in the form of the male lovers who keep the brothel at Port-Arthur: 'Ils

s'habillaient en femmes et se disaient gousses sans avoir renoncés à leurs moustaches et á leurs noms masculins.'[87] In a further oblique link to *Les Mamelles*, Mony declares after sodomising Cornaboeux, if you don't fall pregnant, you're no man: 'Si tu ne deviens pas enceinte, t'es pas un homme!'[88]

The bearded lady and the colossus

Once more, one may note that there are many ways to arrive at the bearded lady. But this notion brings with it the question of provenance: what would it mean to say that we are dealing at any given point with *the* bearded lady? It has been remarked that the figure had a particular currency in popular literature and culture at the time that Apollinaire wrote his play. Evanghélia Stead's dense but illuminating *Le Monstre, le singe et le foetus*[89] documents the figure's association in late nineteenth-century French literature with the fairground, in writings that themselves take on some of the generic indeterminacy of their subject and its setting, without nevertheless citing Apollinaire. Stead cites Véron's *Roman de la femme à barbe* (1863; four editions to 1877), and Jules Vallès's sketch 'Le bachelier géant', in *La rue* (1864), as seminal works.[90] There is also a vaudeville-parade by Elie Frébault of 1866. And the song was made famous by one Thérésa (Frébault and Paul Blaquière, 1865), and later reprised by Marcelle Bordas (1935). One might add that in 1870 'la femme à barbe' figures in Lautréamont's remarkably comprehensive proscription list of 'sophismes' of the literature of the nineteenth century.[91] Furthermore, bearded ladies have a presence in, for instance, arthouse cinema, with Tod Browning's *Freaks* (1933) and Marco Ferreri's *La donna scimmia* (1963) that goes well beyond the alleged period. In any case, the case in terms of thematic and structural homologies is more interesting than any notion of rigid periodisation.

The lists of freaks and fairground attractions cited by Stead frequently closely juxtapose 'femme à barbe' and 'colosse' or 'géant'.[92] The collocation with 'colosse' is remarkably persistent, figuring for instance in a recent French-government-sponsored exhibition on the fair at La Villette.[93] We have already seen this coupling of ideas in a rough form in Apollinaire, with the bearded colossus Cornaboeux from *Les Onze Mille Verges*. More suggestively, in the poem 'Lecture', composed when Apollinaire was just seventeen, when indeed he claims (probably falsely) to have first written *Les Mamelles*, reading an ancient grimoire gives way to decadent reverie, concluding:

> Et je ne sais pourquoi
> Je songe de femme à barbe et de colosse triste
> Et je frissonne d'entendre en ma chambre derrière moi
> Comme un bruissment de soie.[94]

The claim not to know why these particular figures spring to mind appeals, negatively, to a background familiarity with their pairing and the *frisson* – or vague erotic charge – that comes with it. Neither can these collocations of ideas be simply attributed, as they sometimes are, to the peculiarities of Apollinaire's sexual identity. For these elements are, if anything, what links Apollinaire's flirtation with the bearded lady to other instances of the figure in French literature of the period running up to the production of *Les Mamelles*.

Marriage and coupling

A similar *frisson* appears in an erotic verse of Guy de Maupassant. In a letter dated February 1876, Flaubert asks Maupassant to bring two of his erotic poems, namely 'Le Colosse' and 'La Femme à barbe'. Sadly, the former has not survived.[95] But in the latter, the bearded lady arrives for an assignation dressed as a young man, provoking in the male speaker 'des frissons de femme à l'approche du mâle'.[96] Breastless, she is 'un homme, avec un trou'. Latterly, it is the lady that 'inoculates' the speaker with her come, and declares, 'Nom de Dieu, que je viens de tirer un bon coup', placing her in the position of the penetrator. Narratives of this sort thrive on the idea of incongruity in such love matches, but also vaunt the stubborn pride of the bearded lady. In a little verse by Germain Nouveau, a lovelorn hairdresser's attempts to ply the bearded lady with products is met by incomprehension on her part.[97] Elie Frébault's heroine Rosalba wears a fake beard, but sings the song of Theresa, of the fair at Saint-Cloud, whose beard is her 'gloire'.[98] Otherwise, the discrepancy – whether comic, erotic or tragic – of the bearded lady in marriage *is* the drama. Apollinaire's Thérèse has a distinguished forerunner in the shape of Saint Wilgefortis, who grew a beard upon refusing to marry.[99] Marco Ferreri's *Donna scimmia* (often known by its French title *Le Mari de la femme à barbe*) is exploited by her husband as a freak. Clémentine Delait (née Clatteaux) was something of a local celebrity in the Vosges region in the late nineteenth and early twentieth centuries, and has enjoyed a recent return to fame thanks to the discovery of her manuscript memoirs. Accounts of her life tend to light on her pride in her beard, and her rivalry with both another celebrated bearded lady and her brother.[100]

But the Maupassant verse or *Les Mamelles* suggest a yet more involved role for such couplings: the dialectic of exchanged parts and roles discussed above in my analysis of gender in *Les Mamelles* seems to find its 'natural' *mise-en-scène* in an encounter with a 'normal' man whose position is thrown into confusion. There is not simply a juxtaposition of normal and abnormal, with the production of incongruity, but a confusion or exchange of parts. In the Maupassant, more emphatically than in the Apollinaire, the presence of a beard along with the absence of breasts puts the male into the position of a female, without altering him in any other way. A cartoon roughly contemporary with Clémentine Delait and also from the Vosges region, features the tale of a beardless young man who is not happy until he finds a bearded lady to marry: the couple subsequently swap gender roles. This way, they find that they get on very well: they are, as the title of the cartoon has it, 'Un couple bien assorti'.[101] They are well matched because one supplies what the other lacks.

The kinship between Thérèse and the bearded lady of the popular grotesque is thus by no means superficial, for the figure and its *mise-en-scène* are themselves intimately bound up in a shared anxiety over the structure of heterosexual pairing. In broad terms, the bearded lady offers itself as a sort of narrative lever for opening up the centrifugal possibilities of the 'hetero': rather than a balanced system that keeps separate as it unites, marriage merges into a disconcertingly hybrid entity. At the same time, this staging locates the original disturbance, whether desired as in the Maupassant, or rejected as in *Les Mamelles*, in the bearded lady herself. And even where it emerges in the work of a canonical artist, the essay takes place in works of ambiguous tone and uncertain canonical standing.

Apollinaire's characterisation of popular art as an excellent fund from which art can draw runs into difficulties here. It seems that the figures and staging in question have not proved mere material to be seized upon and reworked at will, but have indeed brought along with them, and may indeed be coextensive with, a whole set of ideological patterns. The problem here is not just that the play proves conservative by returning Thérèse to her box at the end, or that such and such a text is more or less sympathetic to the bearded lady. What is at stake is the groundwork that is encoded in the bearded lady and that persists — other differences of handling aside. It is doubtful how far avant-garde techniques of cutting up, pasting together, reducing and magnifying, alter this problem.

Coda: other sorts of bearded lady

It is also worth asking, however, if there is a way of doing the bearded lady that does not amount to a recuperative safety valve for discontinuities in the heterosexual bargain. I want to close with two instances that, although they are not exactly bearded ladies, may suggest different possibilities. René Magritte's painting *Le Viol* (1934) presents a woman's face whose features are delineated by a woman's body, with breasts for eyes, and the pubic triangle for a beard. Along with the title — 'the rape'— these multiple displacements raise troubling questions about the nature of spectatorship, and the limits of violation. Were the face that of a man, one could see here a variant on the 'what is on men's minds' rebus, where the object of spectacle is 'written all over the spectator's face'. The fact that it is the face of a woman, the presumed object of spectacle, in conjunction with the beard, leaves no safe point of view within the frame possible, so extending the threat and the unresolved suggestion of culpability outwards. This quality of unsettling spectatorship distinguishes Magritte's painting from the other instances that I have looked at, where the bearded lady was a clearly delimited spectacle, who perhaps threatened the 'I' of the poem, or another protagonist, but allowed us to leave the tent and continue down the street once the *frisson* had done its business.

As a final, even more oblique, tilt at the bearded lady, I would propose Meret Oppenheim's fur-covered cup, saucer and spoon, *Le Déjeuner en fourrure* (1936). Maya Slater, in her introduction to *Les Mamelles* and the other plays in her selection, uses this as an example of the surrealist practice: 'to shock by juxtaposing objects that were not normally put together', such that 'Presenting these objects invites the public to view them in a new light, and liberates us from our dull, conventional attitudes.'[102] This, I have been suggesting, is something that *Les Mamelles* fails to do, and that no work bearing the surrealist tag can be simply assumed to do. I offer Oppenheim's piece as a concluding image, because of the ways in which its juxtapositions demand reflection on what constitutes their wrongness or rightness. The collision of elements is not instantly explicable, but it is not enough that it be merely absurd: if there is *no* sort of rightness or fittedness, then there can be no tension, no serious challenge to our 'dull, conventional attitudes'. As well as the clash of textures, and the marriage of organic and inorganic, *Le Déjeuner* takes an artefact associable with femininity *qua* gentility, fragility and decoration, and renders it feral. This is not a bearded lady. It does, however, arguably surprise us in an everyday familiar place with many of the questions over gender identity that the bearded lady potentially raises – only deprived of the comforting familiarity of a place in the cheap seats.

Notes

1 Salvador Dali, *Pensées et anecdotes* (Paris: Cherche Midi, 1995), p. 62.
2 My gloss on 'justice' here owes a debt to Jacques Derrida's discussion of the concept in *Spectres de Marx* (see Jacques Derrida, *Specters of Marx, the State of the Debt, the Work of Mourning, and the New International*, trans. by Peggy Kamuf (London: Routledge, 1994) and Jacques Derrida, *Force de loi* (Galilée: Paris, 1994)), but also to Eve Kosofsky Sedgwick's similarly etymological exploration of 'right' and 'straight' in 'Is the rectum straight?' (see Eve Kosofsky Sedgwick, 'Is the rectum straight? Identification and identity in *The Wings of the Dove*', in Eve Kosofsky Sedgwick, *Tendencies* (Durham, North Carolina: Duke University Press, 1993), pp. 73–103).
3 Linnaeus's *Lusus Naturae*.
4 'Carnivale' is created for HBO (a cable channel in the USA) by Daniel Knauf and produced by Bernie Caulfield (the series started in 2003). On a more

light-hearted note, one might cite the BBC Radio 4 female comedy group 'the bearded ladies', who promise a sideways, slightly wacky take on contemporary mores.

5 Guillaume Apollinaire, *L'Enchanteur pourissant, suivi de Les Mamelles de Tirésias et de couleur du temps* (Paris: Gallimard, 1972; reprinted 2000). Hereafter it is shortened to *Enchanteur*.

6 *Enchanteur*, p. 97.

7 *Enchanteur*, p. 94.

8 *Enchanteur*, p. 97; emphases mine.

9 In this respect, *Les Mamelles* fits easily into a loose tradition in modernist theatre from Alfred Jarry's *Ubu* plays, through *Parade* (1917) and Jean Cocteau and Darius Milhaud's *Le Boeuf sur le toit* (1920). The latter two works in particular seem to agree upon a conjunction of colourful figures drawn from carnival and café society, with brash, maniacal marching music, toy instruments, noises made by objects not necessarily thought of as musical instruments, etc. Indeed, Poulenc's later musical adaptation of *Les Mamelles* seems to underscore this kinship.

10 This is not, however, quite the first appearance of the word in print. *Les Mamelles* had its première on 24 June 1917. Apollinaire had already used 'sur-réalisme' in the programme notes to Erik Satie's *Parade* which premièred on 18 May of the same year. See Guillaume Apollinaire, *Chroniques d'art* (Paris: Gallimard, 1960; reprinted 1993), pp. 532–4.

11 *Enchanteur*, p. 94.

12 See e.g. Julia Hartwig, *Apollinaire* (Paris: Mercure de France, 1972), p. 378; Daniel Oster, *Guillaume Apollinaire* (Paris: Seghers, 1975), p. 111. Timothy Mathews refers to the time of *Les Mamelles* as 'a period in his thinking that, with hindsight, has been called pre-Surrealist': in Timothy Mathews, *Reading Apollinaire: Theories of Poetic Language* (Manchester: Manchester University Press, 1987), p. 126.

13 André Breton, *Manifestes du surréalisme* (Paris: Gallimard, 1975), p. 36.

14 Breton, *Manifestes*, p. 32.

15 Breton, *Manifestes*, p. 29.

16 Breton, *Manifestes*, p. 30; emphasis mine.

17 Breton, *Manifestes*, pp. 31–3.

18 Breton, *Manifestes*, p. 37.

19 Breton, *Manifestes*, p. 40.

20 *Enchanteur*, p. 98.

21 Breton, *Manifestes*, pp. 36–7.

22 Maya Slater, *Three Surrealist Plays* (Oxford: Oxford University Press, 1997), p. xxxi.

23 *Enchanteur*, pp. 96–7.

24 Denis Bordat and Bernard Veck, *Apollinaire* (Paris: Hachette, 1983), pp. 206–7.

25 Peter Read, *Apollinaire et Les Mamelles de Tirésias. La Revanche d'Éros* (Rennes: Presses Universitaires de Rennes: 2000), p. 121.

26 Read, *Apollinaire et Les Mamelles de Tirésias*.

27 Read, *Apollinaire et Les Mamelles de Tirésias*, p. 88.

28 Read, *Apollinaire et Les Mamelles de Tirésias*, p. 77.

29 *Enchanteur*, p. 121.

30 *Enchanteur*, p. 122.

31 Read, *Apollinaire et Les Mamelles de Tirésias*, p. 78.

32 Philippe Renaud, *Lecture d'Apollinaire* (Lausanne: L'Age d'Homme, 1969).

33 Renaud, *Lecture d'Apollinaire*, p. 13.

34 Renaud, *Lecture d'Apollinaire*, p. 14.

35 Renaud, *Lecture d'Apollinaire*, pp. 14–15.

36 Renaud, *Lecture d'Apollinaire*, p. 14.

37 Jean-Bertrand Barrère, *Le Regard d'Orphée: ou l'échange poétique* (Paris: Société d'édition d'enseignement supérieur, 1977).

38 Barrère, *Le Regard d'Orphée*, p. 208.

39 Barrère, *Le Regard d'Orphée*, p. 189.

40 Barrère, *Le Regard d'Orphée*, p. 191.

41 Barrère, *Le Regard d'Orphée*, p. 197.

42 Barrère, *Le Regard d'Orphée*, pp. 200–1.

43 Leroy C. Breunig, *Guillaume Apollinaire* (New York: Columbia University Press, 1969), pp. 36–7.

44 David Berry, *The Creative Vision of Guillaume Apollinaire: a Study of Imagination* (Saratoga: Anima, 1982), p. 103; emphasis mine. The reference is to 'Lou mon étoile', but could equally apply to the prologue to *Les Mamelles*, or to *Calligrammes*.

45 *Enchanteur*, pp. 17–20.

46 *Enchanteur*, pp. 31–2. Apollinaire also applies the word 'prolifique' to the Germans in the preface to *Les Mamelles* (see *Enchanteur*, p. 96).

47 *Enchanteur*, p. 56.

48 *Enchanteur*, p. 57.

49 *Enchanteur*, p. 59.

50 *Enchanteur*, pp. 35–6.

51 *Enchanteur*, p. 43.

52 *Enchanteur*, p. 25.

53 *Enchanteur*, p. 48.

54 *Enchanteur*, p. 49.

55 *Enchanteur*, p. 29.

56 Tristan Tzara, *Dada est Tatou. Tout est Dada* (Paris: Flammarion, 1996).

57 Tzara, *Dada est Tatou*, p. 108.

58 Tzara, *Dada est Tatou*, p. 113; emphasis mine.

59 Cf. the famous phrase of Lautréamont, '[beau] comme la rencontre fortuite sur une table de dissection d'une machine à coudre et d'un parapluie!', in *Les Chants de Maldoror* (Paris: Librairie Générale Française, 1992), p. 206.

60 Tzara, *Dada est Tatou*, p. 115.

61 Tzara, *Dada est Tatou*, pp. 108, 121, 228.

62 *Enchanteur*, p. 148.

63 *Enchanteur*, pp. 151–2.

64 *Enchanteur*, p. 144.

65 *Enchanteur*, pp. 155–6.

66 *Enchanteur*, p. 129.

67 *Enchanteur*, p. 131.

68 *Enchanteur*, p. 133.

69 *Enchanteur*, pp. 134–5

70 *Enchanteur*, p. 141; emphasis is mine.

71 *Enchanteur*, p. 135.

72 *Enchanteur*, p. 130.

73 *Enchanteur*, p. 158.

74 Read, *Apollinaire et Les Mamelles de Tirésias*, p. 53.

75 Read, *Apollinaire et Les Mamelles de Tirésias*, p. 176.

76 *Enchanteur*, p. 158.

77 *Enchanteur*, p. 95.

78 Alfred Jarry, 'De l'inutilité du théâtre au théâtre', in *Oeuvres complètes*, vol. I (Paris: Gallimard, 1972), p. 409.

79 Guillaume Apollinaire, *Les Onze Mille Verges: ou les amours d'un Hospodar* (Paris: J'ai Lu, 1976; reprinted 2005).

80 Apollinaire, *Les Onze Mille Verges*, p. 35.

81 Apollinaire, *Les Onze Mille Verges*, p. 58.

82 Apollinaire, *Les Onze Mille Verges*, p. 19.

83 Apollinaire, *Les Onze Mille Verges*, pp. 40–1.

84 Apollinaire, *Les Onze Mille Verges*, p. 59, p. 70, p. 101.

85 Apollinaire, *Les Onze Mille Verges*, p. 24.

86 Apollinaire, *Les Onze Mille Verges*, p. 42.

87 Apollinaire, *Les Onze Mille Verges*, p. 76.

88 Apollinaire, *Les Onze Mille Verges*, p. 53.

89 Evanghélia Stead, *Le Monstre, le singe et le foetus: tératogonie et décadence dans l'Europe fin-de-siècle* (Geneva: Droz, 2004). Stead unfortunately does not mention Apollinaire.

90 Stead, *Le Monstre, le singe et le foetus*, p. 190.

91 Lautréamont [no first name], *Les Chants de Maldoror. Poésies* (Paris: Livre de Poche, 1992), pp. 239–40. *Les Chants de Maldoror* is a key work for Surrealism, liberally quoted by André Breton. *Poésies*, in which the denunciation of the *femme à barbe* quoted above appears, was republished for the first time by Breton in *Littérature* 2 and 3 (April and May 1919).

92 Stead, *Le Monstre, le singe et le foetus*, pp. 176–7, p. 180, p. 213.

93 Zeev Gourarier, *Il était une fois: la fête foraine de 1850 à 1950* (Paris: Réunion des Musées Nationaux, 1996), p. 74. The catalogue makes great play of the virility of the fair. Hence the entry for 'Femme': 'Fière et virile la voici catcheuse, colosse ou femme à barbe'; and for 'Homme': 'La foire est une grande fête de la virilité sous toutes ses formes.' (p. 88).

94 Guillaume Apollinaire, *Oeuvres poétiques* (Paris: Gallimard, 1965), p. 714.

95 Gustave Flaubert and Guy de Maupassant, *Correspondance* (Paris: Flammarion, 1993), p. 101; see also note, p. 380.

96 Guy de Maupassant, *Oeuvres poétiques completes* (Rouen: Publications de l'Université de Rouen, 2001).

97 Germain Nouveau, *Oeuvres poétiques*, vol. 1 (Paris: Gallimard, 1953), p. 128.

98 Stead, *Le Monstre, le singe et le foetus*, p. 190.

99 See J. Gessler, *La Légende de Sainte Wilgeforte ou Ontcommer, la vierge miraculeusement barbue. Notes bibliographiques, archéologiques et folkloriques* (Brussels/Paris: A. Picard, 1938).

100 See Thomas Calinon, 'Une vie de femme à barbe exhumée d'un cahier d'é-
colier', *Libération* (30 June 2005). See also Susan Bell, 'Memoirs of a bearded
lady who noted barbed comments in ink', *Scotsman* (21 June 2005). Mme
Delait now also has an extensive web presence.

101 Unfortunately, no precise date is possible. The image is by the artist Zutna,
and printed by Imagerie Pellerin. Further details are available on a French
government website at: www.culture.gouv.fr/public/mistral/joconde_fr (last
accessed on 25 November 2005).

102 Slater, *Three Surrealist Plays*, p. xi.

6 'That wonderful phænomenon': female body hair and English literary tradition

Carolyn D. Williams

Bringing the terms of the title into relationship with each other is no easy matter. Writing on female body hair *in* English literary tradition goes against the grain: everything below eyelash level has been subject to so much total or partial erasure that it would be easier to write on it *behind, beneath, outside* or even *despite* English literary tradition. The erasure is often redoubled in passages where, realistically speaking, depilation must have been involved: the removal of something whose existence has never been acknowledged cannot be mentioned without a breakdown in logic. Until the late twentieth century, more direct representations are restricted to genres regarded as artistically or socially inferior, or to points where writers are lowering the tone to raise a laugh, or defying contemporary conventions of decency and politeness in an attempt to broaden aesthetic sensibilities. Female body hair may be presented as 'other', distanced from reader and writer by differences in time, space, culture or, where figurative and symbolic writing are employed, species. At worst, it is depicted as repellent and threatening, a warning of perversion or unfeminine rebellion against patriarchal rule. Discussion of this complex subject, which is often expressed in vague and ambiguous language, can be clarified by categorising writing about women's bodies in terms of presence and absence. Present presence indicates natural hair-growth; present absence denotes the processes and effects of depilation; absent absence occurs in situations where only depilation could account for the smoothness of the body described, but it is never mentioned; absent presence, the favoured mode in polite literature from the Middle Ages until the mid-twentieth century, is the product of a society where nearly every woman past puberty is covered with hair, but a conspiracy of silence renders it culturally invisible.

This chapter will begin by examining the erasure of female body hair in general from polite literature, followed by the special status of pubic hair, and the means by which writers seek to convey its presence without incurring charges of obscenity: where appropriate, ancient Greek and Latin sources will be cited. There follows an examination of more direct treatments of pubic hair, ranging from writers of the seventeenth and eighteenth centuries to the modernists James Joyce (1882–1941) and D. H. Lawrence (1885–1930). Special mention is accorded to another project which ran roughly parallel to the lives of Joyce and Lawrence and, while less frequently acknowledged, generated even greater frankness. From 1882 to 1923, new versions of the *Arabian Nights*, in English and French, brought not only body hair but depilation into focus. Nevertheless, their exotic framing suggests that they were still not completely domesticated. Subsequent writing supports this view: the appearance and removal of women's body hair still has disturbing connotations, and it also features in historical or science fiction as something alien and exciting. Writers and their readers are not entirely comfortable with the realisation that 'MOSSY FACE' is 'The mother of all saints'.[1]

Erasures similar to the absences which occur so frequently in English literature characterise many of the ancient Greek and Latin texts which have exerted such a powerful influence on Western culture. Let us inspect the toilette of Hera, Queen of Heaven, in Homer's *Iliad*, the seminal ancient Greek epic which took shape between 800 and 550 BC. She is planning to inveigle her husband, Zeus, the notoriously adulterous King of the Gods, so should surely use every available cosmetic technique:

> Here first she bathes; and round her Body pours
> Soft Oils of Fragrance, and ambrosial Show'rs:
> The Winds perfum'd, the balmy Gale convey
> Thro' Heav'n, thro' Earth, and all th'aerial Way;
> Spirit divine! whose Exhalation greets
> The Sense of Gods with more than mortal Sweets.
> Thus while she breath'd of Heav'n, with decent Pride
> Her artful Hands the radiant Tresses ty'd;
> Part on her Head in shining Ringlets roll'd,
> Part o'er her Shoulders wav'd like melted Gold.
> (XIV, lines 197–206)[2]

This is the translation of Alexander Pope (1688–1744), first published 1715–20, and itself a respected classic of Augustan literature. One of the first things any twenty-first century woman would notice is the absence of depilatory products and processes. We might assume that ancient Greek women and their sexual partners found female body hair attractive, but for surviving evidence of obsessive depilation. The most uproarious dramatisation of present absence is provided by Aristophanes (c. 448–380 BC), who shows that a man who wishes to pass for a woman must have not only a shaven face, but a depilated bottom. Jeffrey Henderson has produced a translation for the third millennium:

EURIPIDES.   Get up so I can singe you; bend over and don't move.
KINSMAN.   Damn the luck, I'm going to be roast pig!

EURIPIDES.   Somebody bring out a torch or a lamp. [*Slave brings out a lighted torch and hands it to Euripides.*]
Bend over. Now watch out for the tip of your dick.

KINSMAN.   I'll watch out, all right – only I'm on fire! Oh no, no! [*to the audience*] Water! Water, neighbours, before somebody *else's* arse catches fire!

EURIPIDES.   Be brave.

KINSMAN.   How am I supposed to be brave when I'm being turbo-vulcanized?

EURIPIDES.   You've got nothing more to fret about; you've suffered through the worst part.

KINSMAN.   Yuk! Oh, the soot! All around my crotch I'm blackened!
(*Women at the Thesmophoria*, lines 236–46)[3]

Presumably goddesses, unlike mortal women, do not have unwanted fuzz. Whatever the reason, Homer gives us a censored image of the female body within a work which has historically enjoyed much wider circulation, critical admiration and social prestige than Aristophanes' satirical comedy.

This stereotype of absent absence was easy to accept because, for millennia, it seemed both appealing and logical. A mental image of an ideal woman with little or no body hair fitted in with medical, psychological and political theories which the classically educated authors of medieval and modern Europe inherited from Greece and Rome. According to Aristotle (384–22 BC), men were born with hairs

> on the head, the eyelids, and the eyebrows; of the later growths the hair on the pubes are the first to come, then those under the armpits, and, thirdly, those on the chin; for, singularly enough, the region where congenital growths and subsequent growths are found are equal in number. (*Historia Animalium*, Book III, 518a, lines 19–24)[4]

Women who resembled men were either menopausal hags or embodiments of impending doom:

> Women do not grow hairs on the chin; except that a scanty beard grows on some women after the monthly courses have stopped; and a similar phenomenon is observed at times in priestesses in Caria, but these cases are looked upon as portentous with regard to coming events. The other aftergrowths are found in women, but more scanty and sparse. (518a, line 32, to 518b, line 38)

Calling attention to any aspect of appearance that differentiated women from men, and tacitly encouraging women to enhance it by declaring it natural and attractive, makes perfect sense in a world where superiority of males to females occurs 'in all genera in which the distinction of male and female is found.' (Book 9, 608a, lines 22–3). Growth of male body hair was believed to be a side-effect of the constitutional heat which allowed males to develop strength, courage, intellect, virtue, public spirit and semen. Women were moister, and cooler in constitution, so that they might be hospitable growing media for the seed which men planted in them. Their consequent smoothness was a sign of physical, moral and intellectual inferiority.[5]

A typical literary application of this belief appears in *The Taming of the Shrew* by William Shakespeare (1564–1616), where Katharina, newly reclaimed from gross insubordination to patriarchal rule, persuades other wives to conform:

> Why are our bodies soft, and weak, and smooth,
> Unapt to toil and trouble in the world,
> But that our soft conditions and our hearts
> Should well agree with our external parts?
> (V, ii, lines 166–9)[6]

In the eighteenth century, the 'defect of heat' theory was still being used to encourage women to identify femininity with weakness, stupidity and complete dependence on men:

> to this defect they owe their whiteness, the softness of their skin, and, what is more, of their manners; that this gentler heat of temperament necessarily exempts them from those laborious works which are the employment of men; that they are regarded as the most delectable part of the commonwealth; nothing is done but for their sake, all labour for them alone, and nothing is requir'd of them in recompense [sic] for all the care which the men take of their fortunes, their lives and their pleasures, than to be just what they are.[7]

This sort of patronising gallantry (which, incidentally, takes no cognisance of women who perform manual labour for a living) receives short shrift in Kate Millett's *Sexual Politics* (1971): she denounces masculine chivalric attitudes as a technique for disguising 'the injustice of women's social position'.[8] The idea of female bodies as naturally cold, soft and waxen did many disservices to women. When a misogynistic character like Pinchwife calls women 'dough-baked, senseless, indocile [unteachable] animals' (*The Country Wife* (1675), IV, iv, lines 118–19), we need not believe that this expresses the author's views, but it is easy to see how the notion of women as constitutionally colder than men could lead to gross underestimation of female intelligence.[9] Belief in the cold female constitution also encouraged the assumption that women were eternally ready to receive sexual advances: when John Vanbrugh (1664–1726) makes a despairing lover complain that his beloved is 'cold as the northern star', his friend consoles him with the reflection that 'So are all women by nature, which makes them so willing to be warmed' (*The Provoked Wife* (1697), II, i, lines 135–7).[10]

The erasure involved in this cult of absent absence is surprisingly thorough. Even writers who wish to depict women as revolting, and would presumably leap at the chance to display something which they could present as monstrously unfeminine, neglect the opportunity. Juvenal (c. 65 to c. 125) makes no mention of female body hair in his *Sixth Satire*, the ground zero of Western misogyny. The only body hair that he mentions appears on eunuchs who have been castrated after puberty, so that they can make love to their mistresses without causing unwanted pregnancies:

> illa voluptas summa tamen, quom iam calida matura iuuenta inguina traduntur medicis, iam pectine nigro. (lines 368–70)[11]
> (But that pleasure is at its highest when the groins handed over to the surgeons are already ripe with burning youth and a black bush.)

Almost equal restraint appears in the writings of Jonathan Swift (1667–1745), who composed several poems in which he deliberately set out to undermine poetic images of feminine glamour by depicting women's bodies, or the substances which emanate from them, or are used to beautify them, as disgusting. Body hair appears most clearly in 'The Lady's Dressing Room' (1732), where an over-curious admirer inspects the lovely Celia's sanctum, and finds it filled with stomach-churning evidence of tooth-cleaning, nail-paring, face-painting and worse. The appearance of a soiled smock, 'Beneath the arm-pits well besmeared' (line 12), implies awareness of underarm hair as a harbour for perspiration and attendant odours.[12] Celia also owns tweezers:

> To pluck her brows in arches round,
> Or hairs that sink the forehead low,
> Or on her chin like bristles grow.
> (lines 56–8)[13]

But facial hair fades into insignificance beside the lover's traumatised howl: ' "Oh! Celia, Celia, Celia shits!" ' (line 118).[14] This line reappears at the conclusion (line 18) of 'Cassinus and Peter: a Tragical Elegy' (1734), where Cassinus, a Cambridge undergraduate, is driven mad by the knowledge of Celia's defecation – an act which he believes no other woman commits. As a good classical scholar, he experiences appropriate hallucinations from Greek mythology, culminating with: 'Medusa, see,/Her serpents hiss direct at me.' (lines 85–6)[15] This glimpse of the snake-haired goddess, the sight of whom turns men to stone, links Cassinus's horror with a vision of the hairy female pudenda, which makes Celia doubly monstrous. As if in the interest of fairness, Swift provides a sighting of male body hair, which is rare in this period, in the opening description of Cassinus's demoralised state:

> Scorched were his shins, his legs were bare,
> But, well embrowned with dirt and hair.
> (lines 17–18)[16]

Cassinus would have been less naive about women if he had thought more carefully about the implications of his own anatomy. In each of these poems, the lover's unrealistic expectations are held up to ridicule: the Celias, despite their unwanted or threatening growths of hair, are beautiful young ladies. The only truly repulsive female in this group of poems is Corinna, the Drury Lane prostitute in 'A Beautiful Young Nymph Going to Bed: Written for the Honour of the Fair Sex' (1734), where lack of hair is a problem. Her routine begins when she 'Takes off her artificial hair' (line 10).[17] Since the rest of this section concerns her head and face, it is safe to assume that Swift is alluding to a wig. She removes her glass eye, then:

> Her eyebrows from a mouse's hide,
> Stuck on with art on either side,
> Pulls off with care, and first displays 'em,
> Then in a play-book smoothly lays 'em.
> (lines 13–16)[18]

The presence of natural hair on any part of her body might have reassured prospective clients about her health, but her 'shankers [chancres], issues, running sores' (line 30) show that she is already suffering advanced venereal disease.[19]

For the most celebrated classical mentions of women's hairy legs, we must turn to Ovid (43 BC to AD 18), in Book III of *Ars Amatoria* (The Art of Love), ostensibly designed to help women catch their men, though it also serves to alert male readers to the devices used to conceal women's physical shortcomings. But leg hair is mentioned only once, and then in the context of its removal: now you see it, now you don't. Depilation, like other personal grooming, fits Roman ladies for their national identity, and their moment in history. Ovid associates anything unkempt with a rustic 'Simplicitas' (line 113) inappropriate to contemporary Rome: 'nunc aurea Roma est,/Et domiti magnas possidet orbis opes' (lines 113–14) [now Rome is golden, and possesses the great riches of the conquered world.][20] His approach to this ticklish subject is extremely tentative:

> Quam paene admonui, ne trux caper iret in alas,
> Neve forent duris aspera crura pilis!
> Sed non Caucasea doceo de rupe puellas,
> (lines 193–5)[21]
> (I was about to warn you not to keep the stubborn he-goat from your armpits, and prevent your legs becoming rough with hard bristles! But I am not teaching girls from Mount Caucasus.)

Roman girls define their nationality by banishing body hair: to do otherwise would not be exotic so much as barbaric. There are other things they can (or must?) do to improve their looks, including another manipulation of hair: extending eyebrows that fall short of perfection: 'Arte supercilii confinia nuda repletis' (line 201).[22] William King (1663–1712), when imitating *The Art of Love*, retains the false eyebrows:

> Who wou'd a charming Eyebrow lack,
> Who can get any thing that's Black.
> (Part XII, lines 82–3).[23]

He omits the depilated legs – probably a case of absent presence, since his contemporaries preferred Roman verse to Roman grooming.[24] More recent literature has expressed greater frankness and tolerance. The jury may still be out where hair on legs is concerned, but at least its attractions on arms have been acknowledged: T. S. Eliot (1888–1965), in 'The Love Song of J. Alfred Prufrock' (1915), makes his frustrated anti-hero muse longingly on:

> Arms that are braceleted and white and bare
> (But in the lamplight, downed with light brown hair!)
> (lines 63–4)[25]

Even this, however, is too much for some readers: one of my students, clearly rattled by the intrusion of body hair into poetry of any sort, interpreted the reference to hair as an indication of the poet's disgust at the female body.

The pubis is the only site on a woman's body where the existence of hair is frequently acknowledged, but this process is often a matter of paraphrase, metaphor and symbolism, to be decoded only by readers already in the know: many male writers appear determined to display their knowledge to fellow initiates, perhaps to advertise their own masculine sophistication. Contempt for ignorance of the female form can be deduced from the definition of 'NICKUMPOOP, or NINCUMPOOP' as 'A foolish fellow; also one who never saw his wife's ****'.[26] Unfortunately, for some potential nickumpoops, the open secret remained closed. There is a popular legend that John Ruskin (1819–1900), distinguished critic of art and literature, failed to consummate his marriage with the beautiful Euphemia Chalmers Gray (1828–97) because he was put off by her pubic hair, never having seen or read about anything like it in the works of which he had so much expert knowledge.[27] This probably did happen to Wriothesley Russell, third Duke of Bedford (1708–32). In August 1725, Lady Mary Wortley Montagu (1689–1762) wrote a letter to her sister, Lady Mar, attributing the bridegroom's revulsion from the marriage bed to ignorance of what he would find there:

> our Duke of Bedford [. . .] by the care of a pious Mother certainly preserv'd his Virginity to his marriage bed, where he was so much disappointed in his fair Bride (who thô his own Inclination could not bestow on him those expressless Raptures he had figur'd to himselfe) that he already Pukes at the very name of her, and determines to let his Estate go to his Brother, rather than go through the filthy Drudgery of getting an Heir to it. [. . .] This comes of living till sixteen

without a competent knowledge either of practical or speculative Anatomy, and litterally thinking fine Ladys compos'd of Lillys and Roses.[28]

How could a writer express his awareness that women were not all lilies and roses without violating decency or politeness? In Pope's *Rape of the Lock* (1714), the solution was to implicate the reader: Belinda, an aristocratic young virgin whose ringlet has been snipped off by the Baron, rebukes him with the cry:

> Oh had'st thou, Cruel! been content to seize
> Hairs less in sight, or any Hairs but these!
> (IV, 175–6)[29]

Read – or written – by anyone ignorant of mature female anatomy, the passage is simply Belinda's statement that the removal of hair from another part of her head would have caused less damage to her coiffure. It is one of those famously iridescent passages in a poem whose every line appears to change colour with the point of view. What do we think Pope meant that Belinda meant? How much are we prepared to admit that we suspect? Has Pope been cruelly misunderstood by dirty-minded critics? Does he mean his fine lady to be a whore? Or is he deliberately creating one of the best-timed double-takes in world literature? Shakespeare uses a similar technique when the mad Lear gives vent to his sexual disgust:

> Down to the waist they are Centaurs,
> Though women all above:
> But to the girdle do the gods inherit,
> Beneath is all the fiends':
> There's hell, there's darkness, there is the sulphurous pit,
> Burning, scalding, stench, consumption; fie, fie, fie! pah, pah! Give me an
>   ounce of civet, good apothecary, to sweeten my imagination'
> (*King Lear*, IV, iv, lines 127–34)[30]

Some audience members might picture women as centaurs in a purely allegorical sense – creatures with human faces who indulge base animal lusts; others would take the parallel more literally, imagining manes and tails.

Among many resorts to metaphor, allegory and metonymy, some have acquired traditional status. A venerable ploy is the parallel between the woman's body and a landscape, usually involving an enclosure, luxuriant vegetation and a source of water. This is how Homer describes the cave in which Ulysses acts as unwilling love slave to the goddess Calypso:

> Depending vines the shelving cavern screen,
> With purple clusters blushing thro' the green.
> Four limpid fountains from the clefts distill,
> And ev'ry fountain pours a sev'ral rill,
> In mazy windings wand'ring down the hill.
> (*Odyssey*, V, lines 88–92)[31]

The most important erotic enclosure in Western culture, however, is not classical but biblical; it appears in Chapter IV of *The Song of Solomon*:

12 A garden inclosed is my sister, my spouse;
A spring shut up, a fountain sealed.
13 Thy plants are an orchard of pomegranates, with pleasant fruits;
Camphire, with spikenard,
14 Spikenard and saffron;
Calamus and cinnamon, with all trees of frankincense;
Myrrh, and aloes, with all the chief spices:
15 A fountain of gardens,
A well of living water,
And streams from Lebanon.[32]

The identification of girl with garden has become an influential literary trope, though the nature of the physical detail suggested by this passage, and the proportion of spiritual to literal interpretation, varies from reader to reader. Shakespeare, by contrast, leaves nothing in doubt when Venus, in hot pursuit of Adonis, draws a direct comparison between her own naked body and the park in which the boy prefers to hunt:

Within this limit is relief enough,
Sweet bottom-grass and high delightful plain,
Round rising hillocks, brakes obscure and rough,
To shelter thee from tempest and from rain.
(*Venus and Adonis* (1593), lines 235–8)[33]

John Milton (1608–74) in *Paradise Lost* (1667), makes Satan describe the location of the Tree of Knowledge to Eve in terms which delicately evoke these sexual gardens:

Beyond a row of myrtles, on a flat,
Fast by a fountain, one small thicket past
Of blowing myrrh and balm.
(Book IX, lines 627–9)[34]

Although the main motive for this allusive approach appears to be the evasion of indecency, there may also be a cosmetic element, as pretty vegetation is substituted for a less-attractive reality. Pubic hair can be so revolting that the metaphor collapses under its weight, as in an otherwise frankly joyous exercise in pornography by Thomas Nashe (1567–c. 1601). His narrator clearly prefers the bare skin of his mistress's belly to the tangles beneath:

A prettie rising wombe without a weame,
That shone as bright as anie silver streame;
And bare out lyke the bending of an hill,
At whose decline a fountaine dwelleth still,

That hath his mouth beset with uglie bryers
Resembling much a duskie nett of wyres.
(*A Choise of Valentines* [before 1597], lines 109–14)[35]

For those who prefer not to represent human hair as vegetation, the muff, made of animal fur, is a favourite stand-by. The cavalier poet Richard Lovelace (1618–57/8) presents his beloved's body as an open secret, to be shared by any reader who knows what's what, in his brief lyric, 'Her Muffe' (first published 1659). After devoting four verses to the accessory used to warm his lady's hands, he abandons such trivia and proclaims his status as an initiate into love's mysteries:

This for Lay-Lovers, that must stand at dore,
Salute the threshold, and admire no more;
But I, in my Invention tough,
Rate not this outward bliss enough.
But still contemplate must the hidden Muffe.
(lines 21–5)[36]

In *Tom Jones* (1749), Henry Fielding (1707–54) makes great play with the heroine's muff. She is delighted when her maid describes the hero's treatment of this richly associative object: 'he put his hands into it, that very muff your ladyship gave me but yesterday; "La," says I, "Mr Jones, you will stretch my lady's muff and spoil it;" but he still kept his hands in it, and then he kissed it – to be sure, I never saw such a kiss in my life as he gave it.' (Book IV, Chapter 14).[37] The meaning is inescapable: 'To the well wearing of your muff, mort' was allegedly an appropriate toast to a lower-class bride.[38] Laurence Sterne (1713–68), whose bawdiness generally takes an original twist, stays with fur, but uses a cap instead of a muff as a means for his narrative persona to express his sexual frustration:

By all that is hirsute and gashly! I cry, taking off my furred cap, and twisting it round my finger – I would not give sixpence for a dozen such!
   But such an excellent cap too (putting it upon my head, and pressing it close to my ears) – and warm – and soft; especially if you stroke it the right way – but alas! that will never be my luck – (so here my philosophy is shipwrecked again).
   No; I shall never have a finger in the pie (so here I break my metaphor).
(*Tristram Shandy* [1759–67], Vol. VIII, Chapter 11).[39]

In lowlier genres, such as the satirical ballad, puns might be called to the aid of imagery. The furry pelt and ambiguous nomenclature of the rabbit (or 'cony') have been of particular service to writers seeking to adumbrate a woman's hirsute gash. Pope was inspired to compose a bawdy ballad when word got about that a Mrs Mary Tofts of Godalming was allegedly giving birth to rabbits, and that the anatomist Nathanael St André (1680–1776) and Samuel Molyneux (1689–1728), Secretary to the Prince of Wales, had inspected the evidence and believed her claims. The result was 'The Discovery: or, The Squire turn'd Ferret, an Excellent New Ballad, To the Tune of *High Boys! up go we*; *Chevy Chase*; Or what you please' (1726).

> On Tiptoe then the Squire [Molyneux] he stood,
> (But first He gave Her Money)
> Then reach'd as high as e'r He cou'd,
> And cry'd, I feel a CONY.
>
> Is it alive? *St. A-d-re* cry'd;
> It is; I feel it stir.
> Is it full grown? The Squire reply'd,
> It is, see here's the FUR.
> (lines 57–64)[40]

In the hands of a master, even lowly forms could accommodate subtlety. When Geoffrey Chaucer (1342–1400) composed *The Miller's Tale*, a verse *fabliau*, he led up to his catastrophe with a nicely judged combination of simile and dramatic irony. A major climax comes when Absolon, the dandified parish clerk so pathetically 'squaymous/Of fartyng' (lines 3336/7),[41] is ambushed by Alison's offer of a midnight kiss out of her chamber window:

> Abak he stirte, and thoughte it was amys,
> For wel he wiste a woman hath no berd.
> He felte a thing al rough and long yherd,
> And seyde, 'Fy! allas! what have I do?'
> 'Tehee!' quod she, and clapte the wyndow to.
> (lines 3736–40)

As in all great literary tragedies (one thinks of Sophocles's *Œdipus Rex*), the ground is prepared beforehand by clues which it is fatally easy for the hero, or even an unprepared audience, to ignore. Chaucer drops repeated hints about the thoroughness with which Alison is armed for Absolon's destruction. He twice compares her to a colt (lines 3263, 3282), declares her body was as slender as 'any wezele' (line 3243), mentions that she plucked her eyebrows (lines 3245), and combines suggestive simile with metonymy by observing that she was:

> softer than the wolle is of a wether.
> And by hir girdle heeng a purs of lether,
> Tasseled with silk.
> (lines 3249–50)

Short of hanging a sign about Alison's neck, saying 'Danger: this woman is hairy', what more could a conscientious poet do?

Writers had to adopt different approaches when dealing more directly, and at greater length, with this subject. In a group of three genteelly

bawdy verse tales, where a woman's pubic hair is the main focus of attention, each author progresses from the problems of representing the hair
itself, to considering what it represents about women. In 'La Chose impossible' (1674), Jean de la Fontaine (1621–95) tells the tale of a man who signs
a pact with a devil in order to gain the favours of his beloved. He may have
his lady so long as he keeps giving the devil orders. As soon as he runs out
of requests, he will lose everything, including his soul. The wretched lover
soon realises that he has underestimated the devil's speed and efficiency;
he confides in his lady, who instantly provides the solution: he must ask
the devil to straighten one of her hairs. The devil gives up, breaking the
fatal contract:

> Il ne put mettre à la raison
> La toison
> (lines 69–70)[42]

William Congreve (1670–1729), in his version, 'An Impossible Thing. A
Tale' (1720), lays great stress on the indefinability, and magical beauty, of
the mysterious object which the lady presents to her lover:

> A Tendril of the *Cyprian* Vine?
> Or Sprig from *Cytherea's* Grove?
> Shade of the Labyrinth of Love?
> With Awe, he now takes from her Hand
> That Fleece-like Flow'r of fairy Land:
> (lines 124–8)[43]

The hair's indomitable curliness is identified with the power of female
sexuality: when the demon tries (and fails) to straighten it with water,
Congreve observes,

> Poor foolish Fiend! he little knew
> Whence Venus and her *Garden* grew.
> (lines 155–6)[44]

The devil becomes obsessed by the mystery of 'That wonderful
Phænomenon' (line 174):[45]

> For never yet was Wool or Feather,
> That could stand buff against all Weather;
> And unrelax'd like this, resist
> Both Wind and Rain, and Snow and Mist.
> What Stuff, or whence, or how 'twas made,
> What Spinster Witch could spin such Thread,
> He nothing knew; but to his Cost
> Knew all his Fame and Labour lost.
> Suubdu'd, abash'd, he gave it o'er;
> 'Tis said, he blush'd; 'tis sure he swore
> Not all the Wiles that Hell could hatch

Could conquer that Superb Mustach.
(lines 179–90)[46]

The demon despairs, confronted by the insatiability of female desire. The third writer, Elijah Fenton (1683–1730), pays more attention to the heroine as a personality. In 'The Fair Nun' (1717), an indecisive young lady takes the veil, regrets her vows, and makes a deal with the devil in order to elope from the convent and marry a handsome young man. She negotiates much better terms than the men in the two previous stories: the contract will simply become null and void if she asks the devil to perform a service he cannot render. She entraps the devil by skilful self-parody, presenting the task as the lightest of girlish whims:

'Sir Nic,' quoth she, 'you know us all,
We ladies are fantastical'
(lines 141–2).[47]

So the curls which had so deviously represented feminine unreason and feminine passion now come to represent feminine wiles. In every case, they give cause for celebration, pledging physical delight while saving the soul. But they are also powerful, mysterious and, consequently, slightly alarming.

Poems like these probably reflected contemporary consumer taste. In real life, under-endowed girls could purchase merkin, 'false pubic hair for whores worn bald by overwork'.[48] But customers apparently preferred the genuine article. Merkin is likened to 'a sapless hedge, where th' land is poor'. (I, i, line 34)[49] In the eighteenth century, John Cleland (1710–89) was the prose laureate of pubic hair. In *Memoirs of a Woman of Pleasure* (1748–49), Fanny Hill's sexual initiation begins when she is in her early teens, and Phoebe, an experienced whore with same-sex preferences, caresses:

the soft silky down that had but a few months before put forth, and garnish'd the mount-pleasant of those parts, and promised to spread a grateful shelter over the sweet seat of the most exquisite sensation, and which had been, till that instant, the seat of the most insensible innocence. Her fingers play'd, and strove to twine in the young tendrils of that moss which nature has contrived at once for use and ornament.[50]

Cleland uses hair growth to distinguish age as well as sex, in men and women. Phoebe, who is at least thirty-five years old, sports 'a spreading thicket of bushy curls' which 'mark'd the full-grown complete woman'.[51] When Fanny first sees Charles, the love of her life, he is a youth on the verge of manhood, whose bosom is 'whiter than a drift of snow'.[52] His burgeoning masculinity is delicately adumbrated by 'the first down over his upper-lip',[53] and triumphantly declared by his magnificent penis: Fanny admires 'the beautiful growth of the hair, in short and soft curls round its root'.[54] Charles's appearance indicates why the pubic area is the one place where female body hair is desirable: in both sexes, hair round the genitalia is a certificate of maturity, guaranteeing satisfaction to a partner; anywhere else, it is prohibited for women, and optional for men. Fanny's next lover, the forty-year-old Mr *H*–, takes up his options to the full. He has a 'rough shaggy breast', as well as 'hairy thighs, and stiff staring truncheon, red-topt, and rooted into a thicket of curls, which cover'd his belly to his navel, and gave it the air of a flesh-brush.'[55] Cleland's simile produces a comically grotesque effect. He appears to be seeking a more serious response to the young whores who display their charms at Fanny's first orgy. When it is the turn of 'that delicatest of charmers, the winning tender *Harriet*', we are told that the company were 'dazzled, surpris'd, and delighted' by the view of her beauties, including 'that central furrow which nature had sunk there: the dark umbrage of the downy sprig-moss that over-arch'd it, bestow'd on the luxury of the landscape, a touching warmth, a tender finishing, beyond the expression of words, or even the paint of thought.'[56] The next girl also arouses general admiration by 'the fringe of light-brown curls [. . .] that with their silky gloss created a pleasing variety from the surrounding white, whose lustre too, their gentle embrowning shade considerably raised.'[57]

A familiar contrast emerges from these descriptions: even writers who are frank and celebratory in their treatment of female pubic hair appear to work on the assumption that these luxuriant displays are mounted on naturally bare legs. Similar effects survive into the twentieth century. Molly Bloom, whose soliloquy composes chapter 18 of James Joyce's *Ulysses* (1922), is a mature, well-endowed woman, like Phoebe, with plenty to spare: 'I think Ill [*sic*] cut this hair off me there [. . .] I might look like a young girl.'[58] But she takes pride in the silkiness of the surrounding thighs: 'look how white they are the smoothest place is right there between this bit here how soft like a peach'.[59] Lady Chatterley follows suit: naked in the gamekeeper's hut, 'She sat on his thighs, her head against his breast, and her ivory-gleaming legs loosely apart', surrounding 'the fleece of soft brown hair that hung down to a point between her open thighs.'[60]

One reason for absenting depilation is the desire to emphasise the connection between women's pubic hair and the natural. This appears in the episode where Mellors, the gamekeeper, gives literal form to the traditional vegetation imagery by turning Lady Chatterley into the receptacle for a flower arrangement:

> With quiet fingers he threaded a few forget-me-not flowers in the fine brown fleece of the mound of Venus.
> 'There!' he said. 'There's forget-me-nots in the right place!'
> She looked down at the milky odd little flowers among the brown maidenhair at the lower tip of her body.
> 'Doesn't it look pretty!' she said.
> 'Pretty as life,' he replied.
> And he stuck a pink campion-bud among the hair.[61]

Soon, however, the return to nature gets out of hand. When Mellors extends the arrangement, his own humanity, including his power to communicate with Lady Chatterley, is partially obliterated:

> he was coming back, trotting strangely, and carrying flowers. She was a little afraid of him, as if he were not quite human. And when he came near, his eyes looked into hers, but she could not understand the meaning.
>
> He had brought columbines and campions, and new-mown hay, and oak-tufts and honeysuckle in small bud. He fastened fluffy young oak-sprays round her breasts, sticking in tufts of bluebells and campion: and in her navel he poised a pink campion flower, and in her maiden-hair were forget-me-nots and woodruff.
>
> 'That's you in all your glory!' he said. 'Lady Jane, at her wedding with John Thomas.'
>
> And he stuck flowers in the hair of his own body, and wound a bit of creeping-jenny round his penis, and stuck a single bell of hyacinth in his navel. She watched him with amusement, his odd intentness. And she pushed a campion flower in his moustache, where it stuck, dangling under his nose.[62]

The implication of male body hair takes this exuberantly intimate communion with nature a step too far. Soon, allergy takes its toll:

> This is John Thomas marryin' Lady Jane,' he said. 'An' we mun let Constance an' Oliver go their ways. Maybe —'
>
> He spread out his hand with a gesture, and then he sneezed, sneezing away the flowers from his nose and his navel. He sneezed again.
>
> 'Maybe what?' she said, waiting for him to go on.
>
> He looked a little bewildered.
>
> 'Eh?' he said.
>
> 'Maybe what? Go on with what you were going to say,' she insisted.
>
> 'Ay, what *was* I going to say?'
>
> He had forgotten. And it was one of the disappointments of her life, that he never finished.[63]

The flowers that inspired Mellors's thought have made him unable to utter it. This celebrated, not to say notorious, passage marks an experiment in living for the characters, and an experiment in aesthetics for D. H. Lawrence. The moments of awkwardness and mutual incomprehension indicate risks that these flower-decked nudes will register, to the reader and each other, as 'not quite human'.

To many readers today, literature where body hair is treated openly and without fuss, whether as an object of admiration or a nuisance to be removed as a matter of routine, offers the welcome familiarity of a homecoming. A century ago, such a notion seemed bizarre, but rather intriguing: the perfect site for these unprecedented presences was found in *The Arabian Nights*. The enthusiasm with which references to these matters were selected, elaborated, annotated and invented by translators and editors shows that this openness was as much a Western creation as an import, and consequently entitled to a place in the history of mainstream and English – and French – literature. Evidence for this claim will be mainly derived from *The Book of the Thousand Nights and One Night* (1923) by Edward Powys Mathers (1892–1939), translated from *Le Livre des mille nuits et une nuit* (1899–1904) by Joseph Charles Mardrus (1868–1949). In order to establish how inventive Mardrus was, comparisons will be drawn with Husain Haddawy's *Arabian Nights* (1990), faithfully translated from Muhsin Mahdi's magisterial edition of a fourteenth-century Syrian manuscript. Where a story appears that is not in Haddawy, recourse will be made to translations by John Payne (1842–1916) or Richard Francis Burton (1821–90). Passages without equivalent in any of these versions will be taken as evidence of Mardrus's resourcefulness in attaching new material to the *Nights* – a venerable tradition in the history of 'the most famous work of narrative fiction in existence.'[64]

Mardrus and Mathers use body hair to add ironic point to a well-known story: in their version of 'The Master of the White Mare', a man who has purchased, but not yet deflowered, a blonde slave wife thinks longingly of her 'body savoury as an apricot plucked in the dew falling, as downed and as desirable.'[65] This highlights the bridegroom's complacency. The lady is a ghoul: rather than being fit for human consumption, she feasts on human flesh. The presence of facial hair as an attractive feature, defying the female stereotype, strikes a convincingly arbitrary note in the realistic tale of 'Blue Salāmah the Singer', where the musician Muhammad of Kūfah reminisces about 'my most beautiful and vivacious pupil, my most fascinating, witty, and most promising. We called this brown child Blue because she bore on her upper lip a blue trace of dainty hair, as if the light hand of an illuminator had rubbed a morsel of musk upon it.'[66] The beauty of pubic hair is also acknowledged. Sometimes, as with Princess Splendour in 'The Tale of Hasan of Basrah', they do not go beyond the source: 'her thighs, though heavy and firm, had the resilience of cushions filled with ostrich down. Between these thighs there lay in its warm nest, like a rabbit without ears, her pretty love tale.'[67] But when Hasan inspects a crowd of naked princesses, the translators become more creative. Payne accurately renders the original, 'he saw what was between their thighs, and that of all kinds, soft and domed, plump and cushioned, large-lipped, perfect, redundant and ample.'[68] Mardrus produces a string of thirty-one adjectives and metaphors, which Mathers tends to group in threes:

> Then, O Hasan, what did you not see? Oh, every colour and every form of little rabbit between the thighs of these kings' daughters! O little rabbits, you were fat and plump and round, and white and domed and big, and vaulted and high and close, [. . .] but you were not to be compared with the little rabbit of Splendour.[69]

But smooth legs are still requisite for perfect femininity. When the heroine passes as a man, in 'The Tale of Kamar Al-Zamān and the Princess

Budūr', doubts about her sex arise when her thighs turn out to be 'softer than butter and sweeter than silk', or, as Payne expresses it, 'fresher than cream and softer than silk.'[70]

There was no mystery as to how this softness was assured – at least, not to readers with access to Burton's unexpurgated translation. In his version of 'The Tale of the Six Different Coloured Girls', a slim girl insults a fat girl as follows: 'If thou go to the water-closet, thou needest one to wash thy gap and pluck out the hairs which overgrow it; and this is the extreme of sluggishness and the sign, outward and visible, of stupidity.'[71] His note reveals considerable interest in the subject:

> This is the popular idea of a bushy 'veil of nature' in women: it is always removed by depilatories and vellication. When Bilkis Queen of Sheba discovered her legs by lifting her robe (Koran xxvii) Solomon was minded to marry her, but would not do so till the devils had by a depilatory removed her hair. The popular preparation (called Núrah) consists of quicklime 7 parts, and Zirník or orpiment, 3 parts: it is applied in loosened [sic] or it burns and discolours. The rest of the body-pile (Sha'arat opp. to Sha'ar = hair) is eradicated by applying a mixture of boiled honey with turpentine or other gum, and rolling it with the hand till the hair comes off. Men I have said remove the pubes by shaving, and pluck the hair of the arm-pits, one of the vestiges of pre-Adamite man. A good depilatory is still a desideratum, the best perfumers of London and Paris have none which they can recommend. The reason is plain: the hair-bulb can be eradicated only by destroying the skin.[72]

Even in 'The Tale of Abū Kīr and Abū Sīr', whose plot hinges on depilation, there is scope for a Western translation to insert a more detailed formula than the original provides:

> Your hammām is admirable, but lacks in one respect of being altogether marvelous. You have no depilatory paste; when you have finished shaving your clients' heads, you either use the razor or tweezers for the hair on the rest of their bodies. I can give you the prescription of a paste which has no equal. Listen: take yellow arsenic and quick lime, pound them together in a little oil, mix in musk to remove the unpleasant smell, and store in an earthenware pot.[73]

The tendency of *fin de siècle* French and English versions to elaborate on references to depilation, or add them when they were not explicit in the original, can be attributed partly to the fact that this was still, in Western culture, an exotic novelty, no aspect of which could be taken for granted. For example, in Mathers's version of 'The Tale of Alā al-Dīn Abū Shāmāt', we find this agreeable account of a husband's homecoming: 'His wife, who knew his usual hour of return and had prepared herself to receive him with bath and perfume and careful depilation, ran to meet him with a smile, saying: "A happy evening attend you!"'[74] All that appears in Payne's translation is 'his wife knew the time of his coming and had washed and made ready for him', but to those familiar with local customs, the rest could be taken as read.[75]

Other aspects of personal care may be expanded at the same time. Mathers gives an extremely elaborate – and inviting – account of a girl's toilette in 'The Tale of Sweet-Friend and Alī-Nūr:

A few days later Sweet-Friend went to the bath in the wazīr's palace, and all the little slaves set themselves to give her such a bath as they had never achieved in their lives before. After washing her hair and all her limbs, they rubbed and kneaded her, depilated her carefully with paste of caramel, sprinkled her hair with a sweet wash prepared from musk, tinted her finger-nails and her toe-nails with henna, burnt much incense and ambergris at her feet, and rubbed light perfumes into her skin. Then they threw a large towel, scented with orange-flowers and roses, over her body and, wrapping all her hair in a warm cloth, led her to her own apartment.[76]

How unlike the perfunctory ablutions of Homer's Hera! But all we find in Haddawy is that 'it chanced a few days later that the girl went to the bath in the palace, where one of the maids washed her. The bath lent her even greater beauty and grace, and when she came out, she was dressed in an attire befitting her youthful charm.'[77]

Against these examples of good Muslim women, who depilate regularly, must be set Mother-of-Calamity, an evil old Christian who acts as tactician and assassin for invading crusaders, and whose grooming is as bad as her morality. She is the chief villain of the epic 'Tale of King Umar al-Numān', and arguably its most interesting character. On some occasions, the original leaves no room for improvement:

She was libertine, faithless, and rotten with curses; her mouth was a cess-pool, her red eyelids had no lashes, her cheeks were dirty and lacked luster, her face was as black as night, her eyes were blear [sic] and her body covered with scabs, her hair was filthy, her back was bent, and her skin was a mass of wrinkles. She was a festering sore among festering sores, and a viper among vipers. [. . .] She used to compel the young male slaves to mount her, and she herself loved to mount the young female slaves. [. . .] Above all things she loved to tickle and rub herself against these virgin bodies [. . .] Ifrizah herself [a beautiful Christian princess] held her in detestation for many reasons: her foul breath, the smell of fermented piss which rose from her armpit and her groin, the putrid aura, like that of rotten garlic, which remained from the many times that she had broken wind, her hairiness which was more than that of a hedgehog, and the palm-fibre-like texture of her skin.[78]

Signs of insufficient femininity on a woman's body can be used to indicate a culture of failing masculinity. Burton seizes this opportunity: in his version of the story, when the Christian king, Afridun, heard bad tidings, 'he fell into a fainting fit with his nose under his feet, and, as soon as he revived, fear fluttered the scrotum below his belly, and he complained to the ancient dame.' His note adds that in Arabic, the ' "curdling of the testicles" in fear is often mentioned.'[79] Mathers' account of the king's discomfiture, though graphic, disappointingly evades the question of gender: 'his stomach turned inside out, and his bowels loosed so that they slid forth from him'.[80] Links between Mother-of-Calamity and the preposterously perverse are made explicit in the account of her death. The original, as rendered by Payne, says merely, 'they crucified her on one of the gates of Baghdad'.[81] Mathers gives her a much more spectacular send-off: 'she was nailed by her feet to the great gate of Baghdad. Thus perished, rendering her stinking soul through her anus to the hell which gaped for it, that disastrous stench, that fabulous farter, the cunning, the politic, the perverse Mother-of-Calamity.'[82] This gusto typifies the translators' eagerness to make female body hair, with all its sexual, aesthetic and political implications, the site of creative collaboration between East and West.

Today, references to the presence and removal of female body hair can be troubling in unexpected ways. It is easy to relish Roy Scadding's speculations about renewing relations with his former mistress in Howard Barker's *Downchild* (1985): 'does she still wear that bra I like – will she shave her armpits – will she leave a little hair – I'll kiss her in this place – I'll kiss her there' (I, i)[83] But Barker gives depilation a sinister significance for Lady Heyday, the object of these speculations. She declares, 'I've sinned against myself [. . .] What I had to do, to triumph. Be dolly on the one hand, giving off the proper smells, well-shaved and shiny, petal calves, underarms like silk for alcoholic tongues to lick, and on the other, brute male sense, to spot an opportunity, to wring it out. Dared not spill my little bit of pity. My female something.' (II, iii)[84] This instance of present absence reverses former conventions: the razor which smoothes a woman's skin becomes a weapon in her fight for masculine power. She would not have left so much evidence of premeditation if she had been naturally smooth. We are not yet quite at home with women's body hair. It is still exoticised, though perhaps time has now become a more effective distancing medium than space. In *The King Must Die* (1958), a historical novel by Mary Renault (1905–83), hair represents unspoiled nature, and shaving corrupt civilisation. Theseus, who has a penchant for Amazons, has dreams in which he will 'wrestle a love-fall against strong slender limbs naked and cool and ringed with gold', and fears he will become a victim of evil magic when a lock of his hair is cut with 'a woman's razor.'[85] Emma Donoghue's short stories on John Ruskin's wedding night and the predicament of Mary Tofts reveal the prevailing interest of this theme.[86] Looking into the future, the science fiction writer Frederik Pohl gives us the gorgeous Dora, one of the hairiest heroines ever created, conceived as a genetic male with female aptitudes, and living a million days after Christ: 'if you were to see this girl, you would not guess that she was in any sense a boy. Breasts, two; vagina, one. Hips, Callipygean; face, hairless; supra-orbital lobes, non-existent. You would term her female at once, although it is true that you might wonder just what species she was a female of, being confused by the tail, the silky pelt or the gill slits behind each ear.'[87] He is determined to leave his (presumably male heterosexual) reader in no doubt of her attractions: 'On Day Million when Dora danced, the people who saw her panted; and you would too.'[88]

Most of the literary evidence examined in this chapter suggests that Pohl is wrong. In contexts where the idea that women have body hair is most readily accepted and openly discussed, the chief focus is often its removal. It appears to be with literature as with life in general: the cultural visibility of body hair exists in inverse proportion to its physical visibility. At this rate, Dora will never happen.

Notes

1 Francis Grose, *Lexicon Balatronicum: A Dictionary of Buckish Slang, University Wit, and Pickpocket Eloquence* (London: C. Chappel, 1811), [K2V].

2 Alexander Pope, *The Twickenham Edition of the Poems of Alexander Pope*, ed. John Butt, 11 vols (London: Methuen, 1939–69), vol. 8, pp. 168–70. See Homer, *The Iliad*, trans. and ed. by A. T. Murray, 2 vols, Loeb Classical Library (London: Heinemann, 1960), Book 14, lines 170–7, vol. 2, p. 78.

3 Aristophanes, *Birds, Lysistrata, Women at the Thesmophoria*, translated and edited by Jeffrey Henderson, Loeb Classical Library (Cambridge, Massachusetts: Harvard University Press, 2000), p. 491. See also Mary R. Lefkowitz, *Women's Life in Greece and Rome: a Source Book in Translation*, 2nd edn. (London: Duckworth, 1997), pp. 1, 89.

4 Aristotle, *The Works of Aristotle Translated into English*, ed. J. A. Smith and W. I. Ross, vol. 4, *Historia Animalium*, trans. D'Arcy Wentworth Thompson (Oxford: Clarendon, 1910), no pagination. All subsequent quotations are from this edition.

5 See, for example, Aristotle, *Generation of Animals*, trans. A. L. Peck, Loeb Classical Library (London: Heinemann, 1943), 748a, line 27 to 748b, line 34 (pp. 256–8), 765b, line 1, to 767a, line 35 (pp. 384–400), 774, line 35, to 774b, line 2 (pp. 452–4).

6 William Shakespeare, *Complete Works*, ed. W. J. Craig (London: Oxford University Press, 1943), pp. 168–9.

7 Edmund Cave (ed.), *The Gentleman's Magazine; or, Monthly Intelligencer* (1731 onwards), vol. 17 (May, 1747), p. 231; see also vol. 68 (Feb. 1798), pp. 111–13.

8 Kate Millett, *Sexual Politics* (London: Virago, 1983), p. 37.

9 William Wycherley (c. 1640–1716), *The Country Wife*, ed. James Ogden (London: A. C. Black; New York: W. W. Norton, 1996), pp. 40–1.

10 John Vanbrugh, *The Provoked Wife*, ed. James L. Smith (London: A. C. Black; New York: W. W. Norton, 1993), p. 25.

11 W. V. Clausen (ed.), *A. Persi Flacci et D. Iuni Iuuenalis Saturae* (Oxford: Clarendon, 1959), p. 86.

12 Jonathan Swift, *The Complete Poems*, ed. Pat Rogers (Harmondsworth: Penguin, 1983), p. 448.

13 Swift, *The Complete Poems*, p. 450.
14 Swift, *The Complete Poems*, p. 451.
15 Swift, *The Complete Poems*, p. 465.
16 Swift, *The Complete Poems*, p. 463.
17 Swift, *The Complete Poems*, p. 453.
18 Swift, *The Complete Poems*, p. 453.
19 Swift, *The Complete Poems*, p. 454.
20 Ovid, *The Art of Love and Other Poems*, trans. J. H. Mozley, Loeb Classical Library (London: Heinemann, 1969), p. 126.
21 Ovid, *The Art of Love*, pp. 130–2.
22 Ovid, *The Art of Love*, p. 132.
23 William King, *The Art of Love: in Imitation of Ovid. De Arte Amandi* (London: Bernard Lintott [1708]), p. 148.
24 See King, *The Art of Love*, pp. 158–9 for the lacuna where the hairy legs should be.
25 T. S. Eliot, *Collected Poems 1909–1962* (London: Faber and Faber, 1970), p. 15.
26 Grose, *Lexicon Balatronicum* [K5R].
27 See John Batchelor, *John Ruskin: No Wealth but Life* (London: Chatto & Windus, 2000), p. 135.
28 Lady Mary Wortley Montagu, *Correspondence*, ed. R. Halsband, 3 vols (Oxford: Clarendon, 1965–67), vol. 2, pp. 55–6.
29 Pope, *The Twickenham Edition of the Poems of Alexander Pope*, vol. 2, p. 194.
30 Shakespeare, *Complete Works*, pp. 934–5.
31 Pope, *The Twickenham Edition of the Poems of Alexander Pope*, vol. 9, p. 176. See Homer, *The Odyssey*, trans. A. T. Murray, 2 vols, Loeb Classical Library (London: Heinemann, 1966), 5, lines 68–71, vol. 1, p. 174.
32 *The Bible: Authorized Version*, ed. John Stirling, printed for The British and Foreign Bible Society (Oxford: Oxford University Press, 1954), p. 543.
33 Shakespeare, *Complete Works*, p. 1076.
34 John Milton, *Poems*, ed. J. Carey and A. Fowler (London and Harlow: Longman, 1968), p. 893.
35 Thomas Nashe, 'A Choise of Valentines', in *The Penguin Book of Renaissance Verse*, selected and with an introduction by David Norbrook, ed. H. R. Woudhuysen (Harmondsworth: Penguin, 1992), pp. 256–7.
36 Richard Lovelace, 'Her Muffe', in: Norbrook *et al.*, *The Penguin Book of Renaissance Verse*, p. 371.
37 Henry Fielding, *The History of Tom Jones*, ed. R. P. C. Mutter (Harmondsworth: Penguin, 1985), p. 197.
38 Grose, *Lexicon Balatronicum* [K3R].
39 Lawrence Sterne, *The Life and Opinions of Tristram Shandy, Gentleman* (New York: Airmont, 1967), p. 391.
40 Pope, *The Twickenham Edition of the Poems of Alexander Pope*, p. 261.
41 Larry D. Benson (ed.), *The Riverside Chaucer*, 3rd edn., based on: *The Works of Geoffrey Chaucer*, ed. F. N. Robinson (Oxford: Oxford University Press, 1987), p. 70. All subsequent references will be from this edition.
42 Jean de la Fontaine, *Contes et Nouvelles en Vers*, ed. Nicole Ferrier and Jean-Pierre Collinet (Paris: Garnier-Flammarion, 1980), p. 356.

43 William Congreve, *Works*, 3rd edn., 3 vols (London: J. and R. Tonson and S. Draper, 1753), vol. 3, p. 362.

44 Congreve, *Works*, p. 363.

45 Congreve, *Works*, p. 364.

46 Congreve, *Works*, p. 364.

47 Alexander Chalmers, *The Works of the English Poets*, 21 vols (London: J. Johnson, 1810), vol. 10, p. 399.

48 See Roger Thompson, *Unfit for Modest Ears: a Study of Pornographic, Obscene and Bawdy Works Written or Published in England in the Second Half of the Seventeenth Century* (London and Basingstoke: Macmillan, 1979), p. 66.

49 *Rochester's Sodom* [1684], L. S. H. M. van Römer (ed.), (Paris: H. Weiter, 1904), p. 11, 1, 1, line 34. This scandalously obscene playlet is often attributed to John Wilmot, Earl of Rochester (1647–80).

50 John Cleland, *Memoirs of a Woman of Pleasure*, ed. Peter Sabor (Oxford: Oxford University Press), 1985, p. 11.

51 Cleland, *Memoirs*, p. 12.

52 Cleland, *Memoirs*, p. 35.

53 Cleland, *Memoirs*, p. 44.

54 Cleland, *Memoirs*, p. 45.

55 Cleland, *Memoirs*, p. 63.

56 Cleland, *Memoirs*, pp. 114, 115.

57 Cleland, *Memoirs*, p. 118.

58 James Joyce, *Ulysses* (Harmondsworth: Penguin Books, in association with The Bodley Head, 1972), p. 691.

59 Joyce, *Ulysses*, p. 691.

60 D. H. Lawrence, *Lady Chatterley's Lover* (Harmondsworth: Penguin, 1960), p. 233.

61 Lawrence, *Lady Chatterley's Lover*, p. 233.

62 Lawrence, *Lady Chatterley's Lover*, pp. 237–8.

63 Lawrence, *Lady Chatterley's Lover*, p. 238.

64 John Payne, *The Book of the Thousand Nights and One Night: Now First Completely Done into English Prose and Verse, from the Original Arabic*, 9 vols (London: Printed for the Villon Society by Private Subscription and for Private Circulation only, 1882–84), vol. 1, p. x. For the history of the *Nights*, see Robert Irwin, *The Arabian Nights: a Companion* (London: Allen Lane, 1994), and Muhsin Mahdi, *The Thousand and One Nights* (Leyden, New York, Cologne: E. J. Brill, 1995).

65 Powys Mathers, *The Book of the Thousand Nights and One Night Rendered into English from the Literal and Complete French Translation of Dr J. C. Mardrus by Powys Mathers*, Revised edition, 4 vols (London and New York: Routledge, 1993), vol. 4, p. 131 (Burton gives the story, but without this episode).

66 Mathers, *The Book of the Thousand Nights and One Night*, vol. 4, p. 477 (not in Haddawy, Payne or Burton).

67 Mathers, *The Book of the Thousand Nights and One Night*, vol. 3, p. 171 (this closely resembles Payne and Burton).

68 Payne, *The Book of the Thousand Nights and One Night*, vol. 7, p. 209.

69 Mathers, *The Book of the Thousand Nights and One Night*, vol. 3, p. 207; cf. *Le Livre des mille nuits et une nuit, traduction littérale et complète du texte arabe*

par le Dr J. C. Mardrus, 16 vols (Paris: Revue Blanche, 1899–1904), vol. 10, pp. 127–8.

70 Mathers, *The Book of the Thousand Nights and One Night*, vol. 2, p. 65; cf. Payne, *The Book of the Thousand Nights and One Night*, vol. 3, p. 182.

71 Richard F. Burton, *A Plain and Literal Translation of the Arabian Nights' Entertainments, Now Entituled [sic] The Book of the Thousand Nights and a Night*, 10 vols (Benares [Stoke Newington]: Printed by the Kamashastra Society for Private Subscribers only, 1885–86), vol. 4, pp. 255–6.

72 Burton, *A Plain and Literal Translation of the Arabian Nights' Entertainments*, p. 256, note. Burton is, of course, wrong about the Queen of Sheba's hairy legs being mentioned in the Koran: see Jacob Lassner, *Demonizing the Queen of Sheba: Boundaries of Gender and Culture in Postbiblical Judaism and Medieval Islam* (Chicago and London: University of Chicago Press, 1993).

73 Mathers, *The Book of the Thousand Nights and One Night*, vol. 3, pp. 19–20; cf. *The Book of the Thousand Nights and a Night, Translated from the Arabic by Captain Sir R. F. Burton*, reprinted from the original edition and edited by Leonard C. Smithers, 12 vols (London: H. S. Nichols, 1897), vol. 7, p. 288.

74 Mathers, *The Book of the Thousand Nights and One Night*, vol. 2, p. 94.

75 Payne, *The Book of the Thousand Nights and One Night*, vol. 3, p. 251.

76 Mathers, *The Book of the Thousand Nights and One Night*, vol. 1, p. 276.

77 Anon., *The Arabian Nights, Based on the Text of the Fourteenth-Century Syrian Manuscript*, edited by Muhson Mahdi, translated by Husain Haddawy (London: David Campbell, Everyman's Library, 1992), p. 384.

78 Mathers, *The Book of the Thousand Nights and One Night*, vol. 1, pp. 447–8; cf. Payne, *The Book of the Thousand Nights and One Night*, vol. 2, p. 156.

79 Burton, *The Book of the Thousand Nights and One Night*, 1897, vol. 2, p. 131.

80 Mathers, *The Book of the Thousand Nights and One Night*, vol. 1, p. 447.

81 Payne, *The Book of the Thousand Nights and One Night*, vol. 2, p. 372.

82 Mathers, *The Book of the Thousand Nights and a Night*, vol. 1, p. 582.

83 Howard Barker, *A Passion in Six Days; Downchild* (London: John Calder; New York: Riverrun Press, 1985), p. 61.

84 Barker, *A Passion in Six Days*, p. 102.

85 Mary Renault, *The King Must Die* (London and Harlow, Essex: Longmans, Green & Co. Ltd., 1958), p. 222, p. 258.

86 See Emma Donoghue, *The Woman Who Gave Birth to Rabbits* (London: Virago, 2002).

87 Frederik Pohl, 'Day Million' (1966), in Edel Brosnan (ed.), *The SF Collection* (London: Chancellor Press, 1994), pp. 256–61, p. 256.

88 Pohl, 'Day Million', p. 257.

7 *Fur* or hair: l'effroi et l'attirance of the wild–woman
Jacqueline Lazú

In an aversion to animals the predominant feeling is fear of being recognized by them through contact. The horror that stirs deep in man is an obscure awareness that in him something lives so akin to the animal that it might be recognized. All disgust is originally disgust at touching. Even when the feeling is mastered, it is only by a drastic gesture that overleaps its mark: the nauseous is violently engulfed, eaten, while the zone of finest epidermal contact remains taboo. Only in this way is the paradox of the moral demand to be met, exacting simultaneously the overcoming and the subtlest elaboration of man's sense of disgust. He may not deny his bestial relationship with animals, the invocation of which revolts him: he must make himself its master. (Walter Benjamin, *One-Way Street*)[1]

In *Fur (2000). A Play in Nineteen Scenes*[2] Migdalia Cruz weaves together a narrative that results in one of the most radical contemporary plays for its womanism and its entry into discourses of colonialism that have been traditionally closed off to voices like her own. While a full study of the play would reveal a far more complex series of tropes, I will focus on four elements which best reveal the tie that binds the seemingly closed symbols of the play. The first and most evident element is the allusion to Shakespeare's *The Tempest*, a metaphor that is canonical to Caribbean and post-colonial discourse in general, and which Cruz turns inside out by revealing and transgressing the limitations of her predecessors. Next, the images of cannibalism and their history expose how Cruz challenges the objectification of women's bodies by inverting standards of 'appropriate female behaviours' related to eating and maintaining the 'ideal body'. This then provides an opportunity to reflect upon the traditions of consumerism and spectacle that have been an integral part of Western history and its relation to individual, racialised bodies. Finally I will offer some solutions to the symbolism of hair versus fur, and its relation to human behaviours that have successfully controlled and defined these bodies. These elements demonstrate that *Fur (2000)* is in fact a text about colonialism, its evolution and how it is incorporated in the female body, creating counter-memories that resist the traditional, masculinist rhetoric of hegemonic and nationalist discourses.

The people and the animals in *Fur*

The prologue occurs in a carnival sideshow where we are introduced to the three characters. The first is Michael, a pet-shop owner, lover of beasts. We also meet Nena, the animal trapper who applies for a job to work for Michael and falls in love with him. He hires her to serve him and help clean and fetch the live animals that sustain the third character, Citrona. Michael purchases this hairy woman from her mother at a sideshow auction for human/animal mutants. We do not actually see Citrona until the second scene in the basement of the pet shop, which he inherited from the former owner with whom it is suggested he had a homosexual and bestial relationship. Michael falls in love with Citrona and tries to force her to love him and marry him by keeping her in a cage in the basement. But Citrona falls in love with Nena when Nena comes in to clean up the excrement, animal guts and blood in Citrona's cage. Nena is both repulsed by and strangely attracted to Citrona. Realising that she could never truly have Nena's love, Citrona tears off a piece of her at the end and eats it. Although the ending is heard and not seen, it is suggested that Michael sees a similar fate. A third scenario used throughout the play is an elevated area designated as No-space, representing the outside world (a Utopia of sorts). This is presumably the source of the sand that pours in constantly through the windows and seems to slowly consume all the characters and spaces. Physically, it houses a three-blade fan that spins in correlation with the loss of hope by the characters. It represents the passing of time, invoking the urgency of the message of the play.

One subjective observation is that *Fur (2000)* is bizarre. Its strangeness manifests itself on various levels of interpretation. Cruz's 'clues' to staging the play in the 'cast of characters' page,[3] as well as the time and place descriptions, seem as much a part of the action of the play as the dialogue. This exemplifies the literariness of the play, yet certainly does not simplify the complex puzzle of the text. The first character on the list is Citrona. Her description is 'a hirsute young woman whose age is hard to tell; a good sense of humor; a great sense of loneliness'. After reading the play and returning to this description, there is no questioning that there is irony in it and possibly some clues to understanding Citrona's character. Her 'good sense of humor' after all takes on a different twist when we learn that she is a prisoner, in effect, a slave bought by Michael, 'a handsome man, older than he looks and acts, who is searching for true love; the owner of JOE's, a pet shop in the desert suburbs of Los Angeles, California. When ever Michael can, He watches and listens'. The final, seemingly positive descriptive trait is also one that should be carefully considered in the reading of the text.

Finally, the character Nena is described as 'a woman other people think is pretty, thirties, an animal trapper and Michael's servant.' 'Other people' implies a privileged subject not Other, and who these subjects are precisely is worthy of consideration, since the presumed protagonist of the play, Citrona, finds Nena attractive. It is fair to say that upon reading these character descriptions a reader (or actor) may be only somewhat prepared for the character's actions that follow. But the descriptions cannot go unnoticed, since they play an important role in the totality of the play.

Like many of Cruz's characters, Citrona does not receive a stated ethnic or racial identity. She is made even more generic by an unidentifiable age, although within the 'young' range. Cruz seems to consciously, perhaps strategically, avoid marginalising her character who, like the fur that she bears on her body, is already historically linked to trade, and political and economic interests. In the 'prologue', while the audience/reader does not actually meet Citrona, the symbolic nature of the anthropomorphic being is first exposed as Nena approaches Michael with a pick-up line, 'Hey, Hi. You come to these things often?' The event is defined in terms of economic hegemony, the consumer and the commodity should be identifiable. This is a space of vice, social encounter, not unlike a bar. However, Nena's next line is 'Hey. Oh. I'm sorry. Can't you – oh, wow, are you one of them?'[4] Suddenly, the clear borders between mutant and 'man' are abruptly distorted. There is something monstrous/mutant about Michael that makes him worthy of being misidentified as 'one of them', although he has yet to reveal the nature of his 'mutation'. From the 'cast of characters', we understand that the mutation is probably not physical. *Despite* Nena's insight, she falls in love with him. The following scenes reveal the sources of these symbolic disjunctures.

In Scene One, Michael is the first to point out the features of the still-hidden Citrona, an 'unseen animal in a sack'. According to this first scene description, we are privy neither to the fact that it is Citrona in the sack, nor that she is in fact in any way human. Michael says, 'Let me stroke you. Let me rub my hands against your fur. I like furry things. They keep me warm. You could keep me warm.'[5] He is engaging the 'subject' in conversation and asking her to allow him to touch her, suggesting an alternative subject position, one with, albeit limited, agency (the human). The line between humanity and animalism is blurred when he addresses the sack, calling it 'beauty' as he would a lover/human, poetically, like a heroine in a fairytale (*Beauty and the Beast*) – or then again, like a horse (*Black Beauty*):

> It's for you. It's fresh beautiful water. I collected it. It's rainwater. It'll make your fur shine and your eyes will go white if they're red when you drink this. All for you. All yours. It's straight from God. Now that you're home with me, you can be my lady friend. You are so pretty. You have soft eyes – soft brown eyes. You make me melt with eyes like that – when you look at me like that.[6]

The only certainty in the monologue and the dialogue that follows is the animalistic nature of 'beauty'. Her fur can be made shiny and her 'red eyes', presumably hungry, angry eyes of a carnivore, can be made white.

Here begins Michael's quest of domesticating the 'beast'. While it is clear that the animal nature of Citrona is what he is attracted to, he simultaneously seeks to domesticate it, that is, make it respond faithfully to his will. But Citrona is no regular animal. The stage directions in Scene Three finally reveal her person 'squatting in one corner, her back to the audience. She shakes uncontrollably.'[7] Citrona is both human and animal, she is a carnivore and a predator. At the very end of the play, she is also finally revealed as the most vicious of all human and animal meat-eaters: a cannibal.

Cruz's politics of meat

Cruz opens the can of worms that holds social anxiety. She slowly reveals the cannibalism in the play, although certainly, when one first 'meets' Citrona, her physical image is already laden with assumptions of who and what she eats and is. Her behaviour also provokes an anxiety that should lead the audience to anticipate the ending. The first thing we have confirmed is that she eats meat. Preferably raw. Scene Seven focuses on the feeding process. While all three characters appear in the scene, most of it is taken up by Citrona's monologue. She is speaking to Nena, who enters the room to feed her but ignores her words. Citrona begins by analysing Nena's physical appearance; checking her out. She employs every tactic possible to get Nena to react. She tries to seduce her; tell her jokes. When Nena runs away she says, 'Hey, I'm sorry . . . I'm sorry you're so beautiful . . . Tell Michael I approve.'[8] Here Nena comes under the scrutiny of Citrona, who is obviously also being judged by Nena. The lines of power are blurred and disturbed. Citrona's words to Nena become progressively more sexual and aggressive, and finally desperate and sad. All the while, she is eating the live rabbit that Nena has brought her:

> I don't like the furry parts. The parts that still have fur. I mean, I do, the stuff right there next to it – that's the good stuff, but I'm too afraid to eat it. Because if I eat it I might find fur in my mouth. And I couldn't stand that. I would choke. I would choke and die. I don't feel like dying anymore.[9]

The sexual reference, invoking the vagina and symbolically the act of oral sex ('eating out') with another woman exposes the agony and marginalisation of Citrona, albeit via comedy. Not only is she seen as a monster, but her presumably unfulfilled desires are monstrous to a society that condemns homosexual relationships and refuses to believe in the possibility of women giving each other pleasure in the complete absence of men. Michael's mini-monologue at the end of the scene, after eavesdropping on Nena (and Citrona) reveals what lies at the heart of male anxiety about women's relationships with one another:

> There was a time when I could only imagine what two women did when they found themselves alone, together. I imagined that they would talk about men.

They would yearn for men together. They would devise plans and systems on how to catch and confine men and how also to do it so carefully that the men would never know they were caught . . . All each man would know would be that he was in love with a beautiful girl. That's what I imagined.[10]

Michael's anxieties and assumptions about women's interactions (and intentions) seem laughable, but are certainly substantiated by the continued discrimination against lesbian relationships and the systematic misogyny in public and private sectors today. Avoidance of 'the furry parts' is thus critical to Citrona maintaining her 'humanity'.

Citrona's relationship to Nena is the antithesis of her relationship to Michael. Nena's job is to sustain Citrona. Michael, on the other hand, sees himself as Citrona's saviour – her guide to 'assimilation' if not co-operation. This is marked time and time again by his attempts to feed her 'cooked food'. Stage directions explain in Scene Eight:

NENA returns with a mop, a sponge, and a bucket of water. SHE cleans the blood and organs of Citrona's meal from the floor and walls. The smell of blood and shit and urine make NENA gasp and gag.[11]

Later in Scene Nine, we see Michael as he enters carrying a barbecued chicken on a tray. He hands it to Citrona. She pretends to be interested in it and then tosses it back to him. She then says 'I don't eat barbecue', to which he responds:

I thought it would be good for a change. A little change is good. It's very good chicken. I made it myself – my own special sauce. It's a sauce with an edge. A big, spicy edge. Don't you even want to try it? It'll wrap inside you like a snake.

CITRONA: The only thing I want wrapped inside me is gone. Where'd you send her? Where are you meeting her? I know you go to meet her. You go at night. You see her in a cheap motel and she puts on a wig and dances for you. She bends over and shows you her panties. She shows you everything. She never bends here – she crawls and kneels. But I like her like that – then she's on my level. But with you, she could never be on your level. You give her things and that makes her love you . . . I can't believe you brought me barbecued chicken! Don't they sell live poultry anymore?

MICHAEL: Not around here. You can pick it out live, but then they kill it. They insist.

CITRONA: I hate when the world changes.

MICHAEL: It changes all the time.[12]

Before there is any indication that Citrona is likely to eat human flesh, it is clear that she has a preference for raw meat. The association that Cruz draws between what is defined as 'attractive' human female bodies and delectable, attractive 'meat' is no accident. This image appeals to the appetitive desires as they have been constructed in our culture, in which consumers must interpret images from a stance of a privileged male identification.

According to many food theorists, meat-eating demarcates individual and societal virility. Men who decide to reject 'meat'-eating are deemed effeminate; failure of men to eat 'meat' announces that they are not masculine. Inevitably, cultural images of 'meat' are aligned to male-identified appetitive desires. The fact that the Nebraska Beef Board hired Gretchen Polhemus as president because her presence 'adds a unique and attractive element that embodies "the New Beauty of Beef"' is a testament to this way of thinking.[13]

For women, however, eating 'too much' meat, or any other 'sinful', rich, exciting food is taboo. This gender ideology can be traced to the Victorian era. Victorians had conduct manuals which warned elite women of the dangers of indulgent and over-stimulating eating and advised how to consume in a feminine way as little as possible and with the utmost precaution against an unseemly show of desire. *Godey's Lady's Book* warned that it was vulgar for women to load their plates; young girls were admonished to 'be frugal and plain in your tastes'.[14] When women are positively depicted as sensuously voracious about food, their hunger for food is employed almost always as a metaphor for their sexual appetite.

According to Bordo, the emergence of such rigid and highly moralised restrictions on female appetite and eating are, arguably, part of what Bram Dijkstra has interpreted as a nineteenth-century 'cultural ideological counter-offensive' against the 'new woman' and her challenge to prevailing gender arrangements and their constraints on women.[15] Mythological, artistic, polemical and scientific discourses from many cultures and eras suggest the symbolic potency of female hunger as a cultural metaphor for unleashed female power and desire, from the blood-craving Kali (who in one representation is shown eating her own entrails), to the *Malleus Malificarum* (for the sake of fulfilling the mouth of the womb, [witches] consort even with the devil),[16] to the 1980s Hall and Oates lyrics 'Oh, oh, here she comes, watch out boys, she'll chew you up.'[17]

Female hunger as sexuality is an image that provokes terror and hate or pain at the very least, even if it is *pleasure–pain*. The 'man-eater': the metaphorical devouring woman, reveals profound psychological underpinnings. Eating is not used as a metaphor for the sexual act, but the act itself, when initiated by a woman, is imagined as an act of eating, incorporating and destroying the object of desire. As a result, women must be controlled for the sake of the man.

In *Fur (2000)*, Citrona appears as the ultimate symbol of a fear-inducing individual. Her body is an individual body, beastly in nature, consuming only raw meat. Citrona, unlike *The Tempest*'s Caliban, has also mastered, consumed and internalised language, philosophy and knowledge about popular culture – as a result, she is able to use 'the master's tools' to rationalise her circumstances and gain control over the anxiety of her spectators. But, by having Citrona control the levels of anxiety – displacing rather than eliminating them – does Cruz inadvertently reproduce the hegemonic structures?

I believe that the answer lies in a series of symbols and thus strategies that Cruz deploys to create in Citrona a counter-hegemonic body – first seen in her relationship to food. Nena is partly a participant in the power held over Citrona, for she is the one in charge of feeding her. By falling in love with her 'feeder' and attempting to seduce her, Citrona is transgressing boundaries of sex and class. She is, after all, giving her what she truly desires. Michael continues the effort to control her body and his anxieties by attempting to feed her cooked food, for which she has no desire and which to her is simply unnatural. By rejecting it, Citrona rebels to the degree that she is able – against social control. She empowers herself by appropriating a powerful symbol of patriarchal dominance and defining for herself what is in fact 'natural' for her as an individual woman. Aware of her own objectification and subordination, she adopts values of domination and exposes the hypocrisy of a society and its supposed 'respect for the natural'.

Similarly, in Scene Eight, Nena describes her process of trapping an animal. Hunting is a man's sport. Nena being an expert hunter could appear to be a threatening inversion of that power structure. But Nena hunts not with arms, but with strategy and skill. She describes it:

> When you want to trap an animal, you feed it first. You watch it and find out what it likes to eat and then you give it what it likes . . . for a time. Slowly, the animal gets to know you. You get a little closer every day. You leave a trail of food, which leads directly to you. At first, it doesn't come that close. But as time goes on it comes closer and closer. One day, it's in your lap and you're stroking it and it is eating out of your hand. One day, as you are stroking it, you let your hand close tightly around its neck. You stroke its jugular until its heart slows down, until it's so calm that it falls faint – a deep sleep. Restful, trusting sleep. Then you kill it.

> [Speaking to a small animal in a sack that SHE raises above her head.]

> Do you think I'm beautiful? When you look in my eyes or smell my smell, do you think I have the look and smell of beauty?[18]

Nena's monologue can be understood to be referring ironically to human relationships as well. It describes a stereotypical act of seduction. This monologue suggests that precisely because eating and intercourse involve this development of intimacy, they become dangerous or threatening when carried out under adverse conditions or with 'untrustworthy' people. This is why, it might be said, all cultures have rules to control food and sex and to define appropriate mates for both.

Nena and Citrona's attempt to bond, including sexually, may suggest a metaphorical act of both material and social survival, in addition to personal survival, under repressive circumstances. In Scene Eleven, the revulsion/attraction is seen, and the former is momentarily overcome with the promise of an unheard type of freedom for Nena that nearly drives her to the arms of Citrona. Among the strategies that Citrona uses, is the suggestion of sharing food and liberating her body from imposed beauty standards and again pointing out the hypocrisy of the popular 'natural' state of things. (During the following monologue, Nena is mesmerised by Citrona, pulled physically closer and closer until a kiss is almost possible.)

> CITRONA: If you were my girl, I'd treat you nice. You wouldn't have to wear lipstick for me. You could go natural. A natural girl. Been a long time since we seen one of those. I mean besides myself, of course. I can't really wear make-up. It sticks to my beard and when I cry or sweat it flakes off into my eyes and makes them screaming red . . . but you. I bet that you could wear it all the time. I bet it even looks good when it melts off you onto white sheets. That's how I want you, baby. On white sheets, not off-white or gray-white, but white/white. Whiter than the hottest Sun. Whiter than Caribbean sand. Whiter than the Holy Spirit – than the heart of Christ. Pure, simple . . . white. I'll stop being messy if you kiss me . . . If you kiss me, I'll eat cooked meat. You could cook it for me . . . you could make us happen, baby. Baby, baby.[19]

The action is broken when Citrona actually attempts to kiss her. But the point has been made. Until now, Nena, by controlling alimentation, has held power over Citrona. She has satisfied the most basic need. By suggesting that she will voluntarily transform her eating habits from raw to edible product, or by putting on clothes, Citrona is conveying another message. She is willing to accept the social boundaries in exchange for the fosterage and 'family'. In fact, a few lines later, Citrona asks, 'Nena, will you marry me?' When Nena slaps her hand and runs out, Citrona says 'Your skin is like Jersey corn – milk and honey. So sweet you can eat it raw'. Citrona 'returns to her senses'. But that is not the final attempt to create a bond. When Nena finally agrees to spend a night with Citrona in her cage, at Michael's request, Citrona tries to welcome Nena by offering, 'Are you hungry? I told Michael to bring us something nice, something – cooked'.

Food is an important cultural concern and symbol for women. Women usually bear responsibility for food preparation and consumption and, in many cultures, for production and distribution as well. They are defined as nurturers and carry out this role mostly through feeding. Patriarchal Western society not only restricts women's economic and political opportunities, but also defines their role within the family as nurturer and food provider, a role compatible with the use of food as voice. Today, commercials, magazine covers and advertisements offer food that – like performers themselves, with make-up, coiffeur and lighting assistance – has been 'stylised', dressed up and staged as a visual projection of consumerist fantasies. Rosalind Coward goes so far as to call these pictures 'food pornography', suggesting that their appeal to the forbidden, their relation to female servitude and objectification, and their repression of the processes of production, resemble the aesthetic and ideological practices of the photos in soft-core mainstream centrefold pictures.[20] Part of the meanings of food in narrative drama is the novelty of its 'realness' when encountered in a medium that is framed as the 'not real'.

The ideal body – the Other in the self

The sexual and sensual references in *Fur (2000)* are the ultimate symbols of the tension between human and beast, and where Cruz most profoundly challenges the roles and spaces assigned to women. In Scene Four, when Citrona physically appears for the first time, she is inside her cage in the basement and speaks one of several monologues throughout the play, that reveal not only her biography, but her dreams, nightmares, desires and the politics of the play. This technique of self-revelation would seem almost untheatrical in nature, relying on a final series of monologues until, in this play, the 'dénouement' emerges only at the end. The omniscience that seems to be offered to the public is a subtle departure from the traditional narrative of realist texts. Although it is already clear much earlier in the play that the play is not in the mode of realism, the monologues do set up a real and an imaginary in a way that politicises an elaborately aesthetic 'speech' and creates revealing but internal peaks in the play that culminate in the ending. By 'aesthetic', I am referring to an elaborate use of figures of speech, symbols, and musical references. There are questions that one needs to ask in order to collect and collate as many of the internal actions of the play as possible to help to 'explain' it.

Conceptually the words in the play are 'rational' (a 'real'). Citrona begins one particular monologue with a type of 'cliché': 'People say you can't get used to some things – but you do.' This may suggest that Citrona has had many 'normal' conversations with 'normal people'. What follows is an explanation that goes from the shocking 'like the smell of your own shit' to the seemingly incomprehensible:

> You sit on it long enough and you want to feel it on your legs. You smear yourself. Because it keeps you warm. It's familiar. It's like your family. My shit and urine is my company. I check it all the time. I look for signs of life. I look for light. I sleep with my face toward the light. I keep track of myself. When I feel the light, I count my fingers. I count them out loud because numbers are a comfort.[21]

The vulgar image conjures both a familiarity that constructs the human (the cliché and the reference to the family) and a visceral vulgarity that distances and 'animalises' Citrona. Like eating, defecation fulfils an essential –

albeit routine and perfunctory – nature here. Citrona's comfort with her wastes disrupts social structures, evokes animalism and challenges the classification system of pure/impure and its structures of subjectivity. In *Purity and Danger*, anthropologist Mary Douglas argues:

> Ideas about separating, purifying, demarcating and punishing transgressions have as their main function to impose system on an inherently untidy experience. It is only by exaggerating the difference between within and without, above and below, male and female, with and against, that a semblance of order is created.[22]

From this argument it can also be deduced that blackness and homosexuality represent what is deemed 'filthy', because of a perceived disruption of social order. They are out of place, and therefore constitutive of a system in which heterosexuality and whiteness represent order.[23]

In *Powers of Horror*, Julia Kristeva reinterprets Douglas's study of pollution rituals. She searches for a connection between social structures like the classification system of pure/impure and structures of subjectivity. She asks, 'Why that system of classification and not another? What social, subjective, and socio-subjectivity interacting needs does it fulfill?'[24] Or more specifically, 'Why does *corporeal waste*, menstrual blood and excrement, or everything that is assimilated to them . . . represent – like a metaphor that would have become incarnate – the objective frailty of the symbolic order?'[25] In search of an answer, Kristeva develops her theory of abjection:

> An extremely strong feeling which is at once somatic and symbolic, and which is above all a revolt of the person against an external menace from which one wants to keep oneself at a distance, but of which one has the impression that it is only inside. So it is a desire for separation, for becoming autonomous and also the feeling of an impossibility of doing so – whence the element of crisis which the notion of abjection carries with it.[26]

As with the dynamic behind Stuart Hall's theory of racism and Francis Affergan's 'exotic Other', the abject both attracts and repels.[27] Yet it is not a 'lack of cleanliness or health that causes abjection but what disturbs identity, system, order. What does not respect borders, positions, rules. The in-between, the ambiguous, the composite'.[28]

If, as Kristeva suggests, every society is founded on the abject – those things it excludes – they must be controlled so that society can develop. For Kristeva, the ultimate prohibition is that against the maternal body. But Doris Witt argues that her theorised maternal body is uninflected by markers of cultural difference such as race, class and historicity, not to mention other taboos and biases. To expand the construction and use of abjection, she suggests thinking about the relationship between the subjective fascination with 'filth' (the abject) and the social stigmatisation of certain peoples and practices as 'dirty' or 'filthy'.[29] Witt suggests looking at 'interlocking prohibitions' and thus 'interlocking abjections'.

As the abject, Citrona searches for her humanity while attempting to make a whole subject out of objectified, imprisoned parts of othered selves. Yet, she finds solace in numbers. She says, 'When I feel the light I count my fingers. I count them out loud, because numbers are a comfort.' This evokes the ritual of human mothers at the birth of their child, counting their child's fingers to ensure 'normalcy'. In this action, Citrona too needs to be reminded of her 'normalcy'; her 'humanity'. It is not ironic that numbers are a comfort, since the other place where she needs to assert and save her humanity is in the economic world; after all, she is both consumer and commodity. The consumer is comically revealed in her fanatical obsession with The Beatles, an ultimate symbol of teen consumer culture. The commodity is multilevelled and complicatedly tied to her value as physical labour, sex object and material goods (fur).

Despite Citrona's position as abject and commodity, Michael does not simply want to 'dominate' her. In fact, in Scene Eight, he says to her:

> You're still afraid of me. That's good for now, but soon you'll learn how not to be. Soon, you'll love me. I'm good to all my treasures. I'll be good to you because you are a treasure. You're a beautiful seed – someone should have buried you a long time ago . . . and then there'd be trees of you. Big ones. And branches would drop you, many yous like ripe, yellow fruit.[30]

According to bell hooks, the desire to make contact with those bodies deemed as Other, with no apparent will to dominate, assuages the guilt of the past, even takes the form of a defiant gesture where one denies accountability and historical connection. Most importantly, it establishes a contemporary narrative in which the suffering caused by the power structures to the Other is deflected by an emphasis on seduction and longing – where the desire is not to make the Other over in one's image necessarily, but to become the Other.[31] Almost directly affirming this idea of 'imperialist nostalgia'[32] Michael says in Scene Twelve:

> People come to this pet shop to buy their pets. Especially at Christmas and Easter. People get pets then because they think it will help them be reborn. They think they'll get holier by buying an animal – that they'll be more like God, by feeding and stroking a little hunk of fur and flesh. And if they need to . . . a lot of stress can be relieved with a pet. Or through a pet. Or on a pet. They can relieve certain types of pain. But is that true for every type of pet? Or only the ones with fur?[33]

Michael is projecting his own desires on these 'people'. He too uses contemporary strategies to keep a continuum of 'primitivism'. Michael's guilt and projection are based on much more than his own privileged position. In fact, from the following monologue from Scene Nine, when he asks Citrona to marry him, we can deduce that Michael's interest comes from a much more powerful desire to repress his own position as abject:

I worked in this pet shop. My first job. The guy who owned it – his name was Joe. I felt tender about his lips. I watched him talk. He especially talked to the rabbits. I don't know why. He liked rabbits, I guess. He liked the straw they lived in. He used to stick pieces of it up his nose. I laughed when he did that. Then he stuck the rabbit down his pants once. With some straw. I thought that was funny too. But it bit him. And he got some weird infection. And then he died. That's what I heard. That he died from this weird thing. But really what he died from was being too close to a rabbit. People aren't supposed to be that close to rabbits. You see, working with Joey taught me a lot. About animals. We had a spider monkey once . . . she climbed all over me and gave me lots of kisses . . . and then she died too. She had the same weird disease. All the other animals started to drop, like dominoes, in a spiral. I got out of its way. I made it stop. I didn't want that disease on me . . . so I bought a wife.[34]

Michael is able to 'control' his *disease* (homosexuality? bestiality?) by attempting to choose a more 'normal' lifestyle (marriage, wife) to disguise his own abjection. Neither attempt has been successful. In Michael's Scene Six monologue, he further reveals his struggle with sexuality in a semi-Freudian interpretation of his desire for both sexes, the root of which is in his childhood relationship with his father. He reveals his adoration of man/women (hermaphrodites) and a lust for the idea of kissing both 'through one set of lips'. Suddenly Michael's humanity peers through in the form of repressed sexuality; his bisexuality. This is a reminder that even those in positions of privilege can be standing in another marginal one; that hegemonic structures and abjections are not vertical but horizontal and interlocking.

Spectacle and consumerism – missing links

In Scene Six we enter the mind-world of Michael in which his conflicts, his *human* struggles are suddenly revealed in another one of these strange locations between histories and nations. He talks about his love of sideshows, proclaiming the ones 'now' better than any before. The study of 'freak shows' provides a perfect opportunity to develop understandings of past practices and changing conceptions of human variation. In the process, I ask what we can learn about current methods of retailing bodies from this sociological encounter with history that may hold another key to its use in Migdalia Cruz's depiction of 'the near future'.

Spectacle questions the relationship of certain types of bodies to particular logics of space. Citrona's naked, hairy body tempts the audience tactically and their desire for passive submission in the event of their choosing. After all, who doesn't like to run their fingers through soft fur or gaze at the 'Wild Kingdom' from a safe distance? *Fur (2000)* invokes different histories to present the public display of colonial bodies as spectacle. However, the characterisations invert major themes, including

Citrona as the controlled savage observing even more than she is observed, and by her being both consumer and commodity. Through an aesthetic of carnivalesque horror, comic relief and *anthropophago*,[35] Cruz begins to formulate in *Fur (2000)* a complex politics of belonging for the marginalised that is profoundly tied to former histories and multiple spheres of belonging at local, national and transnational levels.

The years 1840 to 1940 witnessed the rise and fall of the sideshow ('freak show', 'ten-in-one') in the United States. By 1940, a failing economy, technological and geographical changes, competing forms of entertainment, the medicalisation of human differences and changed public taste resulted in a serious decline in the number and popularity of freak shows, although they continued through the 1950s and 1960s, and vestiges exist even today. In 1969, when the World Fairs Shows opened in North Bay Village, Florida, the freaks were forbidden to appear, on the basis of an anti-pornography law in the city.[36] 'Freak' is a way of thinking about and presenting people – a frame of mind and a set of practices.

Two specific modes of presenting sideshow freaks may be discerned: the 'exotic mode' and the 'aggrandised status mode'. These were constituted by particular techniques, strategies and styles that promoters and managers used to present the exhibits. In the exotic mode, the person received an identity that was formulated in terms of cultural strangeness, the primitive, the bestial and the exotic. Often, US citizens were misrepresented as non-Western foreigners – Ohio-raised dwarfs were said to be from Borneo; a tall North Carolinian black man purportedly came from Dahomia. Favourite themes included cannibalism, human sacrifice, head-hunting, polygamy, unusual dress, and food preferences that repelled Americans (eating dogs, rodents and insects).[37] While the exotic mode emphasised how different and, in most cases, how inferior the people on exhibit were, the aggrandised mode reversed this by proclaiming the superiority of the freak. Social position, achievements, talents, family and physiology were fabricated, elevated, or exaggerated and then flaunted.

The two modes were not always mutually exclusive. Some freaks appeared in a mixed mode, playing on juxtaposing incongruities. A famous example was Krao Farini, a hirsute woman from Laos. In the 1880s, when she was still a little girl, she started her freak career as 'Darwin's Missing Link', portrayed as halfway between human and monkey. The microcosm that Migdalia Cruz creates in *Fur (2000)* is a reproduction of this tradition and its conflicts. The ten-in-one, the Bally platform[38] and of course the 'woman-beast' (The Missing Link), herself a cross between systems of classification, are some of the symbols that Cruz appropriates. Citrona's body is completely covered with hair – different from the freak-show standard 'bearded woman'. Why does Cruz choose to recreate and recover these disquieting images to create and meditate on the state of a society now or in the future?

The discourses of freakdom structure cultural rituals that produced the deviant against a typical, offering a spectacle of somatic features filled with meaning for the gaping spectator. Excess and absence, along with such hybridity, are the threatening organisational principles that constituted freakdom. The freak show made more than just freaks: Rosemarie Garland Thomson argues that the freak show created the 'self-governed, iterable subject of democracy – the American cultural self.'[39] Serving as 'education' and 'entertainment', the institutionalised process of enfreakment united and validated the disparate masses brought together as viewers. The job of the freak show is to make the freakiness of the displayed individual into a hypervisible text that allows the viewer's indistinguishable body to fade into a neutral, invulnerable, independent instrument that, as Thomson puts it, can fit into the uniform abstract citizenry democracy institutes. But there was also a certain amount of reverence and attraction to the popularity of these unique individuals, emotions that created some ambivalence in the spectators regarding their own lack of distinction. Perhaps they too longed in a sense to be interesting in some way, instead of just indistinguishable normality in a confusing cultural moment.

When we consider this, Michael as the consumer suddenly takes on a complex role in the power relations developed thus far. In this relationship between the oppressor and the oppressed, the object and the objectifier, the 'freak' and the spectator, which is which? Is this merely a situation of entrapment? How can the consent that Nena seems to give to Michael to use her as he will, be understood? Could Citrona as the oppressed, herself become an oppressor?

Consenting subjects

At the heart of an understanding of Cruz's characters is the necessity to understand the nature of choice, and the ways in which choice ultimately may or may not be said to be the deciding factor in unforced consent. David Gerber suggests an understanding of choice and consent in the lives of human exhibits appearing in freak shows, an understanding which seems to align well with Cruz's play. He suggests adopting a historically grounded minority-group model. In this model, one has to adopt a hierarchy of priorities and goals in analysing human behaviour, and truth – in this case, acknowledging the imperfections and confusions of people in determining what is in their own interest – has to take priority. This does not suggest that respect or empathy should be sacrificed. Only by understanding the social oppression, exploitation and degradation experienced by the sort of people who become freaks can one understand the choices made – if choices even exist – to appear to give consent to being exhibited (or manipulated, used, etc.). So, according to Gerber, in the case of the freak show, the minority-group model serves to join a respect for social process to the power of social constructionism.[40]

The commodification of Otherness, as bell hooks calls it, becomes an alternative to the 'normal' ways of doing things. This perhaps is analogous to the ambiguous desires that Victorian spectators felt upon gazing at their favourite sideshow anomaly. Hooks argues that within commodity culture, ethnicity becomes the spice that livens up mainstream white culture. She suggests that cultural taboos around sexuality and desire are transgressed and made explicit as the media bombards people with ideas of difference no longer based on the white supremacist assumption that 'blondes have more fun'. The fun, hooks argues, is associated with the surfacing of the 'nasty' unconscious fantasies and longings about contact with the Other embedded in the deep structure of white supremacy. It is, in fact, a contemporary revival of interest in the 'primitive'.[41] This recuperation of the 'primitive' seduces with its temporary relief from the symptoms of imposed sameness by the mainstream. Hooks says:

> To make oneself vulnerable to the seduction of difference, to seek an encounter with the Other, does not require that one relinquish forever one's mainstream positionality. When race and ethnicity become commodified as resources for pleasure, the culture of specific groups, as well as the bodies of individuals, can be seen as constituting an alternative playground where members of dominating races, genders, sexual practices affirm their power-over in intimate relations with the Other.[42]

A type of 'consumer cannibalism' takes place, in which the differences inhabited by the Other are exchanged, displacing the Other and denying her/his history through decontextualisation. The notion of 'crossover' expands the parameters of cultural production to enable the voice of the non-white Other to be heard by larger audiences, even as it denies and appropriates it for its own use.[43] Communities of resistance are replaced by communities of consumption.[44]

Fur versus hair

The final and perhaps most important symbol throughout *Fur (2000)* is fur itself. Throughout the play, hair and fur as descriptive and metaphorical symbols are interchanged in a seemingly indiscriminate way. To Michael, Citrona is covered in fur, which he loves to brush his fingers through. Nena doesn't seem to have 'enough hair' for Michael, although in her opinion, she does usually have 'thick' hair until she washes it (Scene Five). Citrona never refers to herself as having fur, although animals and 'prohibited parts' of their bodies have fur – which, according to her monologue in Scene Seven, could cause death upon being ingested. I believe that the key to understanding the symbol of fur in the play is intimately tied to the historical significance of fur as trade and its political and economic interest, thereby constituting Cruz's strongest commentary on the powerful symbols of exploitation and oppression.

Most studies of fur focus on its material production; its status as a luxury good or article of trade to colonial relations among Britain, France and North America. Julia Emberley, in *Venus and Furs. The Cultural Politics of Fur*, suggests that to address the complex scene of fur's current configurations, cultural studies of fur must go beyond its material production to the symbolic production. She contends that analyses must include the value of fur as a commodity, a luxury good, an article of trade and as an object invested with libidinal desires. She argues, 'More than an object of material culture, a commodity, fashion garment, animal skin, or sexual fetish, fur circulates as a *material signifier* in the transnational discourses of political and libidinal exchange.'[45]

Because of meanings attributed to fur by economic exigencies and modes of exchange, the process of exchange itself has to include the identification of codes of exchange value. According to Emberley, the exchange value of fur exists in our ability to recognise or misrecognise its figuration as commodity, currency or sexual fetish. At a more general level of transaction, codes of exchange would include the larger categories of money, women and natural resources. She proposes a transactional reading that traces the representation of exchange value in various symbolic forms including language, film and literature, as well as the market-place.[46]

In the play *Fur (2000)*, there are codes of exchange ascribed to fur as a cultural artefact; there are social differences encoded in the value of fur. With its long history of trade between domestic and foreign entities, the presence of fur, or choice over hair, for example, mediates social as well as economic relations of reciprocity or contestation. A transactional reading of fur in *Fur (2000)* reveals the differential play of antagonistic oppositions such as human/animal, woman/man, and negotiates and even mobilises them. They may in fact be disassembled to the point where the imperial voice that constructs the distinctions could be displaced and the 'fluidity and permeability of borders set in motion'.[47]

While Michael may see Citrona's fur only in terms of a fetishistic object of exchange coded by sexual difference, Citrona allows us to read it in a transactional way. She infuses it with her own sexual assertions, as we have already seen, displacing the borders set against her sexually, racially and in terms of other hierarchies. In fact, towards the end in Scene Sixteen, Citrona is able to look positively on the same fur that she discarded and feared when she uses it to 'make a bed of fur for her [Nena]' to lie on, when Nena gives in to Michael's coercions and agrees to come into her cage and spend the night with Citrona. She says:

> I'm gonna weave a spell around her. I'll make a bed of fur for her. To lie on and dream . . . of me.

[SHE picks up two pelts, with the heads still on and puts them on her own side of the cage.]
Then she'll have to love me . . .
[Pause]
It's times like these I wish I knew some Marvin Gaye songs.
[Collecting the leftover bones]
I could make her something. A chair, maybe. Ladies like to sit.
[She piles them up neatly.]
I never thought I'd really want someone to smell my real smell. I thought if I covered it up, built a cloud of other animals' smells over me – then I could save the real me – the real smell of me for someone I thought could love me . . . and could stand the smell – maybe even want it on her. Maybe even long for it.[48]

Citrona challenges the history of sexual propriety and hierarchy of social positions associated with the symbolic power of fur, which she herself formerly believed. We can recall her own revulsion against even touching it. In fact, she can use it to cast a love spell or, even better, she could find someone who actually loves it because *she* can relate to it and desire it as a reflection of her own unfulfilled desires. As a *lady* Nena will *surely* love fur.

If fur is infused with symbolic power, its binary opposition to 'hair' in the play should also be read in a similarly transactional way. Most significant to the reading of Citrona's hair is the scholarship on black people and hair. In 1990, Kobena Mercer in 'Black Hair/Style Politics' argued that hair is second only to skin colour as a racial signifier. More recently, Robin D. G. Kelley and Maxine Craig have considered the relationship between constructions of race and gender within the context of African-American hair-styling practices. Several works have been written that engage beauty culture and black women.[49] Here, black people's hair and hair-styling practices are read as political. Ironically, few, if any, writers of the Afro-Latino Diaspora have addressed these profoundly relevant issues in their own work as critics or as creative writers. Migdalia Cruz's use of hair – kinky hair – marks an important entry into the indelible construction of hair as signifier for Latinos, particularly writers in the Spanish-speaking Caribbean who have contributed greatly to theories of race in the Black Diaspora. Citrona understands the distinction, like most members of the Diaspora, between 'good hair' and 'bad hair'. Banks explains that 'good hair' becomes a marker of privilege in the eyes of those who have it as well as those who don't. Both of these understandings speak to the potency of 'good hair' in relationship to 'bad hair'. Individuals who feel special because they have 'good hair' can only feel special through the existence of what has come to be known as 'bad hair'. It is no surprise, then, that hair removal is one of the highest-profit industries in the United States, with technology that evolves faster than much of medical research. Citrona, then, characterises the ultimately disfigured body – beyond remedy. We learn that shaving is completely out of the question for her.

There are, however, parts of the human body, in this case, women's bodies, that generally produce no or minimal hair growth according to the narrative of *Fur (2000)*. Among them, much to Citrona's comfort, is the vulva. We also learn later that she has been sexually mutilated by her own mother. As a result, although she questions ownership of her sexuality, Citrona 'can stand' to allow herself to find comfort in the unnamed part of herself which provides comfort, pleasure, femininity and 'humanity' as long as she stays away from any other part of the body that may remind her once again of the violated and stigmatised self.

Conclusion

With this play, then, Cruz joins other contemporary artists who attack the notion that modernity is something separate and inaccessible to them as people of colour – relegated to the margins of post-modernity. What is most intriguing is not that she is the first to propose these ideas, but that she is able to accomplish this within the limitations of the 'traditional' form of the play. Migdalia Cruz's play appears as a reminder of Richard Schechner's ideas about the living space: including all the space in the theatre, not just the stage.[50] Cruz accomplishes a sophisticated medium for unravelling history, colonialism and its impingement on individual bodies. In much of her work, Cruz uses complicated and disturbing narratives and visual methods to tell complex, disturbing stories. These *monstruas* symbolise the alienation and marginality that Nuyorican women have experienced as part of the two cultural perspectives and/or societies that they belong to, and their economic and social status within them.

Cruz's play is perhaps the most aggressive Nuyorican response to the construction of a gendered and racialised self in the era of globalisation and cosmopolitanism. Although a discussion on the aesthetic classification of the play is beyond the scope of this chapter, I will say that what marks it as distinctly Nuyorican is not so much its consideration of race and ethnicity, but its more nuanced attention to the forces of history that have most shaped the need to articulate new subjectivities, in both a creative and political sense. Cruz follows the contours of Caribbean cultural expression and is influenced by various historical sources, as well as the multiplicity of the individual experience. The result is a contempo-mythography that both travels along, and is grounded in, cultural singularity. *Fur (2000)* is a process of critical resignification; Cruz shows how bodies have been marked with meanings; humanises them; and, simultaneously, empowers them. Cruz questions modern decisions about the nation and its citizens, more specifically, their decisions about the most marginal of beings: dark-skinned people, women, people with so-called 'disabilities', women who desire women, women who do not desire marriage, women who desire.

Notes

1 Walter Benjamin, *One-Way Street and Other Writings*, trans. Edmund Jephcott and Kingsley Shorter (London and New York: Verso, 1979), p. 392, as also quoted by Julia Emberley at the start of her *Venus and Furs. The Cultural Politics of Fur* (London: I. B. Taurus, 1998), p. 1.

2 *Fur. A Play in Nineteen Scenes* (hereafter *Fur (2000)*) was written in the early 1990s and published in Caridad Svich and María Teresa Marrero (eds), *Out of the Fringe: Contemporary Latina/Latino Theatre and Performance* (New York: Theatre Communications Group, 2000), pp. 71–115.

3 *Fur (2000)*, p. 75.

4 *Fur (2000)*, p. 77.

5 *Fur (2000)*, p. 78.

6 *Fur (2000)*, p. 78.

7 *Fur (2000)*, p. 79.

8 *Fur (2000)*, p. 84.

9 *Fur (2000)*, p. 85.

10 *Fur (2000)*, p. 86.

11 *Fur (2000)*, p. 87.

12 *Fur (2000)*, p. 91.

13 Helen Bryant, *Dallas Times-Herald* (n.d.), cited in Carole J. Adams, 'Eating animals', in Ron Scapp and Brian Seitz (eds), *Eating Culture* (New York: SUNY Press, 1998), pp. 60–76, p. 67.

14 Susan Bordo, 'Hunger as ideology', in Scapp and Seitz (eds), *Eating Culture*, pp. 11–36, p. 19.

15 Bram Dijkstra, *Idols of Perversity* (New York: Oxford University Press, 1986), pp. 30–1.

16 *Malleus Maleficarum*, quoted in Brian Easlea, *Witch-Hunting, Magic and the New Philosophy* (Atlantic Highlands, New Jersey: Humanities Press, 1980), p. 8; Hall and Oates, *Maneater* (1982).

17 Bordo, 'Hunger as ideology', p. 20.

18 *Fur (2000)*, p. 86.

19 *Fur (2000)*, p. 95.

20 Deborah R. Geis, 'Feeding the audience: food, feminism, and performing art', in Scapp and Seitz (eds), *Eating Culture*, pp. 216–37, p. 217.

21 *Fur (2000)*, p. 80.

22 Mary Douglas, *Purity and Danger: An Analysis of the Concepts of Pollution and Taboo* (London: Ark-Routledge & Kegan Paul, 1966), p. 15.

23 See: Doris Witt, 'Soul food: where the chitterling hits the (primal) pan', in Scapp and Seitz (eds), *Eating Culture*, pp. 258–88, p. 265.

24 Julia Kristeva, *Powers of Horror: An Essay on Abjection*, trans. Leon S. Roudiez (New York: Columbia University Press, 1982), p. 92.

25 Kristeva, *Powers of Horror*, p. 70.

26 Kristeva, *Powers of Horror*, p. 135.

27 See: Stuart Hall, 'New ethnicities', *Black Film/British Cinema*, ICA Documents 7 (London: Institute of Contemporary Arts, 1988), pp. 27–31 and Francis Affergan, *Exotisme et altérité: essai sur les fondements d'une critique de la anthropologie* (Paris: Press Universitaire de France), 1987.

28 Kristeva, *Powers of Horror*, p. 4.
29 Witt, 'Soul food', p. 267.
30 *Fur (2000)*, p. 88.
31 bell hooks, 'Eating the Other: desire and resistance', in Scapp and Seitz (eds), *Eating Culture*, pp. 181–201, p. 186.
32 Renato Rosaldo, *Culture and Truth: The Remaking of Social Analysis* (Boston, Massachusetts: Beacon Press, 1989).
33 *Fur (2000)*, p. 98.
34 *Fur (2000)*, p. 92.
35 Oswald de Andrade formulated the roots of this concept during Brazil's Modernismo period of the 1920s. It means to devour homogeneity and spew out syncretism: referring to the cannibalising of Europe to produce the heterogeneity of Brazil. It has become an influential term for rethinking New World syncretism and post-modernity as a process (see Oswald de Andrade, 'Anthropophagic manifesto', *Revista de Antropofagia*, 1:1, May 1928 (São Paulo, Brazil)).
36 Robert Bogdan, 'The social construction of freaks', in Rosemarie Garland Thomson (ed.), *Freakery: Cultural Spectacles of the Extraordinary Body* (New York: New York University Press, 1996), pp. 23–37, p. 23.
37 Bogdan, 'The social construction of freaks', p. 27.
38 Carnival terms for 'sideshow' and an elevated platform outside the tent, see Daniel Pratt Mannix (rev. ed.), *Freaks: We Who Are Not as Others* (San Francisco: Re/Search Publications, 1990).
39 Rosemarie Garland Thomson, 'From wonder to error – a genealogy of freak discourse in modernity', in Rosemarie Garland Thomson (ed.), *Freakery: Cultural Spectacles of the Extraordinary Body*, p. 10.
40 David A. Gerber, 'The "careers" of people exhibited in freak shows: the problem of volition and valorization', in Rosemarie Garland Thomson (ed.), *Freakery: Cultural Spectacles of the Extraordinary Body*, pp. 38–54, p. 41.
41 hooks, 'Eating the Other', p. 181.
42 hooks, 'Eating the Other', p. 183.
43 hooks, 'Eating the Other', pp. 186–191.
44 hooks, 'Eating the Other', p. 194.
45 Emberley, *Venus and Furs*, p. 4. For another discussion of fur and hair, see Chapter 9 of this volume, by Sue Walsh, on 'Bikini fur and fur bikinis'.
46 Emberley, *Venus and Furs*, p. 5.
47 Emberley, *Venus and Furs*, p. 6.
48 *Fur (2000)*, p. 104.
49 See, for instance: Patricia Hill Collins, *Black Feminist Thought: Knowledge, Consciousness, and the Politics of Empowerment* (Boston: Unwin Hyman, 1990); Nancy Caraway, *Segregated Sisterhood: Racism and the Politics of American Feminism* (Knoxville: University of Tennessee Press, 1991); bell hooks, *Black Looks: Race and Representation* (Boston, Massachusetts: South End Press, 1992).
50 Richard Schechner, *Environmental Theater* (New York: Applause, 1994), p. 2.

8 Designers' bodies: women and body hair in contemporary art and advertising

Laura Scuriatti

Body hair is constantly mentioned in magazines aimed at a female reading public (but increasingly also to a male readership), and is a relatively recent entry in art. Paradoxically, women's magazines' preoccupation with body hair only relies on a series of images in which female bodies are hairless, except for the genital area.[1] Advertising campaigns about body hair only consider it as refuse that needs to be removed from female bodies, and therefore just *refer* to it, but never show it. On the other hand, in recent years, contemporary artists have been increasingly devoting attention to human hair, and specifically to body hair, as if they were making use of the refuse products that have been disposed of, or deemed unfit for, the world-picture of advertising. While some works challenge and question assumptions about women's bodies through the portrayal and deployment of body hair, often the distance between these two visual codes is not as large as it seems, and when it comes to picturing and representing female bodies, often even the most radical and iconoclastic artworks can be seen as reproducing the same ideal criteria that have their roots in centuries of visual representation, sexual aesthetics and patriarchal ideology. In this chapter, I propose to analyse some examples[2] of images of female bodies with body hair – both in advertising and in contemporary art, discussing possible coalescences and differences. I will investigate the way in which such images might endorse or indeed try to expose the taboo of body hair and the different representations and constructions of female bodies across the diversity of Western cultures.

I would like to start my discussion by comparing two images used in recent advertisement campaigns, and *Mixed Metaphors* (1993),[3] a painting by the artist Dottie Attie (Figure 1), which share a common concern with the female body and its hair. I have decided to consider these three images because of their visual similarity – they all depict female genitals with pubic hair or a semblance thereof. Moreover, they all suggest that female bodies can be constructed according to various aesthetic or artistic criteria: they can be sculpted, reshaped, designed or designed upon, and all this by means of intervention or representation of body hair.

Both advertisements focus on the idea of removal. Body hair on a woman's body – the message seems to be – needs to be kept under control, even in the parts of the body on which it is allowed to exist and be shown. Both images are based on gardening metaphors: in the first example, an advertisement for Kookaï bikini costumes, a miniature man with a lawn-mower is trimming the bikini line of a woman lying on a green satin sheet. In the second picture, the model's pubic hair is being sculpted with a pair of scissors in a fashion which recalls the art of topiary; as in the first example, here too the agent of this reshaping is male: the arm holding the female body is definitely a male arm, not just because it is hirsute and has darker skin, but because of the fact that, despite being hairy, it is allowed to feature in this specific context.[4]

The deployment of gardening images in relation to the female body links it with an idea of 'nature' – nature which needs to be controlled, shaped, made into 'culture' by male hands.[5] But in these pictures the implications of this age-old binarism of nature and nurture which constructs the female body as negative 'other' are manifold and complex; there are in my view three main issues at stake here, which can be used also as starting points for an analysis of Dottie Attie's painting and other works of art considered in this chapter. Firstly, body hair on female bodies is a source of anxiety: it is important to consider the way in which this anxiety is articulated and the reasons that generate it; secondly, it will be apparent that in many of these images this anxiety is inscribed in a sexual context; thirdly, the analysis of this anxiety and its connotations will highlight the mechanisms which inform the cultural production and construction of female bodies as gendered bodies or, perhaps better, *a gendered body*.

I will start with the first point, the recognition of an anxiety which is generated by body hair on female bodies. The anxiety is expressed by the need to remove the hair, which grows outside the specific areas of the body in which it is allowed to be. As in a recent advertisement for a high-street shoe brand in the UK, which suggested that by wearing the brand's ankle-high boots, women would not need to shave their legs, these two advertisements do not negate the presence of body hair on a female body, but strive to convince the observer that, despite its existence, it must not be seen. Visibility, as Karín Lesnik-Oberstein suggests in Chapter 1 of this volume, is seen as extremely dangerous. Dangerous, indeed, to the extent that an advertisement addressing the problem of body hair on legs, bikini-area, armpits and arms, cannot but limit its visual testimony to the usual permitted pubic area trimmed into shape. Why might this be?

Lesnik-Oberstein points out that the danger of body-hair's visibility on female bodies consists in its blurring the gender categories of masculine and feminine, in that 'it reveals femininity as that which hides within itself the potential masculine'.[6] I would like to address this question through a reflection by anthropologist Robin Whitaker, who, in her article on Trish

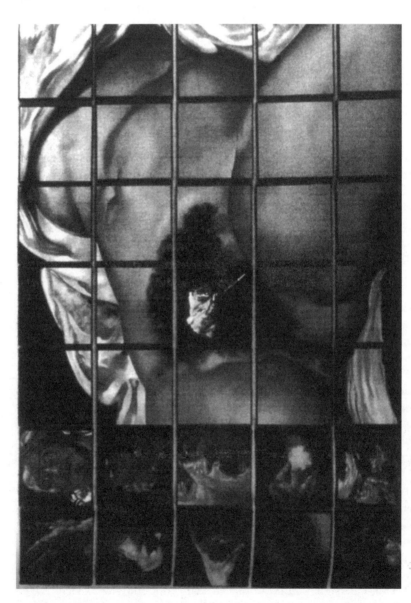

Figure 1 *Mixed Metaphors* by Dottie Attie

Morrissey's photographs *WWM – Women with Moustaches*, comments on the uproar generated by the exhibition of these pictures in London.[7] Morrissey's photos portray, in a style suggestive of fashion magazines' language, a number of women, sometimes very elegant, with precious jewels, styled hair, tweezed eyebrows and full make-up, and sometimes looking just ordinary, with a bit of lipstick and light make-up. They look like well-groomed middle-class women, and they all have more or less evident facial hair. Whitaker maintains that these pictures are unsettling because they 'remind us that the sexed body, as such, does not exist',[8] because they question 'sex as guarantor of gender' and therefore threaten to 'expose as insubstantial the very foundation of our culture's most basic system of categorisation'.[9] This is due, explains Whitaker, to the fact that these women's studied conformity to the conventions of 'feminine' appearance sharpens the paradox created by the presence of moustaches and beards on their faces. Whitaker highlights the double problem that these portraits raise:

> as much as its [facial hair] suggests the precedence of nature over culture, the exoticism of 'women with facial hair' is evidence of culture's habitual triumph over nature – a victory secured by all the mundane disciplines that eliminate any sign of nature's ambiguity.[10]

Yet, adds the author, 'as style, the notion of "women with facial hair" questions our presumption that nature exists somewhere beyond culture. [. . .] These photos unmask the cultural work required to produce sexed and sexable bodies'.[11]

Drawing on Judith Butler's concept of 'bad faith of gender' – the claim that one's womanhood is effortless – Whitaker suggests that Morrissey's photos show 'gender as enabling as well as limiting, opening up certain possibilities for living in the world even as it closes down',[12] and yet they also reinforce the binarism of sex and gender, deriving their transgressive power precisely from the expectations generated by it. Thus, the danger represented by the possible blurring of the categories of masculine and feminine, of sex and gender, not only in Morrissey's images, but also in the previously mentioned advertisements, lies in the fact that these show on the one hand that one 'becomes a woman', to borrow Simone de Beauvoir's words, through a certain styling work. But, on the other hand, they show that should one take for granted that this work is done on a body which is considered 'natural' (therefore needing acculturation), its natural characteristics are also presented as styled and dependent on what is not considered natural. In this way, not only are the categories of masculine and feminine questioned, but also the dichotomies of natural and cultural, of sex and gender. This is perhaps the reason behind the difference between the photographic material used by the advertising industry, which only shows permitted hair, and these artworks, which, because they are perhaps more able to use the transgressive power of body hair to its own advantage, can afford to show facial or other types of body hair. Here I do not use the idea of 'work' to be performed on a body to imply that there is a given, natural and original 'raw' body material which is transformed and made into something else; rather, I want to suggest that bodies are always and constantly being produced. Similarly, I do not intend to enforce an opposition between art and advertising: I will show further on in this chapter how, in both areas, images of bodies are produced by drawing on similar ideas of sex and gender.

Visibility is indeed, as argued by Karín Lesnik-Oberstein, the mark of the body-hair taboo. The reason why fashion magazines do not show 'non-allowed' body hair, even though they mention the work that is necessary to create the conditions for a body to be deemed feminine, is that the bodies regularly shown have a normative quality – they become *the* 'real/natural' female body to which women should aspire. These images should raise no questions about the feminine ideal – an ideal that has generated, as suggested in Naomi Wolf's popular volume *The Beauty Myth*, a gigantic and thriving industry world-wide.[13]

Commenting on the traditional pictorial genre of the female nude, Griselda Pollock and Rosizka Parker write that:

> As female nude, woman is body, is nature opposed to male culture, which, in turn, is represented by the very act of transforming nature, that is, the female model or motif, into the ordered forms and colours of cultural artefacts, a *work* of art.[14]

This assertion seems a fitting description of the narrative of the advertisements considered here. Yet, it needs to be analysed further: even though in both images a male figure performs the work necessary to turn the female body into a feminine one, I think that one should not necessarily stop at this binarism. First of all, the aesthetic of hairless bodies is recently also permeating images of male bodies, not only in gay magazines, but also, and this is an even more recent phenomenon, media products directed towards a (middle-class) heterosexual male public.[15] What is at stake, therefore, is not only a differentiation between female and male bodies, but between bodies that are objectified into objects of desire and bodies that are subjects of that desire. And when this is the case, patriarchal ideals about the body which has been constructed for centuries as an object of desire circulate and become normative, thus being applied also to male bodies, which would traditionally be positioned as the instigators and not the objects of such desire.

Helen McDonald reflects on this problem in a special issue of the British magazine *The Face*, entitled 'Forget the new man. Here come the new boys':[16] in her analysis of images of androgynous-looking male models, McDonald points out that the male model in question, who is apparently also portrayed inside the magazine as vulnerable, and half-naked in seductive poses recalling 'Dionysian prototypes in the paintings of Caravaggio or the sculptures of Michelangelo' – poses in ways 'which are immediately recognisable as ways in which women have looked down the camera for over a century in order to signify "sale"'.[17] Thus, observes McDonald, *The Face* 'aimed to sell teenage products by blatantly eroticising the relationship between the model and the viewer. Whether male or female, adult or adolescent, parent or boy-self, the viewer/reader/buyer of *The Face* entertains erotic fantasies about boys for whom he or she might buy clothes'.[18] What determines the appearance and status of the body in such a display is therefore the position in the relationship between object and subject of desire, viewer and viewed, and ultimately between buyer and object to be bought. In this sense, then, patriarchal criteria traditionally underpinning images of female bodies have been circulating and are now operative in many cases when the bodies in question are represented as objects of desire. Another example of this phenomenon is the iconography of the erotic fragment – images of parts of bodies, such as the amputated statue of the *Venus of Milo*, or the female torso and crotch in Gustave Courbet's *L'Origine du monde* (1866): McDonald points out that this technique, which has been used in art and photography to depersonalise the body of the model, has been 'more recently applied to the photographing of the male body for gay magazines',[19] thus coming to signify the erotic body *tout court*.

Thus, the overt gender dichotomy of the advertisements points to the idea that there are certain bodies which are objects of desire, and certain bodies which are arbiters of that desire and determine the criteria which make a body desirable. As Judith Butler points out, 'Assuming for a moment the stability of binary sex, it does not follow that the construction of "men" will accrue exclusively to the bodies of males or that "women" will interpret only female bodies.'[20] The desired body, male or female, must be made to look hairless, if it wants to be desired, and the whole exchange takes place in a heterosexual regime, and heterosexuality, in both cases, is metaphorically enforced through images of castration. Therefore, as blatantly unfair as they may be, these images are also loaded with a subversive potential, precisely because they, perhaps not intentionally so, thematise the material, cultural and psychological work implicit in sex-based gendered images of human bodies.

Dottie Attie's *Mixed Metaphors* is a reflection on precisely this 'work' on the body, focusing on visual techniques and on the iconographic tradition of the female nude in art history. This installation enacts the artist's/voyeur's gaze as it is pictured in Albrecht Dürer's drawing *Der Zeichner des liegenden Weibes* (*The Artist Drawing a Reclining Female*, 1538).[21] The space of this picture is divided into two halves by a wooden frame, in the middle of which is fixed a grid. To the right, the artist is observing the body of the reclining model on the other side of the divider, measuring her body against the grid which he has also reproduced on to the wooden panel or carton on to which he will draw her image. On one level, Attie's installation plays with the idea of transparency usually associated with perspective[22] and with the neutrality of the grid as a visual aid not only to produce 'realistic' pictures, but also to see 'reality'. By positioning the crotch of Courbet's *L'Origine du monde* on/behind/inside the grid, and by centrally placing the hand holding a scalpel from Thomas Eakin's *Gross Clinic* on the crotch itself, Attie suggests that this is a designed body, or a 'designer's body', drawn but also literally made to fit specific visual techniques, seen through and because of these techniques.[23] Indeed, as argued by Jo Anna Isaac, since Attie is an 'appropriationist' artist, i.e. an artist who copies works of other artists not by photographing them, but by repainting them, she duplicates 'not just the image, but the act of creation itself'.[24] Linda Hentschel reads Attie's artwork as a comment on the coalescence of artistic space with genital space, and on the parallel between the development of central perspective in art and of a voyeuristic gaze;[25] this coalescence, according to Hentschel, leads to a sexualisation of the act of seeing. This is expressed here through the idea of the construction, or design, of female bodies as sexualised bodies *par excellence*.[26]

Thus, to sum up, these three images, although directed to different publics and belonging to different media spheres, highlight through similar depictions of female bodies the problems and ideologies informing their idealisation and construction. These bodies are represented as needing control and shaping, in order to render them fit for assuming their sexualised and gendered role in society. All three suggest that these operations of control and construction take place through biological sex as a guarantor of gender, and all three suggest that an operation of castration might be part of this process. Two of these images also draw attention to the need to remove or clip body hair so that this operation is successful. The association of the idea of castration with the removal or clipping of 'unwanted' body hair, be it of the 'permitted' type or of the 'taboo' type, draws attention to Karín Lesnik-Oberstein's argument that 'body hair [. . .] does indeed reveal femininity as that which hides within itself the potentially masculine. . . . [T]his emphasises the threat that is posed by a female body not constituting itself as "absolute" other: as lack in opposition to the masculine "presence" '.[27] I would like now to elaborate this particular point further by analysing artworks which show female bodies with 'non-permitted' body hair, and reflecting on whether these images or installations do effectively open up a possibility for body hair to become visible, to become a possibility in language, and what kind of ideas about gendered bodies they might propose.

Since the 1960s, art has seen an increasing presence of bodies and body hair as a constituent and material of artworks, from Fluxus performances, to Jordan Baseman's and Rachel Glynne's hair dresses, to Mona Hatoum's hair paintings – in which the artist used her own hair to paint on a surface placed on the floor – and to Robert Gober's waxworks, via body art. There is of course an enormous amount of material, especially photographic, in which body hair features as part of an aesthetic of hyper-realism; in most cases it comes to represent freakishness and is instrumental in suggesting that this type of art should be invested with a subversive or shocking potential. The format of this chapter will allow me to discuss in depth only a few of these works – a selection which cannot be exhaustive or do justice to the complexity of the phenomenon, but that might be useful, I hope, in highlighting a few points about gender performance.

I will start with Zoe Leonard's photographs. This American artist is mostly famous for her *Untitled Installation at Neue Galerie*, set up in Kassel at *Dokumenta IX*,[28] where, after removing portraits of men, she hung close-up photographs of crotches, often being masturbated, as counterparts to seventeenth- and eighteenth-century female portraits. As part of her reflection of the eroticisation of the female body in art, in 1991 Leonard photographed the preserved head of a bearded woman at the Musée Orfilia of the School of Medicine in Paris, and produced a series of photographs of bearded performance artist and circus director Jennifer Miller as a pin-up girl (Figure 2).[29]

In an interview with New York art critic Laura Cunningham, Leonard explained that the photographs of the bearded woman's head were part of a larger project in which the artist took pictures of the rooms and exhibits of several different natural history and medical history museums, as reflections on the way in which the items had been selected and exhibited.[30] These photographs, according to Leonard, are meant to ask questions about the mechanisms of classification and voyeurism which inform these displays, they are 'about our culture, about an institutional obsession with difference'.[31] The *Preserved Head of Bearded Woman* (1991) photographs indeed beg questioning, not only as an exhibit of a medical history museum, but also as photographs. As pointed out by Cunningham and by the artist herself, it is difficult to determine whether the head had belonged to a female or a male body, yet the earrings and the lace collar insert the head in a gender-coded system, which also explains the scientific purpose of its presence in this museum:[32] the bearded woman is a (scientific) curiosity,[33] since its appearance breaks the classificatory rules of gender identification. It has been necessary to add certain accessories to code the exhibit as feminine, as if the exhibitor could not stand the idea of letting the ambiguity perpetuate itself; in turn, this femininity gives the head its status of 'curiosity'. Leonard's photos address the issue of 'exhibition', as well as the voyeurism implied in the display of the head in a glass cabinet, and the construction of gender which underpins the whole operation. As the artist notes in an interview with Anna Blume, 'none of our

Figure 2 Jennifer Miller as a pin-up girl, by Zoe Leonard

recognised rituals of honouring the dead are bestowed on her. No name, no grave, no plaque, just dismemberment and obscurity':[34] if, on the one hand, the separation of the head from the rest of the body serves the purpose of depersonalising what has become an item of scientific observation – which therefore does not need any recognition as a dead human body – on the other hand it communicates that the focus of the observation should only be the beard and its contrast with the expectations about the way that female bodies should look. The various angles from which the glass jar and its content are shown, seem indeed to enact the possible movements of a spectator, who moves around the object in search of further details.

A naturalising operation has been performed on the bearded woman, making the head into a female head; the implements – earrings and lace collar – are cultural artefacts signifying 'female' in French nineteenth-century culture. These implements at the same time create confusion – they signal the rupture of gender expectations – and stabilise this very confusion, by affirming through it the strength and power of gender dichotomy. Something different happens in the Jennifer Miller photographs, where the performer is present with her whole body, which she can move and control to assume certain poses rather than others: while posing for pictures which are modelled on Marilyn Monroe's pin-up photos, Miller's body presents itself as an object of desire, as a sexualised body, and as a body that defies both the conventional criteria for the exposure of female bodies as nudes, and the cultural expectations as to what a woman's body should look like.

Helen McDonald compares Miller's portraits with Jusepe de Ribera's *Magdalena Ventura with Her Husband* (1631), where the bearded Italian woman is shown with her husband and child according to the traditional 'sacra famiglia' iconography, breastfeeding her child. McDonald maintains that, while in Ribera's painting the necessity of proving that Magdalena was female is expressed through a 'naturalisation' of the subject in a social context, using both the family iconography and the motif of breastfeeding, Miller's pictures are not naturalised in this way:

> The particular composition, the pin-up format in general and the image of 'woman' in *Pin-up* are all culturally constructed and, as components of Leonard's parody, are coded as such. In this way the question of excessive hair on Miller's face and body engages the spectator with contemporary discourses on beauty, sexuality, gender identity and eroticism. It points to the ambiguity of the sex/gender distinction.[35]

Despite the obvious parody of Leonard's pictures,[36] I am not sure that it is possible to distinguish between a 'naturalisation' and 'cultural construction' in this way; in fact, both the family context (including breast-feeding) and the pin-up images derive their meaning from the fact that both these roles are typically female roles. I do not want to suggest that we should do away with the important difference in cultural context that separates these two pictures, yet, McDonald's polarisation does not seem to stand: what these pictures derive their shocking or subversive power from is precisely the deployment of iconographic motifs which signify 'female'. These images have to signal in one way or another an anomaly, so that the spectator can perform an operation of comparison, and draw the conclusion that something is not as expected. In this sense, the pin-up pose functions in the same way as breastfeeding in Ribera's painting: it signals femininity in its least equivocal way; it classifies to signal ambiguity, to reinforce classification.

However, Leonard's pictures do portray Miller as an object of desire: these photographs comply with the ideal of female bodies as erotic, healthy, young and available. The conformity to these ideals and the parallel suggestion that these might be valid also for bodies which do not fit into the rigid classification system to which they ought to belong, draws attention to the mechanisms of gender as cultural construction, and to the way in which ambiguity – that is something that does not fit into the prescribed categories – is expelled from it. As Liz Kotz points out, Leonard and other contemporary artists are no pioneers, and work in a tradition that goes back to, just to name a few, Weegee, Diane Arbus and Larry Clark. What is important in these works, however, is the potential for a problematisation of aesthetics in general, and of feminist aesthetics and art in particular.[37] In the 1970s and 1980s, many feminists criticised body art,[38] since they saw the danger of complying with the traditional association of women with the body, and suggested that body art might be read as a sort of acceptance of the female body as spectacle and commodification. Leonard's photographs lend themselves to various interpretations (which would also be valid for Trish Morrissey's portraits): on the one hand it could be argued that in adopting Marilyn Monroe's poses, or fashion magazine aesthetics, Leonard and Morrissey suggest that the only way to promote the acceptance of difference and ambiguity in gender is to adhere to prescribed ideals of representation of the female body, and that in order to do so, the ambiguous body has to become an object of desire. On the other hand, however, this is also a way of exploding these ideals and of creating a space of visibility for unacceptable bodies, marked by a taboo that excludes them from what is defined as norm.

Moreover, by playing with the genre of the female nude, these photographs expose the problems of the sex/gender relation: by showing bodies which do not conform to the assumptions made about the morphological characteristics of female or male bodies, they draw attention to, in Judith Butler's words, 'the presumption of a binary gender system [which] implicitly retains the belief in a mimetic relation of gender to sex whereby gender mirrors sex or is otherwise restricted by it', thereby also questioning the 'immutable character of sex'.[39] In this way, to borrow Butler's words once again, these pictures can be seen as contesting the idea of a 'pregiven sex' and suggesting that maybe after all 'sex was always already gender'.[40]

It is interesting here to link these reflections to the genres of female and male nudes in art history. Among the artworks in which body hair is shown or used as material, numerous examples conform to these traditional iconographic motifs. This should not be labelled as conservative *tout court*. In fact, the use of established aesthetic forms inserts these artworks into an age-old pictorial tradition. By doing so, it is as if these works were saying that not only sex has a history, but that also sex as a pictorial genre has a history, and one that needs to be explored and renegotiated.

It is also interesting in this sense to compare Leonard's portrait of Jennifer Miller with Annie Leibovitz's in her volume *Women*. In this book of portraits of American women, Jennifer Miller is the only completely naked one, and is portrayed sitting on a chair and facing the spectator, brocade wallpaper in the background, as if she was an exhibit in a museum. Even though on its own this photograph might be read as challenging the gender expectations linked to the motif of the 'nude model on chair', so common in nineteenth-century French painting for example, it is difficult to disregard the fact of her nudity. Is Miller nude in order to affirm the right to be a 'female nude' also for a hairy woman? But if so, why should particularly a bearded woman have this privilege? Even if the volume would be claiming to celebrate the diversity of womanhood, this would not dispel a doubt about the use of Jennifer Miller's body in this context as an exotic curiosity, if not a freak. The problem still remains about the contextualisation of the photo in the volume about 'women': this contextualisation, as well as Jennifer Miller's Marilyn Monroe's poses, might be in danger of closing down the problematisation of gender binarism by precisely reinforcing that binarism. At the same time, at least in the case of Leonard's photos, they are parodies of gender binarism, and at the heart of the parody is the repetition of gender characteristics and behaviours. In this sense, they might be interpreted as opening up the possibility for a multiplication of gender performances, as argued by Butler.

Judith Halberstam reads Catherine Opie's and Della Grace's photographs in a similar way.[41] Both these artists, who are active in the 'Drag Kings' movement, focus on ideas of female masculinities. Opie's series *Being and Having* (1991) are close-up portraits of women or transgender persons with sometimes fake, sometimes real, moustaches and beards, and with a masculine look. Often the camera is so near to the faces of the models that the artificiality of beards and moustaches is noticeable, and the models stare straight in the camera, thus foreclosing the possibility of a voyeuristic gaze. Opie has also photographed the backs of 'butch lesbians', including her own. These photos are very similar to Della Grace's *Jack's Back* (1994) and *Jack Unveiled* (1994). In the first photograph, the model, who turns out to be called 'Jackie', is shown with her or his back to the camera, presented according to the aesthetic criteria of certain gay erotic magazines, wearing combat trousers and with an almost total haircut, looking definitely male. In the second picture the same model is shown frontally, taking her shirt off, and showing the viewer her breasts. In Catherine Opie's *Dyke* (1992), the model, who is also shown from the back and closely resembles 'Jack' in form and aesthetics, has the word 'DYKE' tattooed on her or his neck. In both cases, there is a confusion which is created by the presence of breasts or by the word 'dyke', both referring to women. On this point, Halberstam writes that:

> Whether we are confronted with the hormonally and surgically altered bodies of transgender men or the tattooed and pierced and scarred skin of the butch dyke, we look at bodies that display layered and multiple identifications, adding a gender dimension unassimilable within the boundaries of 'man' or 'woman'.[42]

The thing is, it is difficult to determine whether these models belong to either of the commonly accepted biological sexes: as in the case of Leonard's photos of Jennifer Miller, the names – Jennifer, Jack – the breasts, the word 'dyke', do not actually manage to fix a gender identity on to these bodies, which are repeating, reinterpreting and parodying prescribed sexual practices and appearances without fully adhering to them.

Halberstam notes also that Grace's and Opie's portraits are 'stylised portraits in the Mapplethorpe tradition':[43] as in the case with Morrissey's photos, stylisation – that is adhesion to style, its aesthetic norm and canon – does not maintain these pictures' ability to question gender discourse. Of course, Morrissey's pictures are about creating a space for different criteria and definitions of 'woman', and question gender binarism itself; however, Opie's, Grace's and Leonard's works prompt a much more radical rethinking of these categories, without providing any solutions – without suggesting any ideas of a 'third other', but only suggesting that through parody and enactment, a variety of non-fixed gender identities can be created, assumed and rethought again. This, I have suggested, does not work in the same way in Annie Leibovitz's photo of Jennifer Miller, which fixes her as 'woman', but exhibits her as curiosity. A further comparison with one of Leibovitz's photos can be found in the Halberstam article: the critic discusses here Leibovitz's picture of Demi Moore on the cover of the August issue of *Vanity Fair* in 1992; the actress, Halberstam claims, is meant to look masculine, and is naked except for a painted man's suit. Inside the magazine she leans over her sleeping husband, Bruce Willis: 'here the body suit emphasises the femaleness of the female body [which is naked and visibly so], while Grace's and Opie's portraits make no effort of making femaleness visible.'[44] Moreover, the presence of Moore's husband reinforces the strictly heterosexual component of this picture, and of the actress's own body, which therefore does not pose any threats to the sex/gender system; whereas, to quote Halberstam, 'the female masculinity in the work of Opie and Grace [and, I would add, the 'hairy' femininity of Leonard's *Pin-up* series] offer[s] a glimpse into worlds where alternative masculinities [and femininities] make an art of gender',[45] thus questioning, in Butler's words, 'the fundamental ontology of sex and gender'.[46]

Parallel to the work of these artists, body hair has also been used as material to create artworks and installations. I will not be able to cover a broad spectrum of such works,[47] but I would like briefly to discuss some installations by Lebanese artist Mona Hatoum and by the American surrealist Rober Gober. These works have less to do with preoccupations about the function of body hair in the perception and construction of gender difference than with reflections on how bodies enter art, and which criteria regulate their presence and appearance. I will begin with Mona Hatoum's *Recollection* (1995) and *Jardin public* (1993), two installations which, according to Giorgio Verzotti (curator of the exhibition of her work in Turin, Italy), represent 'the female as disturbance'.[48] The first installation was commissioned for the space of a former medieval female convent, the Beguinage St Elizabeth, Kortrijk, Belgium. It consists of the artist's hairs, gathered over a period of six years and woven into little balls then scattered on the floor, or stretched on an old wooden loom, and hanging from the ceilings as if they were old cobwebs. The latter, in particular, apparently annoyed visitors and 'interfere[d] with [their] circulation through the space';[49] the hanging hairs and the hair balls, according to Catherine de Zegher, have also prompted reactions of disgust and anger in some visitors.[50] The hairs in question here are not body hair of the kind that has been discussed so far: they are simply hair which the artist collected, as she explains, from her brushes, combs and sinks. If still attached to a living body, especially to a female body, they would be standing for beauty and sexual appeal (which also explains the nuns' ban on letting their hair grow), but detached from it they become disgusting, or at least are seen as dirty. A homonymous work, which I believe is part of the same project (albeit developed later on in the same year), and *Jardin public*, both reflect on the same question: the first consists of a soap bar on to which pubic hairs are stuck,[51] the second is a metal chair in painted wrought-iron, where pubic hair in the shape of a triangle emerges from holes in the seat. In all these works, hairs are the relics of the presence of a female body, but as such, they are displaced and cause disturbance.

In the case of the Beguinage, hairs are out of place in all possible senses, since it is one of the basic prescriptions for almost all orders of convent nuns to keep their hair very short. On the other hand, both the soap and the chair bear the marks of the presence of hair – a mark that causes anxiety and disgust. This fundamental displacement of a part of a female body[52] not only points to a general reflection on the style which Hatoum adopts and reinterprets: as Verzotti explains, Hatoum seeks to reinsert the body and corporeality in minimalist art, which is seen as 'de-corporealis[ing] the art object, considering it more as a theoretical axiom and abstracting it from any context of meaning'[53]. Also, specifically, it suggests once more how certain parts of female bodies are subject to policing, regulation and scrutiny – procedures on which the status of 'woman' is seen to depend. De Zegher sees Hatoum's work as 'a complex reflection on bodily pollution, involving the relation of order and disorder'.[54]

Indeed, in these works the ideas of dirt and disorder are very much linked with ideas of order and cleanliness: in *Recollection* hairballs are scattered on the floor (dirt and disorder), yet at the same time stretched on the loom in a regular pattern; instead of yarn, the soap, which is supposed to remove dirt, bears the marks of that dirt in the form of relics. Mary Douglas famously defined dirt as 'matter out of place' and suggested that this definition:

> implies two conditions: a set of ordered relations and a contravention of that order. Dirt then, is never a unique, isolated event. Where there is dirt there is a system. Dirt is the by-product of a systematic ordering and classification of matter, in so far as ordering involves rejecting inappropriate elements. [. . .] In short, our pollution behaviour is the reaction which condemns any object or idea likely to confuse or contradict cherished classifications.[55]

Thus, in these works by Mona Hatoum, hair can be read as standing for the enactment of this process of removal and ordering, with its inevitable counterpart of defilement and disorder. The system of classification questioned here is of course those cultural practices which constitute certain body parts as abject, depending on the moment and location of their encounter with another human being. I would suggest, however, that the reflection suggested in these works also involves the classification of gender: in particular, the regulations on female hair, and their 'right' place.

This brings us back to the idea of removal mentioned at the very beginning of this article: Mona Hatoum shows that female bodies are the sites of monitoring and regulation. When the material removed from the body in the process of being defined as female (part of which are the permissions for growing or not growing hair and the effect that this has on the femininity of the individual, or the obsession with female genital hygiene) reappears, subsequent to its removal, it causes disturbance because it draws attention to the process of categorisation and classification of which it is a refuse.

Robert Gober's *Untitled (Hairy Shoe)* (1993) and *Untitled (Candle)* (1991) parody this process: the first object is a wax model of a shoe, which looks very much like a child's shoe, its internal sole covered in hair, as if the wax had been previously used to wax someone's body; the second work is a wax candle on a wax pedestal, in which again body hair is trapped. These objects also present body hair as a refuse, as something that needed to be removed from somewhere, but they suggest that it may find a place elsewhere. Jed Perl suggests that in *Untitled (Candle)* Gober 'is giving an extra little shove to the most obvious phallic analogy. By adding those bits of hair, Gober seems to undress the candle'.[56] The writer refers here to the explication of the phallic metaphor through the presence of the hair; I would like to add that, considered in conjunction with *Untitled (Hairy Shoe)*, the work also comments on the role of body hair in the creation of specifically connotated bodies. Wax is here both an implement for removing body hair from where it should not be, and a raw material for the creation of other objects which contain it. If the candle is readable as a phallic symbol – thus referring to a male body – then the shoe seems to indicate a child's body. In one case, the hair is positioned where it is allowed to be, whereas in the other case it is displaced, not only because it is placed in a shoe, but also because this shoe is metonymically linked to the image of a child. In both cases, however, a displacement is still operative, since the hair has been eradicated from elsewhere. The malleable consistency of wax renders its double function possible, thus drawing attention to the processes of creation not only of the work of art itself, but also of the body images that enter art as representation. It is by removing and adding that bodies are constructed, imagined and depicted. It is this constant process that the works mentioned in this chapter visualise through the deployment and depiction of body hair. By focusing on body hair as an object of disgust, disturbance, taboo, defilement and curiosity, and by linking these reflections to the discussion of gender and body images, these artists have suggested many different ways in which it might be possible to start rethinking the system of classification which, in our culture, divides the human bodies into two permitted categories and kinds of individuals. These works also show that trying to rethink such a system, with roots in the structures of social and political power and hierarchy, and trying to discuss body hair as a site of such a construction, cannot provide fixed solutions and new schemes for classifications. Rather, this should provide a platform of negotiation of such a system and, above all, a niche of visibility and possibility for whatever might exceed definition to become meaningful in discourse.

Notes

1   I would like to thank Astrid Welter for her invaluable suggestions and for drawing my attention to Mona Hatoum's and Robert Gober's work. I also wish to acknowledge the helpful comments of Manuele Gragnolati, Alexander Graf and Francesca Muscau, as well as the kind and competent help of the staff of the Kunstbibliothek in Berlin.

2   The list of images does not pretend to be exhaustive. Apart from the artists and work of which I might not be aware, I will not discuss here the photographs of Terry Richardson and Elinor Carucci, who produced each at least one photograph in which female bodies have body hair (located in the armpit in the case of Richardson's portrait, and on the breast in the case of Carucci's photo).

3   In Linda Hentschel, *Pornotopische Techniken des Betrachtens. Raumwahrnehmung und Geschlechterordnung in visuellen Apparaten der Modern* (Marburg: Jonas Verlag, 2001), p. 29. Oil on canvas, 86.4 × 138.7 cm panels, 15.25 × 15.25 each, PPOW Gallery, NY.

4   This image is part of a desk calendar specially made for the German edition of *Vogue*, with which it was issued as a gift for the readers. The picture in question is the illustration for the month of June; the text at the back of the card focuses on the theme of the month – hair removal – and suggests that with the impending good weather and the increasing uncovering of body parts, body hair must be removed. Hair-removal products which alleviate pain and embellish the skin are also advertised here.

5   See also Chapter 1 of this volume. Lesnik-Oberstein differentiates between hair which is permissible – pubic hair, eyebrows – and taboo hair. Permissible hair needs constant regulation and trimming. On the other hand, she points out that, should taboo hair be permitted to grow, it would not need any type of regulation (as opposed to body fat, for example).

6   See Lesnik-Oberstein, Chapter 1 of this volume, p. 11.

7   Robin Whitaker, 'Women with facial hair', *Source*, online magazine, http://source.ie/issues/issues2140/issue22/is22artwomfac.html. The works were exhibited in London, at the Tom Blau Gallery, 23 November to 5 January 2001. See also the website of f.uk fashion news: www.widemedia.com/fashionuk/news/2000/10/18/news0000711, which shows some of Morrissey's portraits and provides links to the website of the London gallery where the exhibition took place. *Source's* search function also provides links to Morrissey's photographs and related pages.

8   *Source*, http://source.ie/issues/issues2140/issue22/is22artwomfac.html.

9   *Source*, http://source.ie/issues/issues2140/issue22/is22artwomfac.html.

10   *Source*, http://source.ie/issues/issues2140/issue22/is22artwomfac.html.

11   *Source*, http://source.ie/issues/issues2140/issue22/is22artwomfac.html.

12   *Source*, http://source.ie/issues/issues2140/issue22/is22artwomfac.html.

13   Naomi Wolf, *The Beauty Myth: How Images of Beauty Are Used Against Women* (London: Vintage, 1991). Wolf's main argument is that a conservative backlash followed the activism of the 1960s and 1970s, decades in which women gained political and social rights. According to Wolf, this backlash obtained the result of reining-in women, their activism, enthusiasm and demands; one of the ways in which this was possible was the circulation of beauty norms which should occupy women's time, directing their efforts and newly acquired wages towards the achievement of such beauty, rather than towards more active social commitments. Wolf suggests that women's magazines are one of the sites in which the backlash is more evident, in that even those magazines which are renowned for publishing awareness-raising articles for and about women, must depend for their survival on the income

coming from large multinationals which, with their products, promote a dia-metrically opposed image of women. Incidentally, despite its critical and polemical intentions, Wolf's book does not include body hair in her critique of the manufacture of the female body (mostly focused on body weight), except in one instance, where she mentions leg shaving in connection with the sexual confusion felt by women who are not able to discern the difference between feeling sexual and being sexually felt, or sexual looking and being sexually looked at. In this case, she quotes women considering as their first sexual experience the first time they shaved their legs and ran their hands over the smoothly shaven legs (Wolf, *The Beauty Myth*, p. 158).

14 Rosizka Parker and Griselda Pollock, *Old Mistresses: Women, Art and Ideology* (London: Routledge and Kegan Paul, 1981), p. 119, quoted in: Helen McDonald, *Erotic Ambiguities. The Female Nude in Art* (London: Routledge, 2001), p. 8.

15 See on this for instance: Michael Boroughs, 'Body depilation in males: a new body image concern', *International Journal of Men's Health*, 1 (2002), 247–57.

16 McDonald, *Erotic Ambiguities*, p. 86–7. The issue of *The Face* mentioned in the text is no. 83, year 2 (August 1995).

17 McDonald, *Erotic Ambiguities*, p. 87.

18 McDonald, *Erotic Ambiguities*, p. 88.

19 McDonald, *Erotic Ambiguities*, p. 119.

20 Judith Butler, 'Subjects of sex/gender/desire', in Sandra Kemp and Judith Squires (eds), *Feminisms* (Oxford: Oxford University Press, 1997), pp. 278–85, p. 280.

21 The two images have also been compared by Linda Hentschel in *Pornotopische Techniken des Betrachten*, pp. 28–9. The author analyses the theme of per-spectival grids in the two works, considering the construction of the gaze of the spectator as penetration. For a list of the works copied in Attie's *Mixed Metaphors*, see: Jo Anna Isaak, *Feminism and Contemporary Art: The Revolutionary Power of Women's Laughter* (London: Routledge, 1999), p. 60.

22 This is something which Leon Battista Alberti also formulated in terms of a grid-like visual construction.

23 Eakin's painting interestingly also serves as an illustration for the 1994 £1 Penguin edition of *Frankenstein*.

24 Isaak, *Feminism and Contemporary Art*, p. 60.

25 Butler, 'Subjects of sex/gender/desire', p. 280.

26 As Hentschel's study makes clear, this does not necessarily lead to the associ-ation of the voyeuristic gaze with male spectators. Helen McDonald also draws attention to this issue by reflecting on Linda Williams's suggestion that 'as a result of women's participation as both producers and consumers in the [pornographic] industry, the hierarchies governing traditional phallocentric distinctions encoded in pornography were breaking down'. Linda Williams, *Hard Core: Power, Pleasure and the 'Frenzy of the Visible'* (London: Pandora Press, 1990). See McDonald, *Erotic Ambiguities*. Indeed, the difficulty of endorsing the assumption of a male gaze for art and advertisement can be expressed from different points of view, depending on the theoretical approach: these could for example be summarised as either the impossibility of thinking of a unified, essential and recognisable male gaze, which did not

involve also reflections on race and class – categories which would explode the gender dichotomy; or, once recognised that these images are the always evolving and circulating product of Western culture, the impossibility of positioning oneself outside this culture, or any, for that matter, so as to be immune from the ideology that informs it. Indeed, if we consider the position of the designer's hand in Attie's grid, we will realise that the hand is inserted in the grid too, as if to suggest that there is no possible 'outside' to this way of seeing.

27 See Chapter 1 of this volume, p. 11.

28 13 June to 20 September 1992, Kassel, Germany.

29 Some texts describe Jennifer Miller as a 'transsexual'; in others, such as Annie Leibovitz's and Susan Sontag's book *Women*, Miller's transsexuality is not mentioned (Annie Leibovitz and Susan Sontag, *Women* (Munich: Schirmer/ Mosel, 1999), p. 240).

30 See Laura Cunningham's interview of the artist in *Journal of Contemporary Art Online* at: www.jca-online.com/leonard, 1–6. See also Leonard's interview with Anna Blume, 'The bearded woman', in the exhibition catalogue *Secession. Zoe Leonard* (23 July to 14 September 1997), pp. 8–9, p. 8.

31 Cunningham, *Journal of Contemporary Art Online*, p. 3.

32 Cunningham, *Journal of Contemporary Art Online*, p. 3. Apparently this was the head of a woman who worked in a circus and died at the turn of the twentieth century.

33 I put the word in brackets, since bearded women have also been 'curiosities' in the literal sense of the word, most of them participating in 'freak' shows and circus performances.

34 Blume, 'The bearded woman', p. 9.

35 McDonald, *Erotic Ambiguities*, p. 50.

36 I would say that parody is absent in Ribera's painting.

37 Liz Kotz, 'Questions on feminism: 25 responses', *October*, 71 (Winter 1995), 26–7, 26.

38 See, for example, the critique of some of Mona Hatoum's works and of Karen Finley's performances, which were also put under scrutiny by the US federal art funding body NEA and by the Bush Sr and Clinton administrations, which suggested that NEA should only fund artists with a certain standard of decency.

39 Butler, 'Subjects of sex/gender/desire', p. 280.

40 Butler, 'Subjects of sex/gender/desire', p. 280.

41 Judith Halberstam, 'Bathrooms, butches and the aesthetics of masculinity', in J. Blessing (ed.), *Rrose is a Rrose is a Rrose. Gender Performance in Photography*, exhibition catalogue, Solomon Guggenheim Foundation, New York, 17 January to 27 April 1997 (New York: Guggenheim Museum Publications, 1997), pp. 176–89.

42 Halberstam, 'Bathrooms, butches and the aesthetics of masculinity', p. 184.

43 Halberstam, 'Bathrooms, butches and the aesthetics of masculinity', p. 185.

44 Halberstam, 'Bathrooms, butches and the aesthetics of masculinity', p. 187.

45 Halberstam, 'Bathrooms, butches and the aesthetics of masculinity', p. 188.

46 Butler, 'Subjects of sex/gender/desire', p. 285. Leibovitz's photograph of Jennifer Miller, one of Morrisey's portraits and some of Opie's recent works have been exhibited together in an international project by 'Camera Magenta'

entitled *fe/male*: the project involved the installation of these and many other photos in poster format in the underground station Braunschweingasse in Vienna (1–31 August 2001). See the website of the exhibition: http://camera-magenta.com/feMale_home.html.

47 I therefore refer the reader to the following works, which will not be discussed here: Janine Antoni, *Loving Care* (1993–95), performance with hair and hair dye, Anthony D'Offay Gallery, London; Jordan Baseman, *Call Me Mister*, shirt and tie in human hair (1994), exhibited in the New Art Gallery, Walsall, UK; Dorothy Cross, *Stilettos* (1994), first exhibited at the MIT List Visual Arts Center, Cambridge, Massachusetts, from 9 April to 28 June, reproduced in *Art Monthly* 203: 2, (1997), p. 20; Jimmie Durham, *Chemise* (1996), shirt, hair and other materials, Galerie Micheline Szwajcer, Antwerp; Rachel Glynne, *Long Hair Dress Shirt* (1995). See also the cover of this volume: *Hair Book* (1992) by Mary Ellen Croteau, first exhibited at the Artemesia Gallery in Chicago, from 2 October to 1 November 1992 in a solo exhibition entitled 'New Work'.

48 Giorgio Verzotti, *Mona Hatoum*, exhibition catalogue, Castello di Rivoli, Museo di Arte Contemporanea, 24 March to 23 May 1999, trans. Marguerite Shore (Milan: Edizioni Charta, 1999), p. 29.

49 Verzotti, *Mona Hatoum*, p. 30.

50 Catherine de Zegher, 'Focus. Hatoum's *Recollection*: about losing and being lost', in Michael Archer, Guy Brett and Catherine de Zegher, *Mona Hatoum* (London: Phaidon, 1997), pp. 90–104, p. 93.

51 Zegher, 'Focus. Hatoum's *Recollection*: about losing and being lost', in Archer *et al.*, *Mona Hatoum*, p. 103.

52 I refer to the female body, since both the *Recollection* installation and soap were conceived as part of projects on femininity and female bodies, and the hairy shape on the chair suggests the shape of a female pubic area rather than a male one.

53 A tendency that feminist artists have been trying to counteract; see Verzotti, *Mona Hatoum*, p. 20.

54 Zegher, 'Focus. Hatoum's *Recollection*: about losing and being lost', p. 93.

55 Mary Douglas, *Purity and Danger* [1966] (London: Routledge, 2002), pp. 36–7.

56 Jed Perl, 'On art: our Dadaist', *New Republic* (17 and 24 April 2000), pp. 66–70, p. 68.

9 Bikini fur and fur bikinis

Sue Walsh

[F]ur and velvet – as has long been suspected – are a fixation of the sight of the pubic hair, which should have been followed by the longed-for sight of the female member;[1]

In other cases the replacement of the object by a fetish is determined by a symbolic connection of thought, [. . .] no doubt the part played by fur as a fetish owes its origin to an association with the hair of the *mons Veneris*.[2]

In this chapter I want to discuss further the grounds for reading animal fur as body hair, a reading referred to especially in Chapters 4 and 7 of this volume. This is because, both in the texts cited in those chapters and those described there, and in the political actions and discussions that I will also be addressing, body hair and fur are connected with, and substituted for, each another in a variety of ways. So what grounds are given for making these connections and substitutions? Firstly, fur and hair are seen as having an *obvious* relation to each other: they are claimed to look and/or feel similar, and yet, if this similarity is a given, and uncontestable, why, nevertheless, does a distinction remain between fur and hair? The second of the two quotations from Freud prompts a question about what constitutes a 'symbolic connection of thought', a question that I will return to later in the chapter, but in the meantime I will note that it is precisely in the notion of 'association' or similarity that an idea of difference is preserved, and so it seems that, secondly, fur and hair can be read as serving to mark radical distinctions: the most obvious instance being a distinction between humanity and animality. To help me to think through the question of the grounds of the comparison between fur and hair, I want to turn firstly to an advertisement for an anti-fur campaign launched by PeTA (People for the Ethical Treatment of Animals) in 1999/2000. The advertisement in question features, in PeTa's own words, 'a woman in pink panties whose bikini line is in dire need of waxing, with the caption, "Fur trim. Unattractive."'[3]

The outcry surrounding this particular PeTA campaign advertisement peaked in the publicity around an open letter of protest written by Galen Sherwin (the then President of the New York City Chapter of the National

Organization for Women) and the response by Ingrid Newkirk (the President of P*e*TA), both of which were published in the April/May 2000 issue of *Ms. Magazine*.[4] This episode may be seen, however, as yet another in what has become a long-running saga of disagreements between P*e*TA, which is staffed by a number of self-defined feminists,[5] and various (other) feminists and feminist animal advocates. In 1994, feminists writing for and on behalf of FAR (Feminists for Animal Rights) critiqued P*e*TA's use of naked models for its 'I'd rather go naked than wear fur' campaign, and also censured its apparent willingness to accept substantial donations from the soft-porn industry,[6] as did prominent feminist animal-rights advocate Carol Adams, who bemoaned what she characterised as P*e*TA's cynicism in 'sid[ling] up to pornographers (specifically *Playboy* and *Penthouse*), and compliment[ing] them by imitating them'.[7]

Though the complaints against P*e*TA's 'Fur trim. Unattractive' and 'I'd rather go naked than wear fur' campaigns turn on the way that the advertisements and promotions seem to produce an equivalence between animals and women, this is not to say that what feminist animal advocates are unhappy about is simply that P*e*TA makes such a connection, since writers like Carol Adams and groups such as FAR see just such a link, and indeed argue that 'The oppression of women and animals comes from the same source – patriarchal, hierarchical domination and control'.[8] The problem is rather, that where feminist animal advocates such as Carol Adams see this connection in the way that animals and women are produced as a cultural construction, P*e*TA is regarded as simply contributing to the construction of that connection, neither producing an analysis of it, and nor, therefore, able to mobilise a radical reading of that cultural construction for the benefit of either women or animals.

P*e*TA's 'Fur-trim-ad' shows, on the left (occupying about a third of the advertisement space), the pelvic area of a woman, from just below the navel to the top of the thighs. She is wearing a small pair of pale-pink knickers with what appears to be pubic hair, or at any rate a dark shadow line (about as thick as the thickness of the knickers over the figure's hips) showing around the edge of the knickers. I have tried to choose my words carefully in describing the advertisement, in the effort to distance myself from normative interpretations such as P*e*TA's own 'bikini line [. . .] in dire need of waxing';[9] however, the awkwardness of my description might be said to indicate the difficulty of finding the appropriate language. The remaining two-thirds of the ad-space is occupied by large black letters which read:

Fur trim.
Unattractive.

These words are then followed, at the bottom, in much smaller type, of about a third of the size, with the P*e*TA logo in white on a grey background, followed by '1–800–FUR-AWAY (bullet point) www.FurIsDead.com'. This advertisement thus draws an analogy between pubic hair and fur. In Chapters 4 and 7, as with the quotations from Freud that open this chapter, instances of the appearance of fur are read as standing in for body hair, but here the reverse is the case, here the pubic hair stands in for fur, and I am interested in whether, because of this, the 'Fur-trim-ad' and the reaction to it can help me understand further the relationship between fur and hair.

In the first place it seems to me that this advertisement could be read in two apparently contradictory ways. One interpretation would read the pubic hair as 'excessive' and thereby as analogous to the fur 'trim' or edging on the collar or cuffs of a coat or jacket. Where the fur trim would be an unnecessary addition to a coat, the pubic hair is already in itself excessive, unnecessarily adding itself to the female sex ('a surplus, a plenitude enriching another plenitude, the *fullest measure* of presence')[10] and therefore there is a requirement that it should be made absent, removed or indeed 'trimmed'. This, I would argue, has therefore a point of connection with the second interpretation that I will offer.

In this second interpretation, the *'trimming'* or removal of pubic hair would be read as paralleling the removal of fur from the animal body for the purpose of producing the fur 'trim' for a coat or a jacket. This would involve an entirely different reading of the pubic hair, not as excessive, but as integral and 'natural' to the female body – as the fur is to the animal from which it is harvested. However, Ingrid Newkirk's defence of the advertisement in no way suggests that she herself reads it in this manner – rather the reverse. She claims, 'PETA's ad speaks to something the overwhelming majority of women worry about – grooming. Since we left the 60's style of unshaven leg hair and bushes [. . .] most people, regardless of gender, like the groomed look better. It's not sexist, it's just fact'.[11] Here then Newkirk's defence proclaims as 'fact' what could be read as the naturalising force of the 'overwhelming majority', and so follows my first interpretation of fur/hair above: pubic hair as an excess that it is natural to want to be rid of. However, Newkirk also implicitly acknowledges *fashions* in the appearance of pubic hair; and while she might attribute 'style' to the past, in the shape of the 1960s, and thereby implicitly construe in opposition to this style the look of the moment as not style but 'just fact', the 'groomed look' is nevertheless (and necessarily) acknowledged through her language precisely as a 'look'. At the same time, Newkirk's statement slides away from the initial connection set up between pubic hair and fur, thus disrupting any apparent inevitability that there may seem to be in such a connection, and moves towards a gardening analogy through the use of the word 'bushes', which would allow the 'trim[ming]' of the advertisement to be read as a regulatory activity (like 'grooming' or 'pruning') which keeps what is there under control, rather than an entirely eliminatory one. This tends to lead to the question of whether the body hair in question here falls into the category of the permissible or the impermissible; how this is determined depends also on how the relation of fur to hair is read.

However, even those responses that could be read as showing a predisposition to interpret the advertisement in the second of the ways that I outlined above, nevertheless suggest that this reading is not felt to be unequivocally available. The following quotations from the letters collated by *Ms. Magazine* can all be read as linguistic interventions intended to reorient or limit the reading of the advertisement to the second of my two interpretations, and these interventions are presumably felt to be necessary because of what is perceived to be the overriding discursive power and influence of the 'mainstream media'[12] and the 'sexist superstructure of our society'[13] and their 'normative' constructions of the female body, on any discussion of female body hair:

> Please allow me, like my nonhuman relatives, to wear my own fur!
> (Lynne Pashal: Westcliffe, Colorado)
> [. . .]
> How about featuring naked crotch shots of a man and woman next to a beaver with the headline, 'Fur only looks good where it grows naturally'?
> (Lethea Erz Takaka: New Zealand)
> [. . .]
> Change the ad to: 'Trimming Fur. Unattractive. Wear your own with pride.'
> (Colleen Kirby: Melrose, Massachusetts)[14]

In one sense then, Sherwin and the respondents quoted above could be seen as occupying a position diametrically opposed to that of Newkirk; however, in another sense they could be read as founding their disagreements in what are fundamentally similar kinds of perception. In all of the cases above, through ideas of commonality between humans (particularly female humans) and animals, a certain appeal is made to the 'natural'. Likewise, Sherwin argues that the advertisement presents 'women's *natural* state'[15] as unattractive, while Newkirk appeals to the 'majority' (who apparently 'worry about' grooming) and enlists the naturalising powers of the status quo and the market: 'In fact, if you're like the majority of women, you have probably thought "that's a nice push up bra" and cut out the sales ad for panties. If women didn't do and think those things, the stores would stop running the ads'.[16] Furthermore, Newkirk goes on to appeal to an idea of the 'naturalness' of sexual display and attraction: 'If you see a picture of a cool-looking man in BVDs, do the women in the NOW office all pitch a fit, or do the heterosexual staff linger over it? If you're a lesbian, substitute some hot chick for a guy and tell me the harm in enjoying the scenery'.[17] Thus, both Sherwin and Newkirk view their own versions of 'women' as 'natural', as an account of the reality of women beyond or beneath the obfuscations of culturally or environmentally determined meanings, whereas the version subscribed to by the other is seen precisely as a construction. Similarly, both spokeswomen seem to regard it as entirely possible to separate 'women' from their environments and determine what they really are outside of (beyond, beneath) the cultural meanings that they negotiate and also produce.[18] Newkirk's assertion that preference for the 'groomed look' is 'not sexist, [. . .] just a fact' is the clearest expression of this position, and it is challenged as such by one of the *Ms. Magazine* respondents:

> None of our preferences for appearance are 'just fact' – they are actually bolstered by values and norms, which are usually unstated. They are socially constructed. If Newkirk thinks she can feed off social construction without feeding into it she is sadly mistaken. An analogy is how when we tell a racist joke, we rely on stereotyped images of the group we present; in telling the joke, we also reinforce those images.
> (Susan Hylen: Decatur, Georgia)[19]

Susan Hylen's argument here might be said to have something in common with Clifford Geertz's observation that while 'religion rests its case on revelation, science on method [and] ideology on moral passion; [. . .] common sense rests its on the assertion that it is not a case at all, just life in a nutshell'.[20] Newkirk's claims, in Geertz's words, construe themselves as 'present[ing] reality neat'[21] without any sense of their cultural or historical specificity.

Even so, Hylen's riposte to Newkirk here itself sets up a 'real' or 'actual', through the notion of the 'stereotype', which is always both more than – excessive – and less than a presupposed 'reality' which is always prior to the stereotype and which the stereotype inherently fails to represent. Pubic hair then is further produced and defended as 'natural' in the letters to *Ms. Magazine* by its association with the 'fur' of the animal, and so while the animal is constituted as the 'natural' *par excellence* (a notion that none of the correspondents seems to want to challenge),[22] it functions both to naturalise body hair and, conversely, to naturalise its removal. Though not as such part of the debate on the 'Fur trim' advertisement, the way that the 'animal' functions to lay claim to the 'natural' and the 'true' can be seen in Cathleen and Colleen MacGuire's qualified approval of PeTA actions involving naked protesters who are not models of any sort: 'The participants in the "naked stunts" are presumably displaying their *true animal bodies* – not the false, technological makeovers constantly marketed to the public as *natural women*'.[23] This may be read as pointing towards another reading of 'fur', which, drawing on the connection with 'animal', produces a relation in which the MacGuire's 'natural' body, the supposedly non-culturally constructed body, can slide into becoming another marker of the supposedly non- or pre-cultural: the 'primitive'. An instance of this can be found in the *Ms. Magazine* correspondence: 'Do an ad showing a really hairy prehistoric man, and next to him, a man in a fur coat. The caption would say, "Fur. Some people haven't evolved yet." (Nicole Mertens: Plymouth, Minnesota)'[24] In this example, the connection between fur and body hair serves to produce both as markers of the primitive via the notion of evolution, where the fur coat is figured as a reminder and remainder of a past hairiness, which in this instance means uncultured or uncivilised.

The way in which fur can be used to mean 'primitive' can also be seen in various discussions of the film that has as one of its features perhaps the most famous of all fur bikinis:[25] the one sported by Raquel Welch in *One Million Years BC* (1966).[26] There are in fact a large number of websites devoted to this film or to merchandise associated with it (posters of Welch in the said bikini). Interestingly, part of the fascination with the film seems to stem from its 'artificiality' (a number of the websites featuring discussions of the film are devoted to 'special-effects' motion-pictures), since it was directed by Don Chaffey who was also responsible for other early special-effects films such as *Jason and the Argonauts* and *Creatures the World Forgot*, with stop-motion animation by the famed Ray Harryhausen. One online review puts it this way: 'Raquel Welch in a strategically upholstered bikini gets to fight the dinosaurs and other anachronistic beasties in this anthropologically dubious reworking of the 1940 Hal Roach/D. W. Griffith prehistoric potboiler (alas, no Victor Mature in this one). Nobody knows how to speak, but they sure know how to apply make-up'.[27] Here then, the focus would actually appear to be on artificiality and the non-natural, given the references to 'strategic "upholstery"' and the 'application' of 'make-up'. What is read here as the non-naturalistic covering (a 'technological make-over'?) with make-up and fur bikini, of the thereby 'naturalised' female body of Welch, is allied with the film's non-naturalism as it is defined in other respects: its 'anachronism' and 'dubious' anthropology. According to the review, 'speech' is an event that should take place *before* 'make-up', and so the film is characterised as disrupting the natural progress of evolution by (among other things) its use and prioritisation of the latter over the former. Potentially, the claim seems to be that such things as 'make-up' and 'strategic "upholstery"' are less 'natural' than 'speech', or are contingent upon the anterior existence of 'speech'. In any case, language and an activity which is defined as an adornment or addition to the natural body are, in this review, closely related.

Another review, which can be found on Bruce V. Edwards' 'Bad cinema diary' website, consists of a stream of criticisms of the film's lack of dialogue, poor plot and general lack of interest, punctuated by five interjected repetitions of 'Raquel Welch in a fur bikini'.[28] These repetitions function as *non sequiturs* to what it seems is being presented as the main argument; but through these mock eruptions into the text of a desire that is figured as beside-the-point or irrelevant-to-rational-argument, Edwards' text asserts the desire claimed to be elicited/provoked by the female body clothed in the fur bikini as natural through its positioning as unconscious.

The review ends accordingly: 'To be honest I find this flick rather dull. Raquel Welch in a fur bikini. There is, however, one special thing about it that makes me want to see it again & again.'[29] In these comments on *One Million Years BC*, the fur bikini functions to claim a naturalised woman beneath, in the first case by being 'upholstery' for the 'natural' female body, and in the second case because there the fur bikini can be read as both veiling and yet pointing to her sex through the connection of fur to body hair.

What remains constant between the reviews of *One Million Years BC* cited here, and the reactions of the *Ms. Magazine* correspondents is the connection, made via fur, back to the notion of a 'natural' or 'real' female body. In Julia Emberley's *Venus and Furs* (1998), considerable disquiet is expressed about the consequences for the First Nation peoples of Canada of this kind of 'fur-bearing animal' and the 'natural woman' equation. Emberley's analysis of 'sumptuary legislation' in the Middle Ages can be read as a challenge to any idea that 'fur' can or should always be read as referring to female body hair, since there she reads 'fur' as meaning 'wealth' and social status. All the same, Emberley affirms the meanings of 'fur' as differently inflected in relation to gender:

> Clearly noblewomen did not possess the same privileges as the men of their class and were able to secure only a re-presentation of such privileges through the ideological power of symbolic display. Thus, these noble/bourgeois women participated in creating a symbolic code of female economic power that could be *misread* as identical with the economic and political realities of their husband's material wealth and social power.[30]

Here Emberley invokes a distinction between 'economic and political *realities*' of male 'material wealth and social power' and fur worn by women as a 'symbolic display', which while it may be read as *claiming* an equivalent power can – and should, according to Emberley – at the same time be read as pointing to a lack of such power. For Emberley then, the 'symbolic' is an important notion, for in her analysis, even while it claims and points to a 'real' or actual connection between one thing and another ('fur' and 'wealth/power'), it is a 'code' in which one thing ('fur') can substitute for, in the sense of replacing, an absent other ('wealth/power'), and as such it marks the boundary between a material reality and a system of meaning that is based upon that reality, even if negatively so.

In the last chapter of her book, Emberley goes on to claim that, 'The symbolic dimension of Inuit fashions must be foregrounded because too often the assumption is that such clothing functions solely in a utilitarian manner and indeed lacks the signifying capacities already associated with "Western Dress"'.[31] Here, Emberley's use of 'symbolic' again both cleaves to a distinction between material reality and systems of signification, and simultaneously wishes to retrieve for the Inuit the 'capacity' for signification that is diagnosed as all too frequently denied because of the equation of fur with an unsupplemented (uncivilised) nature. However, by combating the 'utilitarian' with the 'symbolic', Emberley's position ends up implicitly accepting the notion that the 'utilitarian' is, in fact, non-symbolic. Later, Emberley tries to address this problem and so challenge the developmental and evolutionary narratives of historiography that she sees as precisely producing such divisions as 'practical' versus 'symbolic':

> Utilitarian values are often attributed to aboriginal cultures, and often this attribution conforms to a type of 'primitivism' [. . .] Fur's utilitarian value for aboriginal cultures is often said to supersede symbolic value. Conventional historiographies demand that a chronologically delineated line be drawn for fur from the practical to the symbolic, to trace through an 'earlier' culture what, if inescapably lost, has never been entirely erased. This Eurocentric bias raises a question about history and the place it allocates for indigenous peoples. [. . . But t]he point is that no clear, historically developmental line can be traced to mark a shift from the practical to the symbolic values attributed to fur. For indigenous cultures, past and present, fur has symbolic value as well as, for example, value for survival in a cold climate. The utility of fur is often constructed in a way that creates this spurious developmental logic from the 'primitive' to the 'civilised,' from the practical to the symbolic, from use value to exchange value.[32]

Even while this analysis diagnoses a certain problem, however, it also reinstates the very terms that are supposedly under critique: 'symbolic values' here become an add-on, an 'as well as' and, as such, the 'utilitarian' as 'utilitarian' is not under question, and neither is its a priori positioning *vis-à-vis* the 'symbolic', which remains here as a secondary system of meaning imposed on a 'material reality'. Fundamentally, I would argue that the question here turns on the meaning of 'symbolic' in Emberley's text, where it is used to discuss the meanings of 'fur'.[33] For her the 'symbolic' fundamentally seems a system predicated on a 'reality' which is 'material' and which is implicitly anterior to it. As such, it claims a real relation between 'fur' and that 'reality', just as, in the 'Fur trim' advertisement debate, the repeated reconstitutions of 'fur' and 'body hair' as similar also produce the idea of a natural connection between fur and hair, in which 'hair' is figured as a kind of evolutionary residue of animal 'fur'.

In general terms then, the relation between 'fur' and 'hair', and the consequent connection made through these ideas 'back' to a notion of the 'natural', apparently tends to reify these connections as essential or inherent. At a key point in the *Course in General Linguistics*, Ferdinand de Saussure points to an analogous issue, which is the problem posed by the notion of the symbol for his argument that the linguistic sign is arbitrary:

> No one disputes the fact that linguistic signs are arbitrary. [. . .] The word *symbol* is sometimes used to designate the linguistic sign, or more exactly that

part of the linguistic sign which we are calling the [signifier]. This use of the word *symbol* is awkward, [. . .] For it is characteristic of symbols that they are never entirely arbitrary. They are not empty configurations. They show at least a vestige of natural connexion between the [signifier] and its [signified]. For instance, our symbol of justice, the scales, could hardly be replaced by a chariot.[34]

De Saussure continues to maintain the claim that 'signs' are arbitrary, but also distinguishes 'symbols' from them and allows for a 'vestige of natural connexion' between the latter and the meaning or concept to which they refer. This notion of a 'vestigial' 'natural connexion' seems to carry with it an idea of an origin or a 'reality' upon which the symbol is based. It could be read as positing a language that develops evolutionarily from objects which thus constitute the 'vestige' or remainder/reminder of that development. But this move would be entirely contrary to the main thrust of de Saussure's argument.[35] However, the instances or elements that are connected are not 'things' here, that is to say that one need not read de Saussure as claiming that a symbol refers to a 'reality'. Rather, what is connected through the symbol might be said to be two systems of making meaning (two 'languages'). The scales only work as a symbol of justice in a context in which justice *means* even-handedness ('*our* symbol of justice'); in a context where 'might' is avowed and accepted as 'right', a chariot could quite conceivably function as just such a symbol.[36] This, however, leaves the question unanswered and unexplored of what constitutes the connection that is nevertheless assumed to exist.

At this point then, I must turn to Freud, who asked the question that de Saussure seems to avoid – the *nature* of the connection that, in the case of the second of the two quotations opening this essay, is addressed both as a '*symbolic* connection of thought' and as associating fur with pubic hair. The origin of the connection there then is presented as 'thought', and the act of 'association' can be read as a mental process of connecting ideas of fur and hair. Again, as with de Saussure, this does not necessarily entail an assumption of an intrinsic or essential relation between two 'objects'. A problem, however, remains. While the similarity that 'association' claims can be between ideas or concepts and need not be between 'things', the notion of the 'symbolic' begs some questions of my interpretation and its implicit insistence on the arbitrariness of the 'association'.

In Freud's tenth introductory lecture on 'symbolism in dreams', the issues that the notion of the 'symbolic' brings into play are made clear, when Freud discusses '"mute" dream-elements', that are somehow not amenable to the '*associative* technique'[37] of dream analysis in which the meaning of a dream-element is interpreted through its relation to ideas raised by 'free association'.[38] Where the associative technique seems to deliver no dividends, Freud remarks on the *temptation* to 'set about translating [. . .] with our own resources' such '"mute" dream-elements'.

However, he goes on to make the argument that such a method of inter-pretation cannot 'replace or compete with the associative one', rather, 'it forms a supplement to the latter and yields results which are only of use when introduced into it'.[39] Before this, Freud makes a fundamental point about 'translations' which are not based on the associative technique; he claims that they are 'constant' and that in this respect they differ radically from the kind of interpretation arrived at under free association: 'You will not have forgotten, of course, that when we use our *associative* technique constant replacements of dream-elements never come to light.'[40] The rela-tion of constancy between a dream-element and its translation is named by Freud as a 'symbolic' relation between the dream-element and the '"genuine" thing behind [it]'.[41] Here then is the crux of the problem: on the one hand Freud favours free association which challenges the notion of a constant or inevitable relation between a specific dream-element and a particular meaning. Moreover, even where he discusses '"symbolic" rela-tions', he refers to them as 'translations' (albeit 'stable' ones), which, by the very fact of bringing in the notion of different languages to analogise the relationship between a dream-element and its ('translated') meaning, resists the notion that that meaning can indeed be claimed to be 'the "genuine" thing'. However, Freud's reference to 'stable' or 'constant' translations does, on the other hand, seem to allow that certain 'symbols' do have a predetermined meaning that in some sense could imply an intrin-sic connection with the 'thing behind' it.

My readings of both de Saussure and Freud have suggested that in neither case does 'symbol' *necessarily* suggest an intrinsic or inevitable connection to, or with, a realm that we might call the 'real' or the 'natural'. Even where de Saussure writes of a 'natural' connection, the linkage posited is between an element in one system of meaning-making and an element within another such system. However, this leaves a question as to what precisely then constitutes the *difference* between 'symbols' and other 'signs' in de Saussure's schema, and between 'symbolic' and other dream-elements in Freud's discussion. The following quotation from the tenth introductory lecture again foregrounds the issue:

> [The] symbolic relation [. . .] is a comparison, though not a comparison of *any* sort. Special limitations seem to be attached to the comparison, but it is hard to say what these are. [. . .T]he concept of a symbol cannot at present be sharply delimited: it shades off into such notions as those of a replacement or repre-sentation, and even approaches that of an allusion.[42]

Here the notion of 'comparison', while bringing in notions of similarity between the 'symbol' and what it appears to refer to (or what Freud calls a 'common element'),[43] also necessarily brings in the notion of difference. The notion of 'comparison', which necessarily invokes a system of 'limita-tions', is here subject to '*special* limitations', which thus seems to state which possible similarities count as acceptable or perhaps meaningful: 'Not everything with which we can compare an object or a process appears in dreams as a symbol for it'.[44] The 'symbol' then seems to be defined by the 'specialness' of the 'limitation', but here that 'specialness' seems not to relate to a hierarchy of difference between 'objects' or 'things', since meaning or significance seems to be anterior to the 'symbols' in which it is expressed, and yet that 'meaning' does not *ground* the symbol, since it too is 'language'. Indeed 'Symbolism in dreams' goes on to suggest that 'the symbolic relation can go beyond the limits of language',[45] in the sense of not being bound by or limited within any *particular* language, but this still does not seem to constitute resorting to a notion of a base-line 'reality', as Freud goes on rather to suggest 'that what we are faced with here is an ancient but extinct *mode of expression*'[46] or, with reference to Senatspräsident Schreber, 'the phantasy of [. . .] a "basic *language*" of which all these symbolic relations would be *residues*'.[47] For Freud then, the symbolic connection does not go back to a 'real' relation, but to a 'language': a system of making meaning in which 'things which were once called by the same name as the genitals could now serve as symbols for them'.[48] In other words, the idea of similarity between 'things', 'objects', 'ideas', 'concepts' is *set up* by a linguistic connection here, rather than an intrinsic similarity being at the root of the link or connection: 'the signified of a signifier is always another signifier.'[49]

Freud's discussion, because it raises the question as to what constitutes connection, and tends towards addressing similarity as a *process* or *dynamic* rather than an already existent relation between delimited 'objects', is vital to the political project of this volume as a whole. Diagnosing the cultural enforcement of shaving, waxing and depilating as the problem can only result in an equally culturally determined unshaven body, as long as the notion of the connection to the natural body remains inviolate. To begin to think in terms of a process that can acknowledge that the issues raised within this volume are not a matter of freely conscious choice can perhaps lead to a political dynamic that reaches beyond an entrapment within hierarchies of value.

Notes

1   Sigmund Freud, 'Fetishism' [1927], in Sigmund Freud, *On Sexuality: Three Essays on the Theory of Sexuality and Other Works*, Pelican Freud Library, vol. 7, trans. by James Strachey and Angela Richards (London: Penguin, 1977), pp. 345–57, p. 354.

2   Sigmund Freud, 'Three essays on the theory of sexuality' [1905], in Sigmund Freud, *On Sexuality: Three Essays on the Theory of Sexuality and Other Works*, pp. 31–169, pp. 67–8.

3   PeTA's news release for 19 October 2000, entitled 'PETA's undies hit furriers

below the belt', concerns the use of the 'Fur trim. Unattractive' leaflets: www.peta.org/news/newsitem.asp?id=126 (accessed 18 April 2002). The advertisement itself can be seen at: www.msmagazine.com/aug00/ wildpussy.html or at http://youanimal.net/Animal%20Rants/FurTrim.htm (both accessed 25 March 2002). The news release refers to an action scheduled for 20 October 2000. By this time the advertisement was already current and *Ms. Magazine* had asked its readers to give their views of it in its April/May 2000 issue, and back in January–February of 2000, the New York chapter of the National Organization for Women had called for a letter-writing campaign in protest at the advertisement (see NOW-NYC, 'Stop degrading images of women' www.nownyc.org/news/janfeb2000/actnow.htm and NOW-NYC, 'PETA's ad degrades women' www.nownyc.org/alert.orig.htm (both accessed on 23 April 2002)).

4   Galen Sherwin's open letter and Ingrid Newkirk's response can be found on the following website: http://youanimal.net/Animal%20Rants/FurTrim.htm (accessed 25 March 2002) and in the April/May 2000 issue of *Ms. Magazine*.

5   In her response to Sherwin, Newkirk referred to herself as a 'longtime feminist'. See: http://youanimal.net/Animal%20Rants/FurTrim.htm. Similarly, in answer to Nikki Craft's protest against the 'pornographic' content of PeTA's campaigns following an advertisement featuring Kimberley Hefner, Heather Moore made the claim on behalf of PeTA that, 'As an organization staffed largely by feminist women, we would never do something that we felt contributed to the very serious problems that women face' (see Nikki Craft, 'PeTA: where only women are treated like meat' (December 2001), *ACLU (Always Causing Legal Unrest) NoStatusQuo.com*: www.nostatusquo.com/ ACLU/PETA/peta.html (accessed 23 March 2003)).

6   See Batya Bauman, 'Editorial comment: PETA tarnishes its own good name' (1994), *FAR*: www.farinc.org/newsletter/v8_n3–4_94/editorial.html (accessed 23 March 2002); Cathleen and Colleen McGuire, 'PeTA and a pornographic culture, I: a feminist analysis of "I'd rather go naked than wear fur"' (1994), *FAR*: www.farinc.org/newsletter/v8_n3–4_94/petaporn1.html (accessed 25 March 2002). This article can also be found at http://eve.enviroweb.org/ perspectives/peta.html (accessed 23 March 2002). See also, Carol Adams, 'PETA and a pornographic culture, II: a feminist analysis of "I'd rather go naked than wear fur"' (1994), *FAR*: www.farinc.org/newsletter/ v8_n3–4_94/ petaporn2.html (accessed 23 March 2002); and Carol Adams, 'Do feminists need to liberate animals, too?' (Spring 1995), *On the Issue Online, Dialogue*: www.echonyc.com/~onissues/carola.htm (accessed 22 October 2001). In his 1996 book, *Rain Without Thunder: the Ideology of the Animal Rights Movement* (Philadelphia: Temple University Press), Gary Francione, Professor of Animal Rights Law at Rutgers University School of Law in Newark, also attacked the 'I'd rather go naked' campaign (see also Francione, 'Sexism and animal rights' (21 March 1996), *Animal Rights Law: Animal Rights Commentary*: www.animal-law.org/commentaries/mr21.htm (accessed 25 March 2002)). A selection of other website-based critical reactions to PeTA and its campaigns can be found at Nikki Crafts's website, 'PeTA: where only women are treated like meat', in *Ms. Magazine*'s selection of letters from its readers in response to the 'Fur trim' advertisement www.msmagazine.com/aug00/wildpussy.

html, in *Citypaper.net*'s interview with Gary Francione (see Vance Lehmkuhl, 'Animal logic: interview with Gary Francione, part 1 and 2' (7–14 September 2000), *Philadelphia citypaper.net Cover Story:* www.citypaper.net/articles/090700/cs.cover1.shtml, and www.citypaper.net/articles/090700/cs.cover2.shtml (both accessed 22 October 2001)), and in the archives of the Utah Animal Rights Coalition message board: www.chat.uarc.com/uarc/ (see 'Archives', p. 2, listed backwards from 4 January 2002 to 16 May 2001: these include contributions by Nikki Craft and Daniel Hammer, accessed 25 March 2002). The latest controversy that PeTA has been involved in is its use of a touring photographic exhibition entitled 'Are animals the new slaves?', in which images featuring the torturing and murdering of black people are juxtaposed with images of the mistreatment and slaughter of animals in various settings. The PeTA exhibit can be seen at: www.peta.org.AnimalLiberation/slavery.asp (accessed 6 November 2005). Critical reactions to it, some of which also mention previous controversies over PeTA's use of 'T&A' (see Lee Hall, 'Civil rights groups to PETA: you have used us enough' (3 September 2005), *Reclaim the Media*: www.reclaimthemedia.org/stories.php?story=05/09/03/0637999 (accessed 6 November 2005)), can be found as follows: Tim Wise, 'Animal whites', in Alexander Cockburn and Jeffrey St. Clair (eds), *Counterpunch*, 13/14 (August 2005): www.counterpunch.org/wise08132005.html (accessed 1 November 2005); Dana Williams, 'New PETA campaign sparks outrage' (15 August 2005), *Fight Hate and Promote Tolerance – Tolerance.org: a Web Project of the Southern Poverty Law Center* www.tolerance.org/news/article_tol.jsp?id=1266 (accessed 6 November 2005); Marina Hyde, 'Diary' (Thursday, 11 August 2005), *Guardian Unlimited*: http:// politics.guardian.co.uk/columnist/story/0,9321,1546843,00.html (accessed 6 November 2005). Support for the exhibition can be found on the website of the Animal Liberation Front (see Andrew Christie, 'PETA throws bombs in New Haven: shall I compare thee to a freaking cow? Common dreams' (19 August 2005): www.animalliberationfront.com/News/2005_8/BlackPetaExhibit.htm (accessed 1 November 2005)), and a critique of the logic of Tim Wise's article is presented on the *Non Sequitur* blog, which claims a concern with 'logical analysis' as 'a first line of defense against the hijacking of our political discourse by cynical manipulators' (http://thenonsequitur.com/static/about.html (accessed 6 November 2005)) and can be found at: http://thenonsequitur.com/?p=124 (accessed 6 November 2005). This blog also includes Tim Wise's riposte.

7   Carol Adams, 'Fur and the homeless', *Satya: A Magazine of Vegetarianism, Environmentalism, and Animal Advocacy* (February 1998), at: www.montelis.com/satya/backissues/feb98/homeless.html (accessed 23 March 2002).

8   Batya Bauman, 'Blaming the victims' (1994), *FAR*: www.farinc.org/newsletter/v8_n3–4_94/blaming.html (accessed 25 March 2002).

9   www.peta.org/news/newsitem.asp?id=126 (accessed 23 March 2002).

10   Jacques Derrida, *Of Grammatology*, translated by Gayatri Spivak, corrected edition (Baltimore and London: Johns Hopkins University Press, 1998), p. 144.

11   Newkirk in response to Sherwin's letter of protest about the 'panty ad': http://youanimal.net/Animal%20Rants/FurTrim.htm (accessed 25 March 2002).

12 Sherwin's letter of protest: http://youanimal.net/Animal%20Rants/FurTrim. htm (accessed 25 March 2002).

13 Katica Jacob: www.msmagazine.com/aug00/wildpussy.html (accessed 25 March 2002).

14 www.msmagazine.com/aug00/wildpussy.html.

15 Sherwin, letter of protest. Emphasis is mine.

16 Newkirk, letter in response to Sherwin.

17 Newkirk, letter in response to Sherwin.

18 On the subject of bodies as 'made' rather than 'born', see Lesnik-Oberstein's Chapter 1 in this volume.

19 www.msmagazine.com/aug00/wildpussy.html.

20 Clifford Geertz, 'Common sense as a cultural system', in Clifford Geertz, *Local Knowledge: Further Essays in Interpretative Anthropology* (New York: Basic Books, 1983), pp. 73–93, p. 75.

21 Geertz, 'Common sense as a cultural system', p. 76.

22 The final letter quoted by *Ms. Magazine* reads as follows:

    'Don't you see what's really going on here?! The sexism debate raised by the PETA ad in question is intended to distract us from PETA's true agenda. And this is: to wipe out wild pussies around the globe! Long on the list of endangered species, the wild pussy is racing toward extinction at an alarming rate. Yet what does PETA do? It hunts down one of the few wild pussies left!' (Minerva Gow: Montreal, Quebec, Canada), www.msmagazine.com/aug00/wildpussy.html.

23 McGuire, 'PeTA and a pornographic culture, I: a feminist analysis of "I'd rather go naked than wear fur"'. Emphases mine.

24 www.msmagazine.com/aug00/wildpussy.html

25 A search for 'fur bikinis' on the web will reveal no dearth of commercial sites offering such items in both real and synthetic or '*faux*' fur. See for example: www.alaskrafts.com/pix-ethel.htm and www.sirensecrets.com/fauxfurbikinis.html (both accessed 21 November 2005).

26 See the British Film Institute's *Screenonline* for a full cast list and credits and a synopsis, along with the original poster featuring Raquel Welch in the said bikini, production stills and video clips: www.screenonline.org.uk/film/id/443654/ (accessed 6 November 2005).

27 Pat Graham from the *Chicago Reader* in: http://65.201.198.41/movies/capsules/06685_ONE_MILLION_YEARS_BC.html (accessed 21 November 2005).

28 www.cathuria.com/bcd/bco01.htm (accessed 21 November 2005).

29 www.cathuria.com/bcd/bco01.htm

30 Julia V. Emberley, *Venus and Furs: The Cultural Politics of Fur* (London: I. B. Tauris, 1998), p. 56.

31 Emberley, *Venus and Furs*, p. 178.

32 Emberley, *Venus and Furs*, pp. 181–2.

33 A related point is made by Chantal Nadeau in *Fur Nation: from the Beaver to Brigitte Bardot* (London and New York: Routledge, 2001), pp. 16–17. However, while Nadeau sees work such as Emberley's as being in danger of 'further condon[ing] the separation perpetuated by traditional histories of fur between the material production of fur and its symbolic production' (p. 16),

'materiality' resurfaces in her formulations too, but here it is the materiality of 'skin' which seems to anchor the meanings of 'fur', or at least function as their a priori: 'I argue that fur per se has no value without the raw materiality of skin' (p. 17).

34 Ferdinand de Saussure, *Course in General Linguistics*, trans. and annotated by Roy Harris (London: Duckworth, 1983 [main text by Editions Payot, Paris, 1972]), p. 68. NB I have replaced Harris's translations of *signifiant* (signal) and *signifié* (signification) with the now more common English usage: signifier and signified.

35 That argument in the first place refutes the notion that 'language . . . is a nomenclature: a list of terms corresponding to a list of things' on the grounds that this 'assumes that ideas already exist independently of words' (de Saussure, *Course in General Linguistics*, p. 65). In addition, de Saussure wishes to privilege neither ideas nor sounds (words) because for him:

no ideas are established in advance, and nothing is distinct, before the introduction of linguistic structure . . . what happens is neither a transformation of thought into matter, nor a transformation of sounds into ideas. What takes place, is a somewhat mysterious process by which 'thought-sounds' evolve divisions, and a language takes shape with its linguistic units in between those two amorphous masses (de Saussure, *Course in General Linguistics*, pp. 110–11).

36 See Friedrich Nietzsche, *On the Genealogy of Morals*, trans. with an introduction and notes by Douglas Smith (Oxford and New York: Oxford University Press, 1996); and Michel Foucault, *Discipline and Punish: the Birth of the Prison*, trans. Alan Sheridan (London: Penguin, 1991).

37 Sigmund Freud, 'Symbolism in dreams: Part II. Dreams' [1916 (1915–16)], in Sigmund Freud, *Introductory Lectures on Psychoanalysis*, Penguin Freud Library, vol. 1, trans. James Strachey and edited by James Strachey and Angela Richards (London: Penguin, 1991), pp. 182–203, p. 183.

38 Freud, 'The premises and technique of interpretation: Part II. Dreams' [1916 (1915–16)], in Freud, *Introductory Lectures on Psychoanalysis*, pp. 129–42.

39 Freud, 'Symbolism in dreams', p. 184.

40 Freud, 'Symbolism in dreams', p. 183.

41 Freud, 'Symbolism in dreams', p. 184.

42 Freud, 'Symbolism in dreams', p. 185.

43 Freud, 'Symbolism in dreams', p. 186.

44 Freud, 'Symbolism in dreams', p. 185.

45 Freud, 'Symbolism in dreams', p. 197.

46 Freud, 'Symbolism in dreams', pp. 200–1. Emphasis mine

47 Freud, 'Symbolism in dreams', p. 201. Emphases mine.

48 Freud, 'Symbolism in dreams', p. 202.

49 Jacques Lacan, 'The agency of the letter in the unconscious or reason since Freud', in Jacques Lacan, *Écrits: a Selection*, trans. Alan Sheridan (London: Routledge, 1997 [1966]), pp. 146–79, p. 150.

10 Women with beards in early modern Spain

Sherry Velasco

The cover of the Summer 2005 issue of the fashion magazine *V* (known as the 'style bible') features the supermodel Kate Moss with a full beard. While the image undoubtedly provides an unexpected shock to the typical consumer of high fashion, William Van Meter (writing for the *New York Times*) argues that with the strange photo, 'bearded ladies finally leave the freak show and enter the limelight.'[1] Van Meter also cites a few recent female rockers (such as Peaches and J. D. Samson) who also display full facial hair on their album covers, music videos and live performances, in an attempt to challenge the belief that facial hair on women is a problem. In similar fashion, the lesbian performance artist Jennifer Miller for years has been using her beard to encourage women to reconsider these preconceived notions of beauty:

> Miller's act borrows the freak show format to couple entertainment with political consciousness raising in the form of entertainment . . . Calling herself a woman with a beard rather than a 'bearded lady,' she explains to the crowd, emphasises that she is not a freak but an extreme example of a common condition that affects many, if not most women.[2]

While this recent trend seeks to challenge the tradition of exhibiting 'bearded ladies' in early circus freak shows, the image of a woman with a moustache or beard has not yet broken free from the shock value assigned to the condition that has endured for centuries. In fact, the numerous representations of hairy women in early modern historical, literary and iconographic texts in Spain reveal the popularity of the theme, as well as its significance for the understanding of how gender identity, sex assignment and sexuality were configured during that time. Most often, the representation of hirsutism involved a visual spectacle, which in turn required a narrative to interpret the transgression of cultural norms regarding gender and sex categories. An analysis of these texts indicates that both word and image underscore the fluid and unstable nature of ambiguously sexed bodies, which ultimately serve to police and reinforce the superiority and dominance of the traditional male gender and sex conflation, as well as patriarchal heterosexual values.

Historically, women with excessive facial and body hair have been presented as monsters, anomalies and human prodigies. In Ambroise Paré's 1579 teratology *On Monsters and Marvels*, for example, the birth of a 'furry girl' is attributed to the impact of visual stimulus on the mother's imagination during conception:

> Damascene, a serious author, attests to having seen a girl as furry as a bear, whom the mother had bred thus deformed and hideous, for having looked too intensely at the image of Saint John [the Baptist] dressed in skins, along with his [own] body hair and beard, which picture was attached to the foot of her bed while she was conceiving.[3]

Paré likewise features an illustration of the hairy girl to reinforce the visual impact of the monstrous spectacle inherent in all monster gazing.[4] Accordingly, the etymology of the term 'monster' (from the ancient Greek root of the word *teras*, which implied both aberration and adoration, as well as from the Latin *monstrum* 'to show') indicated the ambivalent and visual nature of the monster. As Lawrence D. Kritzman notes, the deviance from the normative that monsters represent is portrayed as a visual effect – 'rarity attributed to the object of the gaze.'[5]

Visual imagery of women with beards during the early modern period was also frequently reproduced as examples of androgynes and hermaphrodites, who were believed to possess both male and female primary and secondary sex characteristics.[6] However, the description of androgyny in Sebastián de Covarrubias's 1610 collection of didactic emblems featuring both word and image (*Emblemas morales*) underscores a third category created by the hybridity of combining (and thereby erasing) the two-sex model for anatomical sexual identity. The emblem depicting androgyny reveals an illustration of a bearded lady accompanied by the motto 'Neither and Both' and the following text:

> I am masculine, feminine, and neuter. I reveal myself.
> I am man, I am woman, I am a third,
> which is neither one nor the other, and it is not clear
> which of these things I am. I am a third,
> one of those shown to be rare and horrendous.
> I am believed to be evil, an omen.
> Take heed all who have seen me,
> For you are like me if you are a female-male.[7]

The text and image together provide the reader/spectator with an exhibitionistic invitation for voyeuristic gazing, as the first-person narrator is willing to reveal her or his 'rare and horrendous' condition. While this verbal–visual spectacle may seem ambivalent ('it is not clear which of these things I am'), it carries a clear warning for those who may also identify as 'afeminado' (effeminate male): androgyny is something to be feared (an evil omen). Interestingly, while the verbal text refers to a feminine male, the pictorial image is that of a masculine woman.

Covarrubia's bearded lady, in fact, is based on the image of Brígida del Río, whose portrait was painted by Juan Sánchez Cotán in 1590.[8] According to a seventeenth-century account, Brígida del Río travelled to Valencia and received monetary compensation for exhibiting her anomalous condition, and thereby indicating that the image of a woman with a beard (either live or pictorial) was marketable and thus could be circulated for financial profit.[9] Not surprisingly, paintings of women with beards were frequently included in important collections of monstrous and rare cultural artefacts, such as that of the Marqués de Pozas at the end of the sixteenth century in Madrid.[10]

The more famous portrait of 'La Mujer Barbuda' (The Bearded Lady) Magdalena Ventura, painted by José de Ribera in 1631, reveals many of the strategies that promote and exploit people with sexual ambiguity. The portrait was commissioned by the viceroy of Naples, Duque de Alcalá and, according to comments made by the Venetian ambassador, people were allowed to observe the artist at work while he painted the portrait of Magdalena. The ambassador's enthusiastic remarks emphasise the importance of the curious gaze for the exhibition of gender indeterminacy: 'His Excellence had the graciousness to let me see her, given the unbelievable sight, which it truly is.'[11]

Magdalena Ventura's portrait also displays other features that contribute to how those who possess ambiguous secondary sex characteristics are visually represented. Magdalena, with full beard and hairy chest, posed breast-feeding a child while standing near her husband. To further emphasise the sensational duality of the 'bearded lady', the painting also displays a spindle (alluding to women's work in the home) and a snail, symbolic of hermaphroditism.[12] Interestingly, Ribera's painting also seems to foreshadow a common practice in 'freak portrait photography', as described by Rachel Adams in her study of sideshows in the United States. Adams argues that these portraits juxtaposed the freak and a normal person to confirm deviance within the social order:

> adopting the conventions of expression, pose, and setting dictated by portrait photography, the carte de visite enhanced the freak's wondrous features by situating her within a familiar context: . . . [such as] a woman standing with her husband in a Victorian parlor, her face covered by a plush, ample beard.[13]

While facial hair on women may have been explained by a monstrous, androgynous or hermaphroditic condition, early modern scientific theory based on classical Aristotelian and Galenian concepts attributed masculine physical appearance and behaviour in women to a sudden prenatal transmutation in the womb of a pregnant woman. Juan Huarte de San Juan's medical analysis in *Examen de ingenios para las ciencias* (*Examination of*

Humors for the Sciences) (1575), for example, documents the cultural construction of gender and sexuality as well as the mutability of one's physiological sex assignment. Huarte describes how masculine women, feminine men and homosexuals were originally destined to be born of the opposite sex, but the temperature of the bodily 'humours' changed during gestation and caused the genitals to 'transmute' before birth: 'Often Nature has made a male with his genitals on the outside, and with an onset of coldness, they are transformed to the inside and a female is created. She is recognised after birth by having a masculine nature, in her speech as well as in all her movements and behaviour.'[14] Although all women are composed of cold and moist liquids, not all have the same level of these humours. These levels are assessed by observing different categories such as intellectual capacity, habits and behaviour, voice tenor, body fat and musculature, complexion, body and facial hair and physical beauty or ugliness.[15] Huarte clarifies that:

> having a lot of body hair and a bit of a beard is a clear indication of low levels of coldness and moisture, since all physicians agree that the source of hair and beard is heat and dryness; and if the hair is dark then even higher levels of heat and dryness are present. The opposite temperature creates a woman who is smooth, without beard or body hair. The woman of average levels of coldness and moisture has a little bit of hair on her body but it is light and blonde.[16] Of course, the woman who has much body and facial hair (being of a more hot and dry nature) is also intelligent but disagreeable and argumentative, muscular, ugly, has a deep voice and frequent infertility problems.[17]

In his 1601 treatise, *Libro de fisionomía natural* (*Book of Nature Physiology*), Jerónimo Cortés includes lasciviousness in his account of masculine women: 'The woman who has much hair on her face and chin is of a strong constitution, has a terrible nature, and has the highest levels of heat, which makes her lustful and masculine in nature.'[18] Not surprisingly, while the hot–dry masculine traits are seen as virtuous when possessed by anatomical men, when observed in women they become physical and moral defects (terrible, ugly, infertile, lustful, etc.).

In fact, the presence or absence of facial hair frequently becomes the external clue to ambiguous sex assignment. For example, according to Antonio de Torquemada's accounts of ancient and contemporary cases of female-to-male sex transformations cited in his 1570 *Jardín de flores curiosas* (*Garden of Curious Flowers*), one woman named Arescusa, 'whose feminine sex having turned masculine, grew a beard and married a woman' and Phetula, whose 'body became male, completely hairy. He grew a beard and his voice became raspy.'[19] However, after a woman named María Pacheco suddenly transformed into a man, he began to live as Manuel Pacheco, went to the New World and later returned to Spain rich and famous. Although he had married a respectable woman, the author was not sure if they had children since Pacheco 'had never grown a beard.'[20]

The belief that postnatal sex mutations only happen to women and not men (since, as Paré explains, nature tends to perfect itself by becoming more masculine, as opposed to the inferiority of femininity) is important for understanding the occasional celebratory reaction to and interpretation of newly acquired primary and secondary male sex characteristics. A news pamphlet published in Granada in 1617, for example, tells the 'true story' of a thirty-four-year-old nun, María Muñoz, who suddenly developed male genitals, dark facial hair and a deep voice. Reminiscent of sensationalised tabloid news, this *relación* describes how her naturally masculine nature drew suspicions and therefore she was examined by the prioress and found to be female. Nonetheless, later, when involved in heavy labour, she suddenly discovered a swelling in her groin and, three days later, male genitalia came forth through a small hole where female genitalia were normally located. A new examination revealed that she was now a man and 'although she was thirty-four years old her chest was as flat as a board.'[21] She confessed that she had never menstruated but used blood from her ascetic mortifications to create the illusion so that the other nuns would not call her *marimacho* ('manly woman' or as Covarrubias defined the term in 1611: 'a woman who looks and behaves like a man').[22] Six or seven days later she began to grow a beard and her voice became deep, so they removed her from the convent and sent her home to her father. Despite the scandal, the shocking case has a happy ending and thus underscores the preference for male identity: 'Her father is very pleased because he is rich and had no son to inherit his wealth. Now he has a very manly son who can marry; and she is also happy because after twelve years of incarceration she enjoys freedom. Having been transformed from woman to man, nature could not have bestowed upon her any better material blessing.'[23] Although the ex-nun is now a man, the author (Father Augustín de Torres) continues to refer to 'her' with female gender markers, thus denying Muñoz an authentic male identity, undoubtedly to emphasise both the shock value of the story and the cultural practice of privileging sex determinacy at birth. Of course the official interpretation of the nun-turned-man story deemed her case a success since there was no longer an issue of sex or gender ambiguity, despite the fact that the new man is still a 'she' in the narrative. However, when the secondary male sex characteristic of facial hair appears on an otherwise 'normal' woman, the result is tragic, comic, shocking or a combination of these.

Undoubtedly, one of the best examples of how hirsutism can evoke a multiple of responses is found in Cervantes's best-selling seventeenth-century classic *Don Quixote*. The protagonist's inspiration for his beloved lady Dulcinea is, in fact, a very butch farm girl named Aldonza Lorenzo, whom Sancho Panza describes as the ultimate *marimacho* (manly woman): 'I can tell you that she pitches a bar as well as the strongest lad in the whole village. Praise be to God! She's a brawny girl, well built and tall and sturdy, with hair on her chest and she will know how to keep her chin out of the mud with any knight errant who ever has her for his mistress. O the wench, what muscles she's got, and what a pair of lungs!'[24] Sancho's enthusiastic characterisation of Aldonza may indicate that he also shares a special affinity for masculine women, especially considering his frequent narrations of *hombruna* (manly woman) types, such as his description of Torralba in chapter 20 of part I of *Don Quixote* as 'rather mannish, for she had a slight moustache' and his references to Dulcinea's manly activities and stature, and her 'rather mannish' odour in chapter 31 of part I.[25]

Orchestrating the theatrical scenes in part II of *Don Quixote* based on their reading of part I, the Duke and Duchess likewise play their own games of sexual and gender reconstruction. It is not by chance that in chapter 35 of the second part, the role of the outspoken and demanding Dulcinea, who has been transformed from 'a highborn lady into a rustic village wench', is played by a page 'with a masculine assurance and in no very lady-like tones.'[26] Similarly, just as the bearded priest in part I was initially prepared to play the role of the Princess Micomicona, the tragic curse that has befallen both the Dueña Dolorida (Distressed Lady-in-waiting) and her attendants is precisely the sudden appearance of excessive facial hair. While this melodramatic performance was intended to portray to the uninformed spectators such as Don Quixote and Sancho Panza the shocking and tragic consequences of facial hair on otherwise 'normal' (i.e. 'feminine') women, its actual purpose was to provide comic entertainment for the Duke and Duchess, as well as for the reader.

Clearly inspired by part I of *Don Quixote*, those in part II who orchestrate the 'hairy' plots also had plenty of supporting material from popular culture, since hirsutism and the 'hairy maiden' motif maintain an established tradition in medieval hagiography. Stories of bearded female saints were well circulated during the Middle Ages. For example, women such as Saint Galla and Paula of Avila grew beards in pious attempts to avoid marriage. The most famous bearded female saint, nonetheless, was Wilgefortis or Uncumber, also known as Librada in Spain.[27] As Leslie Fiedler reminds us, women prayed to St Librada when they were 'eager to get rid of their husbands.'[28] Since Librada's prayers were answered when she suddenly grew a long curly beard (which was revealed when she let her veil slip during the unwanted nuptials), this hairy sight prevented her betrothed from completing the wedding ceremony.[29] Despite the dramatic use of the veil in both cases, Librada's facial hair saved her from obligatory participation in heterosexuality, while Cervantes's bearded ladies-in-waiting lament that their hairy curse would preclude welcome opportunities to unite with the opposite sex: 'For even when she has a soft skin and tortures her face with a thousand sorts of lotions and cosmetics, she can scarcely find anyone to like her. So what shall she do when she reveals a face like a forest?'[30]

Considering the seventeenth century's fascination with 'monstrous' anomalies, Sancho's apparent interest in women with beards and the awareness that facial hair on women could be a deterrent to heterosexual desire were not lost on Alonso Fernández de Avellaneda in his apocryphal continuation of Cervantes's work. When describing what type of lover he would prefer, Avellaneda's Sancho insists that 'she must be beautiful and have pretty hooves and a mustache, so that nobody will lure her away from me or lead her astray.'[31] Of course the old and ugly prostitute Barbara disagrees with Sancho's hairy preferences: ' "You are stupid to want her to have a mustache" said Barbara. "No Barrabas would approach a woman like that".'[32]

Given that gender transgression was believed to cause physical alterations of sex assignment, others insisted that women's beards were the result of unpoliced gender infractions, and therefore it was men's responsibility to control women and prevent them from acquiring a beard – the visual sign of strength and power. The Clerk of Enghien, for example, wrote: 'Boldly keep your wives, that their beards do not descend to their waists. Women ought not to be bold. They have no beards and don't you doubt it a bit. A bold woman is against nature, for a woman ought not to have a beard either by law or by natural reason.'[33] Similarly, the author of *El libro de buen amor* (The Book of Good Love) warns his readers about hairy women: 'Take care your lady has no whiskers on her lip or chin,/To Hell with such! for that is one unpardonable sin.'[34]

Considering, then, the association between women with beards and sin, it is not by chance that the early modern *pícaras* or female rogues and witches were frequently described as having facial hair. For example, Celestina, the old bawd and protagonist of the number-one best-selling fictional work during the early modern period in Spain is first introduced in the text as the 'bearded old lady named Celestina: an astute witch who is wise in all that is evil.'[35] Like Celestina, Cervantes' memorable old witch Cañizares (from the 'Colloquy of the Dogs' from his collection of short stories *Novelas ejemplares* (*Exemplary Novels*)) is also known for her diabolic talents and disagreeable physical appearance, which includes facial and body hair:

> The people went off cursing the old woman, adding the name of witch to that of sorceress, and saying not only that she was an old hag but that she was a hairy old goat to boot [. . .] Her bones stuck out all over, covered with dark, hairy, hard skin; . . . As I looked at her, all of a sudden I was overcome by fear, as I thought of the ugliness of her body and the evil to which she had abandoned her soul.[36]

Perhaps it was this implicit call to enforce the surveillance of women's transgression of traditional gender roles that inspired Francesc Fontanella in the seventeenth century to write the satirical verses about the best-selling author María de Zayas. Although no portrait or other reference to the

author's physical appearance have survived to date, the verses satirise Zayas'
literary activity by commenting on her masculine nature and facial hair, and
by playing on the homonyms 'sayas' or 'skirts' and her surname 'Zayas':

> Miss Mary of Skirts
> has a manly face,
> although she wore 'skirts,'
> she played with her moustache proudly.
> She looked like a man, but it will soon be discovered
> that a sword is not easily hidden
> under feminine 'skirts.' [. . .]
> Oh, Lady Miss Skirt, as reward for your fine desires
> from the circle of a hoopskirt
> you will have your noble crown.[37]

While Kenneth Brown found these verses to be in 'bad taste', Mary Gossy
reads the satirical poem as another reference to lesbian desire associated
with Zayas.[38]

Like the 'fine desires', moustache, manly face and sword mentioned in
Fontanella's verses, the early modern scientific link between masculine
women, feminine men, and homosexuality ('such men are inclined to
behave like a woman and they frequently fall prey to the sin of sodomy . . .
She is recognized after birth by having a masculine nature, in her speech
as well as in all her movements and behaviour')[39] indicates cultural
assumptions about ambiguously sexed bodies, non-traditional gender
behaviour and transgressive sexuality. It is not surprising, then, that masculine women such as the seventeenth-century transgendered celebrity
Catalina de Erauso (otherwise known as the 'Lieutenant Nun') were con-
sistently associated with same-sex desire.[40] Even though Erauso (when
younger and living as a man) was believed to be a eunuch due to a lack of
beard, she was described at age fifty-five as being of 'strong build, somewhat stout, swarthy in complexion, with a few hairs on her chin.'[41] A few
years later, the third and last news pamphlet based on Erauso's life was
published and is primarily characterised by the lesbian desires attributed
to the famous gender-bender. Given the support of both the King of Spain
Phillip IV and the Pope Urban VIII, her case was celebrated, mainly due to
her nobility, military service to the Spanish Crown and her alleged virginity. At the same time, however, Erauso's story also reveals the contradictions inherent in female masculinity, as it provoked a response to the
violation of traditional gender proscriptions while reaffirming the patriarchal assessment of male-centred identity as superior.

Consequently, when reviewing these fascinating images, we discover
that the sensational and hugely popular display of women with masculine
traits, such as facial and body hair, during the early modern period created
a visual spectacle intended to shock and entertain but ultimately proved
also to control non-conforming bodies. While this was achieved through

both humour and fear (by attributing the physical anomaly to male-biased causes such as the danger of women's imagination during sexual intercourse or to nature's way of trying to improve the inferior state of being female), these misogynistic narratives reveal the cultural anxieties inspired by the fluidity of sexual identities, and therefore the need to exploit and control bodies that reject traditional notions of femininity.

Notes

1 William Van Meter, 'These kittens have whiskers', *New York Times* (30 June 2005), E4.

2 Rachel Adams, *Sideshow U.S.A. Freaks and the American Cultural Imagination* (Chicago and London: University of Chicago Press, 2001), p. 221.

3 Ambroise Paré, *On Monsters and Marvels*, intro., trans. and notes by Manis L. Pallister (Chicago: University of Chicago Press, 1982), p. 38.

4 See Jeffrey Jerome Cohen (ed.), *Monster Theory: Reading Culture* (Minneapolis and London: University of Minnesota Press, 1996).

5 Lawrence D. Kritzman, 'Representing the monster: cognition, cripples, and other limp parts in Montaigne's "Des Boyteux"', in Jeffrey Jerome Cohen (ed.), *Monster Theory: Reading Culture*, pp. 168–83, p. 173.

6 Sebastián de Covarrubias, *Tesoro de la lengua castellana o española* (Barcelona: Editorial Alta Fulla, 1989), p. 118, pp. 530–1.

7 Cited in Paul Julian Smith, *The Body Hispanic: Gender and Sexuality in Spanish and Spanish American Literature* (Oxford: Clarendon Press, 1989), pp. 16–17.

8 See Alonso E. Pérez Sánchez, *Monstruos, enanos y bufones en la corte de los Austrias* (Madrid: Amigos del Museo del Prado, 1986), p. 9.

9 Pérez Sánchez, *Monstruos*, p. 68.

10 Elena del Río Parra, *Una era de monstruos. Representaciones de lo deforme en el Siglo de Oro español* (Madrid: Iberoamericana, 2003), p. 32.

11 Cited in Pérez Sánchez, *Monstruos*, p. 9.

12 Pérez Sánchez, *Monstruos*, p. 80.

13 Adams, *Sideshow U.S.A.*, p. 115.

14 Juan Huarte de San Juan, *Examen de ingenios para las ciencias*, ed. Guillermo Serés (Madrid: Cátedra, 1989), p. 609.

15 Huarte de San Juan, *Examen*, pp. 613–17.

16 Huarte de San Juan, *Examen*, p. 617.

17 Huarte de San Juan, *Examen*, pp. 614–18.

18 Cited in Nelson I. Madera, 'La relación entre la fisionomía y el carácter de los personajes en Don Quijote de la Mancha', PhD dissertation (Florida State University, 1992), p. 211.

19 Antonio de Torquemada, *Jardín de flores curiosas*, ed. Giovanni Allegra (Madrid: Castalia, 1982), p. 188, p. 189.

20 Torquemada, *Jardín*, p. 189.

21 Cited in Henry Ettinghausen (ed.), *Noticias del siglo XVII: relaciones españolas de sucesos naturals y sobrenaturales* (Barcelona, 1991), n.p.

22 Covarrubias, *Tesoro*, p. 790.

23 Covarrubias, *Tesoro*, p. 790.

24 I added the phrase 'with hair on her chest' to Cohen's translation on page 209 (Miguel de Cervantes, *Don Quixote*, trans. J. M. Cohen (New York: Penguin Books, 1980)) in order to reflect de Cervantes' original 'de pelo en pecho'.

25 De Cervantes, *Don Quixote*, p. 153, p. 269.

26 De Cervantes, *Don Quixote*, p. 700, p. 701.

27 See Valerie R. Hotchkiss, *Clothes Make the Man: Female Cross Dressing in Medieval Europe* (New York: Garland, 1996), p. 23.

28 Leslie Fiedler, *Freaks: Myths and Images of the Secret Self* (New York: Anchor Books, 1978), p. 145.

29 Vern L. Bullough and Bonnie Bullough, *Cross Dressing, Sex, and Gender* (Philadelphia: University of Pennsylvania Press, 1993), pp. 56–7.

30 De Cervantes, *Don Quixote*, p. 721.

31 Alonso Fernández de Avellaneda, *Don Quixote de la Mancha* (Part II), trans. and edited by Alberta Wilson Server and John Esten Keller (Newark: Juan de la Cuesta, 1980), p. 232.

32 De Avellaneda, *Don Quixote*, p. 232.

33 Cited in John Block Friedman, *The Monstrous Races in Medieval Art and Thought* (Cambridge, Massachusetts and London: Harvard University Press, 1981), p. 129.

34 Juan Ruiz, *The Book of Good Love*, trans. Elisha Kent Kane, intro. John Esten Keller (Chapel Hill, North Carolina: University of North Carolina Press, 1968), p. 70, see also Augustin Redondo, 'Del personaje de Aldonza Lorenzo al de Dulcinea del Toboso: Algunos aspectos de la invención cervantina', *Anales Cervantinos*, 21 (1983), 1–22, 13.

35 Fernando de Rojas, *Celestina*, ed. Dorothy Sherma, trans. James Mabbe (Warminster: Aris & Phillips, 1987), pp. 67–8.

36 Miguel de Cervantes, *Exemplary Novels*, ed. B. W. Ife (Warminster: Aris & Phillips, 1992), pp. 227–8, p. 236. See also Jacobo Sanz Hermida, 'Aspectos fisiológicos de la dueña dolorida: la metamorfosis de la mujer en hombre', *Actas del Tercer Coloquio Internacional de la Asociación de Cervantistas* (Barcelona: Anthropos, 1993), pp. 463–72.

37 Cited in Kenneth Brown, 'Context i text del Vexamen d'academia de Francesc Fontanella', *Llengua i Literatura*, 2 (1987), 173–252, 231.

38 Brown, 'Context i text del Vexamen d'academia de Francesc Fontanella', 231. See also Sherry Velasco, 'María de Zayas and lesbian desire in early modern Spain', in Librada Hernandez and Susana Chavez-Silverman (eds), *En el ambiente: Queer Sexualities in Latino, Latin American, and Spanish Writing and Culture* (Madison, Wisconsin: University of Wisconsin Press, 2000), pp. 21–42.

39 Huarte de San Juan, *Examen*, pp. 608–9.

40 See Sherry Velasco, *The Lieutenant Nun. Transgenderism, Lesbian Desire, and Catalina de Erauso* (Austin, Texas: University of Texas Press, 2000).

41 Cited in Catalina de Erauso, *Lieutenant Nun. Memoir of a Basque Transvestite in the New World*, trans. Michele Stepto and Gabriel Stepto (Boston, Massachusetts: Beacon Press, 1996), p. 44.

11 On Frida Kahlo's moustache: a reading of *Self-Portrait with Cropped Hair* and its criticism
Neil Cocks

Introduction

Margaret A. Lindauer, in her recent monograph *Devouring Frida*, offers what I would suggest is the most rigorous and sustained assessment of Frida Kahlo's various texts yet published. Lindauer's declared intent is to rescue these texts from a critical tradition that casts them in a tradition of 'female' painting that eschews the political in favour of the personal. This is not to suggest there is something intrinsically wrong with an art that declares itself to be personal, or to endeavour to conceive of femaleness only in terms of notions of *the* public and the political. Rather, it is to question any critical discourse that can read in no terms other than autobiography. According to Lindauer, all previous critics have read the texts as either narratives of Kahlo's revenge upon or desire for her husband Diego Rivera; wishes for the children she could not have; narcissistic meditations on pain; or aesthetic objects divorced from any wider social and cultural meaning.[1]

Lindauer states that a successful move away from such narrow readings requires an 'examination of Kahlo's paintings [that is] directed at casting aside powerful binary categories that are so ubiquitous as to seem natural'. These categories, for Lindauer, include 'man/woman, active/passive, phallus/lack', those upon which 'masculine discourse is constructed.'[2] In addition there are other oppositions at work, most importantly that of 'artist = corpus'.[3] With this opposition, critics have offered readings of Kahlo's texts that 'discover' that she is obsessed by her own biography and then condemn her for it. This opposition sits uneasily with other recurrent oppositions, that of artist/wife, for example, in which Kahlo is placed firmly in the second category.

Lindauer's readings of Kahlo's texts seek to disrupt such oppositions by demonstrating how certain 'signifiers', for example the scissors held at crotch height in *Self-Portrait with Cropped Hair* (1940), resist any easy or stable position within the 'masculine' oppositions. They can and have been read both as a phallic symbol and as a symbol of castration – both the phallus and its lack. Lindauer plays out the move by which the supplementary term (woman/passive/lack) attributed to Kahlo in the biographical readings of her texts is always also a suppressed term of mastery (man/active/phallus). That which is the lack is also the lack of a lack. Lindauer charts the play of these 'shifting'[4] or 'floating'[5] signifiers in the text in order to disrupt the 'naturalised' dichotomies of patriarchy: 'I demonstrate how it (a given signifier) has been employed in the service of patriarchal prescription and argue for reconsidering it as a signifier for subverting patriarchal prescription.'[6]

However, as Karín Lesnik-Oberstein has argued in Chapter 1 of this book, there is a danger inherent in such readings. Just as feminist discourse on 'fat' can never liberate itself from the patriarchal text that it reads, so Lindauer's reading of the oppositions of artist/wife and phallus/lack is always indebted to those oppositions.

I will not be arguing that it is possible to free the discourse of Frida Kahlo from the critical assumptions that have so far constructed it. This chapter is indebted to these assumptions, just as surely as Lindauer's arguments are. Rather, I will be arguing that Lindauer's moves involve a certain critical blindness to some of the oppositions already working within the 'masculine' discourse on Kahlo that she reads. Lindauer's moves centre on the oppositions introduced above. Yet, in so doing, they ignore other oppositions that are at play. These are oppositions that are not addressed as such by the critics that she reads, yet, I will argue, they are oppositions that still function as part of 'masculine discourse'. By focusing on one of these oppositions – by bringing it into play, I will suggest that it is not only in destabilising the permitted oppositions of patriarchy that one may question 'naturalised' or 'ubiquitous' cultural constructions. One can also return repressed oppositions to the centre of discourse, oppositions regarded as too irrelevant, comic or grotesque to be of any real value. One such opposition is that between head hair and body hair. Such a move does not only offer the opportunity of questioning 'patriarchal prescription', it also allows us to engage with some theoretical problems with Lindauer's work. My close analysis here of one ambitious critical consideration of one artist's work serves to demonstrate, then, the wide range of effects that I read of hair in theoretical framings of bodies and gender.

Lindauer is very good at questioning the context that Kahlo's texts are ascribed: that of the purely aesthetic, totally domestic and utterly neurotic wife and would-be mother, rather than that of the culturally aware Mexican artist. However, Lindauer makes such a move to finally 'correctly' contextualise Kahlo. In doing this, she leads us, in the words that appear on the back cover of her text, 'to the real significance of the *oeuvre*'. The problem, for Lindauer, is that Kahlo has been put in the wrong context. Which means there is a *right* context, a right place where Kahlo's true meaning may be read correctly. The project of correctly 'recontextualising' Kahlo sits as uncomfortably with the notion of working through the play of an ever-shifting signifier as the idea of Kahlo as the aesthetically obsessed biographical artist sits with that of Kahlo as domestically obsessed wife. There will always be a tension in a text that both celebrates the idea of an ever-'floating' signifier and attempts to ground each signifier with a 'correct' cultural context.

Lindauer does not engage with the question of how one chooses the 'signifier' one is to work with: how one isolates the object of study. It is all well and good to demonstrate the instability of a given signifier in the oppositional systems of masculine discourse, but in Lindauer's reading the signifier never shifts enough to be located as something else. It is always anchored to that which patriarchy has deemed important. The 'shifting signifiers' of Frida Kahlo include 'scissors', 'hair', 'blood' and 'wife'. The list is finite. For Lindauer, Kahlo's moustache is not a shifting signifier, because it has not been declared a 'signifier' at all. The moustache is not important enough to the tradition to need to be destabilised. Yet, as we will see, the moustache can be read as important to the tradition. All it lacks is the status of 'signifier'.

The problem of 'shifting' signifiers is not limited to an idea that the choice of signifiers places limits on the possible readings of a given text. Lindauer praises the idea of the 'shifting signifier' because it disrupts certain assumptions made by patriarchy. She argues that although meaning is flexible, patriarchy requires it to be fixed in order to preserve and reinforce gender inequalities. Lindauer claims that a signifier such as 'hair' is too bound to notions of sexuality and gender in the work of previous writers on Kahlo, but to her too it must be 'hair', even if in ways which oppose these previous readings of the term. Lindauer's readings place limits on the signifier just as surely as those readings she criticises.[7]

Introducing *Self-Portrait with Cropped Hair*

A figure sits upon a chair in front of a background divided into two unequal parts, the smaller and lower of the two a brown floor, the larger and higher a white, plaster wall. The floor and wall have a flat perspective that sits at odds with that of the chair and body that are turned at a forty-five-degree angle to the right. The figure on the chair is dressed in a large dark suit, a red shirt buttoned up to the collar, an earring and a pair of high-heeled shoes. In the figure's right hand, at crotch level, is a pair of scissors, blades pointing upwards. The left hand rests upon the left thigh, and underneath it there is a large lock of brown hair. Similar locks are scattered upon the floor and the chair. At the top of the painting are a few bars of music, above which, in twisting brown paint, are the words of a popular song that reads 'See, if I loved you, it was for your hair, now you're hairless,

I don't love you anymore'. This is a reading of *Self-Portrait with Cropped Hair* by Frida Kahlo.

Lindauer reads earlier critics such as Hayden Herrera and Robin Richmond as reading this text as an act of revenge by Kahlo upon Rivera, who had recently issued a divorce.[8] In this 'vengeful picture' Kahlo does not wear the Tehuana dress that Rivera so loved and that was such a recurrent feature of previous works. Kahlo has also cut the long hair that Rivera loved. In doing so, Kahlo is read as refusing the passive feminine role of object of attraction for her husband. In his absence she has cast herself in a new role, that of the husband who has departed. Yet this attempt at empowering herself by taking on a male persona is read as doomed to failure. The suit is too large for her. She cannot fill the role that she wishes. This 'enormous suit' 'is Rivera's' suggesting that 'Rivera is the intended audience for this self-portrait' – Kahlo having no idea of a wider, more general public for her art.[9] Herrera reads the scissors as Kahlo's attempt to hold the Phallus, again, a doomed attempt at taking on a male position, 'to be a man without her man',[10] one that only leads to her self-mutilation. Richmond claims that because Kahlo is wearing Rivera's suit she may be read as an aggressive woman threatening castration on her husband.[11] The crotch that the scissors are held over is his crotch. This act of mutilation upon Rivera is pointless – 'a vengeful act that only heightens her loneliness'[12] as it will only really be an act of violence against Kahlo's own body, just like the loss of her hair. The song points up the absurdity of Kahlo's actions. Kahlo's impotent revenge is, finally, nothing more than an illustration of a popular song, an act of supreme triviality, a 'rueful jest'.[13]

In her criticism of this reading of *Self-Portrait with Cropped Hair*, Lindauer reads how in reading the text previous 'researchers draw upon ubiquitous metaphors and paradigms, which themselves are constructed with gender codes'.[14] These readings cannot allow Kahlo to have painted herself as active or self-controlled; neither, as a female artist, can she have created something with a complex social or political meaning for an audience wider than Rivera. Rather a 'one to one association of life events to the meaning of a painting' (back cover of Lindauer's book on Kahlo) is set up. Rivera has divorced Kahlo; Kahlo feels pain; she paints an 'irrational reprisal'.[15] Such readings of art as corresponding in a stable way to the biographical 'truth' of the artist's life are dependent on a certain set of signifiers in that art being read as stable symbols. The suit *is* Diego's. The song *is* trivial. Lindauer disrupts this stability by working through the 'contradictory female stereotypes' that are 'inscribed' in the text, demonstrating how one particular signifier will shift its meaning depending on the assumptions that a given reading makes about gender. The scissors, as I have suggested, are a good example of this. Their meaning changes 'depending on gender association'. If Kahlo is a man, or attempting to occupy a male position, they are a phallus; if Kahlo is a vengeful woman, they are the tools of castration.[16] For Lindauer, Kahlo's short hair is another 'shifting signifier', although one that can be 'correctly' contextualised. 'Hair', for Lindauer, 'is a highly charged physical feature'. Previous critics have read the artist's hair as representing 'sexuality' and 'emotional "strength"', a move that Lindauer claims 'essentialises Kahlo according to her feminine attributes, with their ability to attract male sexual attraction'. This relegates Kahlo 'to the feminine, emotional realm of private experience and limited audience', excluding her from 'the realm of paradigmatic artist'. The text is read by critics prior to Lindauer as a foolish rejection of female sexuality; hair embodies female sexuality and that sexuality is simply the ability to attract men.[17]

Lindauer counters this reading by 'contextualising' hair. She claims that in Mexican culture sexuality is constructed in terms of 'acts' rather than 'object choice'. 'Masculine' acts are 'active'; and 'feminine' 'acts' are 'passive'. 'In Kahlo's painting, the "active" quality of her cut hair is clear'.[18] Rather than an act that indicates a refusal of her sexuality, Kahlo's haircut is one that actively takes on a sexual role, one not dependent on essentialised ideas of sexuality.

Facial hair and cropped hair

In 'Fetishizing Frida', a chapter of *Devouring Frida* on the popular image of Frida Kahlo, Lindauer briefly mentions that there is a refusal on the part of the fashion industry, when attempting to dress models with 'a Frida-look',[19] to adopt the facial hair that is such a recognisable part of that style. Lindauer's critique of the fashion industry is that even Kahlo's most ardently patriarchal of critics acknowledge the importance of this physical feature to her work:

> Dan Hofstadter dramatises the artist's 'neglect' of her toilette as he muses, 'there is a moment in the early life of Frida Kahlo that uniquely illumines the evolution of her myth . . . it is the moment, apparently in her eighteenth year, when, gazing into a mirror, she decides to stop trimming her eyebrows'. . . her paintings are distinguished from the Frida-look when critics note that the artist emphasised her facial hair in portraits.[20]

This is one of the few times that 'facial hair' is addressed by Lindauer in *Devouring Frida*.[21] For now, I will limit myself to comparing this quotation with another from Lindauer, one concerning Kahlo's *Self-Portrait with Thorn Necklace and Hummingbird* (1940): 'Blood drips from each wound, transforming into fine, hair-like lines on her chest, thereby adding another masculine feature to her already exaggerated facial hair'.[22]

From these quotations we are led to understand that Kahlo's initial refusal to trim her facial hair is an important moment for the critical discourse. It is important because it brings into being a feature that will eventually distinguish Kahlo's art from patriarchal capitalism's attempts to copy it with the 'Frida look'. The facial hair is that which makes Kahlo's work unique, and this hair is both a 'masculine feature' and an 'exaggeration'. Thus patriarchy is refused through a masculine feature, the act of not cutting one's hair.

There is a difficulty here. In her reading of *Self-Portrait with Cropped Hair*, Lindauer claimed that Kahlo's cutting of her hair was a 'masculine' 'act', yet here Kahlo's refusal to so act results in a 'masculine' 'feature'. The move from 'act' to 'feature' is one that 'essentializes Kahlo'[23] in exactly the way that led Lindauer to criticise previous critics of *Self-Portrait with Cropped Hair* when they 'essentialised' head hair as 'feminine'. It also suggests that placing the cutting of hair in its correct Mexican context as a 'masculine' 'act' is only relevant to certain types of hair. It is precisely when the discourse of hair cutting introduces the idea of body hair, that the idea of a socially constructed sexuality gives way to an essential gendered property, a 'feature'. If cutting hair is an 'act' of 'masculine' sexuality, one would think not cutting hair should be the opposite of this – a thing of 'passive' 'feminine' sexuality. Growing the moustache, or rather not cutting it, is set up as a passive act. In this we have an example of a 'shifting signifier' that is not acknowledged by Lindauer.

There is, however, another way to read facial hair as a 'masculine' feature within the discourse of Frida Kahlo's moustache. It might be that the refusal to cut facial hair is in itself an act. It is because Kahlo has deliberately decided not to cut the hair in this defining moment that gives the act the 'masculine' status, the idea of Kahlo acting out a scene of self-creation. This leads to further problems. There is an idea here that it is in some way 'natural' for women to shave facial hair, and that allowing it to grow must be an act of intention. Conversely, female head hair grows 'naturally', and any attempt to cut it must involve intent. Lindauer writes that 'in a Latin American sexual system, it is not the biological sex of Kahlo's sexual partners that is important but rather her sexual identity was determined by the acts she performed or wished to perform'.[24] From this, there is the idea that it is Kahlo's painting of self-portraits that goes beyond the domestic, personal and 'feminine' role in which she is cast by previous critics through its status as 'act'. Kahlo's repeated painting of self-portraits is a repeated act of self-creation not dissimilar from her act of refusing to shave. Although useful in reading Kahlo's texts as something more than 'one on one association(s) of life events to the meaning of paintings' where life events are relegated to the domestic, romantic and maternal, this also constructs all creativity as 'masculine'. Lindauer claims that 'the self-portrait presents one possibility for liberating the female from patriarchally defined gender tyranny, not in order to become a man, but to have available some of the social privileges symbolically reserved for men'.[25] Constructing her identity through a 'masculine' act, Kahlo can liberate herself from the gendered role in which she has been cast. Through introducing the idea of facial hair into the discourse, however, we can begin to question the whole notion of 'act' having 'masculinity' as its stable signifier. Through facial hair we can read that 'passivity', at a certain stage, is available as a signifier for that which is 'masculine'.

'Shifting signifiers'

The critics of *Self-Portrait with Cropped Hair* that Lindauer refers to in *Devouring Frida* read the cut hair that rests on chair, floor and figure as something that is at odds with the rest of Kahlo's text, although such readings are put in terms of the different features having different stable meanings. The text is, in part, constructed through certain straight lines, both vertical and horizontal. There are the lines of music at the top; the line that joins wall and floor; and the horizontal and vertical lines of the chair, in the very centre on which sits the straight-backed figure, on whose legs, set at a forty-five-degree angle, are trousers with rigid, vertical creases pressed into them. Compared to this rigidity, the hair is read by Lindauer as 'strewn' about, and by Richmond as being 'all over the floor, like spilt blood'.[26] In a later essay, Gannit Ankori has this 'animated' hair 'writhe' around and 'litter the ground'.[27] These quotations attest to a randomness that can be found nowhere else in the text. The frame cuts many of the loose strands in half – the hair threatening to exceed the frame and break away from the text entirely. The hair is therefore not properly contained, and is opposed to a formal structure. Because it is in the wrong place – not on the head of the figure in the centre of the text, it has no right place in the structure, hence the idea of it being 'strewn'. The words above the five straight lines that form the bar of music at the top of the text are the other element that refuses to obey the strict line of the text. They are rendered in the same curling style as the hair, and in the same brown colour. The hair, not satisfied with covering figure, chair, floor and moving beyond the frame, has been repeated in the style of writing; its influence has seeped through the defensive bars of music, breaking the bounds between writing and picture, collapsing the distinction between the text and the title, the art and its supplement.

Lindauer states that according to previous critics the 'artist (personified by her writing style)' is 'on the one hand [. . .] dainty and delicate; on the other troublesome and untamed, analogous to the child who is not yet properly socialized'.[28] The quotation could equally be referring to the unruly, cut hair. The cut hair, despite resulting from an act of 'masculine' sexuality, is open to a reading of 'feminine' sexuality, being 'delicate', 'untamed' and intimately linked to the artist. The shifting signifiers at work are such that I could be referring to something other than the cut hair or the artist 'Frida Kahlo'. These terms could also adequately describe the faint moustache that the figure wears. It is in the wrong place because a 'masculine' 'feature' should not appear on the 'feminine' face; it is 'delicate' because faint; 'untamed' because it is a 'natural' growth that has not been removed by human agency; and 'feminine' – because it has not been shaved off, therefore it is a signifier for a 'passive' sexuality.

Thus the cut hair, rather than a stable symbol of 'feminine' sexuality, may be read as interchangeable with facial hair, a 'masculine' feature. More than that, the cut head-hair may be read as interchangeable with facial hair that is not cut. The text is always collapsing the two. Both types of hair are breaking and escaping from the frame, going where they should not go. Both types appeal to an idea of 'masculinity': one because it is not cut and remains a 'masculine' 'feature'; the other because it is cut, and therefore is both a rejection of the feminine and the victim of the castrating scissors. Both also appeal to ideas of 'femininity': one because it is the result of a passive refusal to cut hair; the other because in mourning the loss of the hair the critics may recover a total 'femininity' from a text that they construct as centred on its loss.

Lindauer does not want to allow such confusion of sexual identity. Hair may be read as 'shifting' its meaning, yet limits must be placed upon the signifiers that allow this 'shift' to take place. Facial hair may not be introduced into the discourse, because it will disrupt the neat shifts in meaning that Lindauer has established. Her disruption of gender 'stereotypes' is reliant on limits being placed on meaning. One such limit is that cutting one's hair is a 'masculine' 'act'; another that 'hair' may only relate to head hair. Despite this, Lindauer does want to avoid the trap of substituting a stable 'feminine' identity for Kahlo with a stable 'masculine' one. To this end, Lindauer is very keen to distance herself from the idea that *Self-Portrait with Cropped Hair* simply demonstrates a rejection of 'femininity' in favour of an active masculine identity: 'Kahlo has not, in the painting, "violently rejected femininity"; she wears earrings and women's shoes'.[29] 'Femininity' here is constructed wholly in terms of adornments and additions, an earring, a shoe. Lindauer has previously criticised readings of the text that claim that the cutting of 'feminine' hair is a 'symbolic cutting away of vulnerability and attachment'.[30] Yet Lindauer only manages to redefine 'femininity' as a different kind of 'attachment'. Because the figure's hair is always already cut; because there is no access to a 'before' of this text – a scene where the hair is attached – the hair becomes an 'attachment', just as the earring is an 'attachment'. The hair is only ever available as something to add on rather than something to take off. The idea of 'feminine' sexuality offered by Lindauer is only ever one of the attachable 'feminine'. This could be read as a positive idea, attacking the kind of essentialised notions of female sexuality described above. However, any comfort in this move must be questioned by the idea of 'masculinity' as an activity that detaches the 'feminine' excess and leaves in its place a 'masculine' sexuality. That is not to say that I am forgetting that Lindauer is talking about sexuality as 'act' rather than essentialised 'truth'. Rather, I am stating that this 'act' is one that detaches the 'feminine', the additional, and, through this act alone, transforms into a 'masculinity'. Because this 'masculinity' is the result of a removal, it is regarded as a norm. 'Femininity' may only be asserted through attaching objects to a prior 'masculinised' body. Lindauer reads Kahlo as attacking such a notion in her texts. In a reading of *Self-Portrait with Thorn Necklace and Hummingbird*, we read that Kahlo's 'hair is decorously arranged and adorned with ribbon and butterflies, as if mocking the viewer by juxtaposing customarily feminine embellishments with unaccountable torture'.[31] Here the detachable feminine that was a signifier for Kahlo's lack of a 'violent' 'rejection of femininity' in *Self-Portrait with Cropped Hair* becomes, unaccountably, an act of violence towards the female. Jewellery shifts from being the attached feminine identity that Kahlo refuses to give up, to a patriarchal creation that injures women.[32]

Through introducing facial hair into the discourse, one can begin to read which signifiers need to be 'grounded' – instead of 'floating' or 'shifting' – for Lindauer's arguments to be sustained. Rather than endlessly charting the play of gendered terms, Lindauer's criticism must 'blind' itself to some of the moves that it makes on gender. One is that 'feminine' hair is that which may be detached, whereas 'masculine' hair is that which stays on the body. Again, through the moustache, we read that 'masculinity' is passive, and 'femininity' active; 'masculine' hair is that which stays, 'feminine' hair is that which is cut. This cannot be recognised, as it brings into question the notion of a 'correctly' 'contextualised' sexuality. This is not a finalised move on gendered oppositions. There is a sense, as there will be for such supplementary terms, that 'masculinity' is also a repressed term of detachment. *Self-Portrait with Cropped Hair* is, after all, read as 'a classic invocation of castration fear'.[33] It is worth turning to this in some detail, to allow a reading of the extent to which gendered terms 'shift'.

According to Lindauer, critics of *Self-Portrait with Cropped Hair*, such as Richmond, read 'long hair' as a property of female sexuality, and the cutting of it as a rejection of that sexuality.[34] The cut hair that is strewn around the painting is 'feminine', including that which rests under the left hand at crotch level. Yet the hair also signifies the loss of 'femininity', as it is no longer attached to the female body. Just as the scissors are read as 'masculinity' and its loss, so the cut hair is both the absence of 'femininity' and 'femininity' itself. The link between scissors and hair is not only one of their being both the presence and absence of a given sexuality. The scissors that threaten mutilation on the Phallus also mutilate 'feminine' hair. Lindauer claims that 'cutting hair is active (masculine)' and that Kahlo takes 'revenge through castration upon herself', but Lindauer never works through the difficulties that these two statements allow. If the scissors are castrating, then the hair is, at one stage of the shifts in meaning, castrated. Hair, which signifies 'femininity' and its lack, also may play the part of the Phallus and its lack. Like the idea of a castrated Phallus, 'hair' in this text plays constantly between the two terms of presence and absence, a thing of totality and utter lack. Hair, as the recoverable feminine sexuality of male attraction, is also the recoverable masculine sexuality of the Phallus.

Presence and absence

So far I have limited myself to reading ideas of presence and absence as related to the idea of a shifting signifier. Anything in the text that is read as lost – whether 'the Phallus' or 'long hair' – can also be read as that which is set up as its opposite. There are, however, many other ways in which presence and absence are negotiated. I will limit myself here to readings of the two terms that relate to hair.

The words to the song at the top of the painting refer to someone who has a complete absence of hair, someone who is 'without hair'. Love was there when hair was there, the song states, but now that hair has gone completely, so has love. Despite these words, the figure that sits in the chair holding the scissors is not bald. The figure not only has hair on its head, it also has hair on its face. The hair that has been cut has not disappeared. It is there, on the chair and on the floor, and held at crotch level. The words of the song mourn an absence, yet the text does not allow such an absence. That which is lost is still there, either as the cut hair, or the facial hair, or the curling, brown lines of the words to the song. The text can be read as claiming that once an idea of hair, or an idea of love, has been introduced, it cannot be totally absented. The text that focuses on the loss of something, can never totally lose that thing as its subject.

The idea of the presence of that which is totally lost to the text is constructed in other, slightly different, ways. For example, critics of *Self-Portrait with Cropped Hair* construct an idea of attached 'feminine' hair, despite there being no attached hair in it. When Richmond states that 'the artist's "sexuality" and "strength" are represented by her hair',[35] Lindauer's only objection is that this constructs female sexuality as that which attracts men. She does not begin to question what hair is being discussed by Richmond, and how a reading of that hair is possible. Are 'sexuality' and 'strength' properties of cut hair? No, because it has been established that cut hair rids itself of those qualities. Yet the hair in the text is cut, short or facial. So Richmond is either reading the qualities of 'strength' and 'sexuality' in the hair that is set up in opposition to the attached 'feminine' head hair, or is reading an idea of attached hair that is never available to him in any other form but a recoverable fantasy of a 'prior' narrative event.

There is a further problem here, and that is that although the text is engaged with certain types of hair, this hair is never totally present, because it is painted hair (although, I would argue, an engagement with 'real' hair rather than 'painted' hair would not give one access to the 'reality' of it, it would allow one to engage with the discourse of the 'real'). Any claims to the 'real' (Kahlo cut her own hair around this time) are always compromised, because Lindauer has set up the discourse of 'hair' as one centred on 'activity' and 'passivity'. The fact that this hair has been painted gives it a very specific meaning in biographical readings of the texts, Lindauer's included. Kahlo's 'activity' is read by Lindauer as the key for understanding the play of gendered meaning in the texts. There is a sense that all the 'hair' in the text results from artistic 'activity'. That is not to say that I am making a move on artistic intention. Rather, Kahlo as artist is a part of the discourse that Lindauer sets up and, because of this, it is impossible, at a certain stage, for there to be any 'passive' (and therefore 'feminine') hair in the text that Lindauer reads. Perhaps this is why the idea of 'feminine' hair is a fantasy placed in a narrative moment prior to the text. To be 'passive' is to be placed outside of textuality.

This relates to some of the most necessary theoretical problems in *Devouring Frida*. The texts set out to question the notion of 'artist = corpus'. Yet this move is constantly staging a return. There is a refusal to break away from an idea of grounding the text in the 'real'. Therefore Lindauer will criticise 'author-equals-the-work criticism'[36] that focuses on interpretations of the 'paintings that naively perpetuate Kahlo's presumed social stigma by incorporating comments by friends and colleagues whose explanations for the couple's divorce inscribed gender stereotypes'.[37] However, Lindauer's readings never escape from the 'author-equals-the-work criticism', as they are constantly collapsing ideas of art and artist.[38] Although Lindauer constantly questions the gendered assumptions about the meaning of the figure with the cropped hair, she never questions that the figure in the chair *is* Kahlo: 'Kahlo has not, in the painting, "violently rejected femininity"; she wears earrings'.[39] The figure in the painting is indistinguishable from 'Frida Kahlo' the artist. A 'correct' reading of the figure will be a correct reading of the artist. The return of the 'real' couples this collapsing of 'artist' and 'art' with a reading of the text as narrative. For Lindauer, Frida Kahlo, the figure in the painting, exists in a narrative 'real', where events constructed as 'prior' to the scene – 'Kahlo' having a full head of hair, the 'frenzy'[40] of shaving prior to the quiet repose, can be recovered and witnessed.[41] Added to ideas of narrative and author = corpus is a notion of 'audience'. The art is extended into the 'real', and coupled to a stable meaning through an appeal to the unbending truth of a particular interaction between 'audience' and 'painting'. Thus, we read that in *My Nurse and I* there is no 'passionate exchange between Kahlo and the nurse or between the painted subject and the viewer'.[42] Every instance of the text being read is known by Lindauer, and all are exactly the same. There is no difference between the exchange between the two painted figures and the reading of a text. The figure in the text *is* Frida Kahlo. Despite Lindauer's appeals to the 'shifting signifier', meaning and the reading of meaning are incapable of change.

This 'blindness' on Lindauer's part to the way that *Devouring Frida* grounds its shifting claims in an unalterable 'real', also results in that text being unable to engage with many of the problems that I read in the work of the critics whom it aims to question. For example, in reading *Self-Portrait with Cropped Hair*, Richmond states that Kahlo 'looks out of the painting at Diego with a slight smirk on her face. He, too, loved her hair, and now, like him, it is gone'.[43] This is attacked by Lindauer as a reading that limits the intended audience of the text to Rivera, therefore placing Kahlo in the 'feminine' role of the artist of the private, romantic and domestic. In doing so, Lindauer misses the idea that, in Richmond's reading, Kahlo is looking out of the painting at a present audience who is not there; Kahlo 'looks' 'at Diego' who 'is gone'. Rivera is both an absence and a total presence – both the audience that makes the painting meaningful and the absolute lack that the painting attempts to fill. In one sense, there is the idea that the text allows Kahlo access to the total presence of that which she has lost, and that Rivera will, at some point, stand in front of the painting and make the meaning complete. There is another sense in which this refers to a hallucinated audience. It is the look that constructs Diego as its object, yet Diego is not there. Richmond constructs an audience that is at once both irreducibly present and absent. Lindauer wishes to recontextualise Kahlo's 'audience' as one that it is 'wider' than Rivera, but does not stop to question what 'Rivera' allows this text, or how the hallucination of audience is repeated in her own readings. She regards this 'wider' audience as one that is ultimately knowable, falling back, as we have read above, on an idea of audience as a way of giving the text a stable meaning.

These moves on the 'real' are indicative of a general problem with *Devouring Frida*. Throughout the text, the presence of a 'true' meaning is always returning, and that is one grounded in the 'real'. This leads to the tensions outlined in the introduction to this chapter: the necessary impossibility of grafting an idea of an ever-'floating' signifier to a project that attempts to ground each signifier with a 'correct' cultural context.

What counts as hair?

We are now in a position to return the idea of facial hair to a reading of *Self-Portrait with Cropped Hair* that has so far ignored it. As well as a text concerned with baldness, or loss of hair, this is also a text about the presence of hair. The figure has not lost its hair. The figure has a full head of hair, has a moustache and joined-up eyebrows. On the figure's left leg, under its hand, is a lock of hair. This is the 'feminine' hair that has been lost by a 'masculine' action. If the scissors are phallic because of the location in which they are held, then this hair could also be read as pubic hair, because it is held in the pubic area. The long 'feminine' hair has, in this sense, become 'masculine', because of the 'action' of cutting. It is also available as a masculine 'feature', because it is body hair, rather than 'feminine' head hair. Yet this shifting game of meaning cannot simply be stopped at this point. This same lock of hair on the left leg is also 'masculine', because it has been the victim of the castrating scissors. The masculine 'act' of cutting hair is also the same emasculating act as castrating. However, the 'masculine' act of cutting hair has also once more constructed the 'feminine' hair as 'feminine', because it has made it detachable. The 'feminine' cut hair also shares the qualities of the masculine facial hair – being 'untamed', 'unsocialised' and 'natural'. Yet all this hair is not hair, it is paint. This paint is read as applied in an act of intent by a female artist, further questioning the stability of the relationship between 'masculinity' and 'acts'. There is a refusal here to recognise that all terms are actively constructed, and that active construction is, at certain stages, gendered 'feminine' rather than 'masculine' because of the assumptions about the biographical relationship between text and artist that Lindauer relies upon. Some readings of the text now enabled might be: 'one that disrupts certain oppositions to construct body and head hair as equal terms'; 'one that seeks to read all apparently absented terms as present'; and 'one that questions the idea of passivity and activity as gendered terms'.

If Lindauer's attempt to disrupt previous patriarchal readings may be disrupted in turn by questioning the limits placed upon the term 'hair' (that it may refer to facial hair or paint), how far can we take those limits? If hair is not tied to an idea of 'real' hair, and if a signifier is signified by its shifts in meaning, then hair could refer to many things. What is it that limits what those things can be? What, in short, counts as hair in this text?

In the criticism of *Self-Portrait with Cropped Hair*, we read that the lock of hair on the figure's left thigh 'hang(s) between her legs like a murdered animal [symbolising] a violent rejection of femininity'. We also read that hair is 'all over the floor, like spilt blood'.[44] Hair is, therefore, animalistic, dead, blood, a symbol. The first of these ties in with the notion of the cut hair being 'untamed' – a quality shared with uncut facial hair. There is also an idea of head hair as something other than an 'embellishment'. By expanding the notion of hair beyond the notion of head hair, Lindauer echoes the critics whom she attacks. She also makes a connection between 'blood' and 'hair'. We have already read her comment that in Kahlo's paintings 'blood drips from each wound, transforming into fine, hair-like lines on her chest, thereby adding another masculine feature to her already exaggerated facial hair'.[45] Blood here refers to body hair. So blood, in the criticism, is both cut head hair and kept body hair. We have also already read Lindauer reading a juxtaposition of two different kinds of ornamentation in *Self-Portrait with Thorn Necklace*. There, Kahlo is read as linking 'decorously arranged' hair with the necklace and the 'hair-like' blood that flows from it.[46] Thus, the blood flowing from the thorn necklace and the arranged hair are both fulfilling the same function – female decoration being read as an act of violence towards women. Thus, distinctions between body and head hair are collapsed once more – head hair and bloody body hair being comparable.

Lindauer's criticism of another text, *Two Nudes in a Forest* (1939), also refers to blood:

> The red shawl encircling the Indian Woman's head metaphorically represents the barrenness of the lesbian womb as it drips blood into a dry riverbed. The blood, signalling a perpetual barrenness associated with lesbian sexuality, also signifies the brutality of conquest that led to obstructing pre-Columbian cultural practices.[47]

Is this a different blood to that which is linked to body hair? Or are the terms exchangeable? Is body hair an indicator of lesbian barrenness?, or of the brutality of conquest? If hair equals blood at one stage, what stops it being blood elsewhere? If hair can be blood, what is it that stops blood being hair? The 'masculinist' discourse that Lindauer reads may only continue in any semblance of sense as long as hair is that which grows on the head. To disrupt the difference between body hair and head hair is to let a given signifier 'float' that little too far; the hand relinquishes control of the string and, grounded no longer in its correct context, the 'signifier', buffeted by contradictory claims, becomes less and less discernible as an object in its own right.

Lindauer's celebration of the 'shifting signifier' is one that cannot allow the shift that it professes to champion, as it will lead to interminability and absurdity. To include the notion of body hair – a term also regarded as absurd and dangerous – into the discourse of *Self-Portrait with Cropped Hair*, is to begin to allow this shift to happen. Then 'masculine' becomes 'feminine'; 'hair' becomes 'barrenness'; and all attempts to securely fasten the text to a stable context become futile. Just as the text constructs hair as that which escapes its boundaries; just as it falls randomly over everything; just as it escapes its correct place on the figure's face, so 'hair', if regarded as a 'shifting signifier', escapes any attempt to close its meaning, to restrict its significance to that which is proper, i.e. head hair.

This move of introducing a repressed term to a discourse is not itself free of the kind of problems that I have been reading in this chapter. I read the moustache as a repressed term in the discourse of *Self-Portrait with Cropped Hair* – a term of lack in Lindauer's reading. I have attempted to read how this term can be returned to a discourse. Yet only when I introduce the idea of the moustache as a mastery term does it enable a reading of it as a lack. There is a slippage of terms of presence and absence every bit as problematic as that allowed in Lindauer's reading. Ideas of repression and lack are conflated. When a term is repressed, where has that meaning gone to before its return? Is it a lack?, the conditions of its being simply ceasing, or has it remained in some knowable form of potential? The move to construct it as total lack requires the hallucination of a knowable time when the subject of discourse ceased to be – the idea that a discourse can be known to have, at one point, totally lacked the ideas that it enables. On the other hand, to construct the discourse of the repressed term also involves a projected hallucination on my part – one that has access to an instance when a term has been inaccessible, although active.[48] The question of how a 'signifier' can be both present and absent in a discourse is related to the idea of 'what counts as hair?', 'how can hair be blood?', 'when we read hair in one way, where do the other possibilities of hair go?' Such questions relate to that of repression, what that term might mean, and the variety of moves that might be allowed to it. As Lindauer reads all prior critics as repressing certain aspects of Kahlo (her Mexican culture, her politics, her genius, her artistry, her sexuality), this is a question that her text needs to attend to in more detail.

Notes

1   Margaret A. Lindauer, *Devouring Frida* (London: Wesleyan University Press, 1999), p. 44. I would argue that Julie Taymor's *Frida* (Miramax, 2003) is a recent example of such autobiographical reading. For this film, all Kahlo's texts must be read as exact copies of moments of experience, even down to decisions on framing, perspective, proportion and colour. Thus, Kahlo sees her dress hanging at the window of her New York apartment and, in the next moment, has completed *My Dress Hangs There* (1933). Lindauer's criticisms of such moves have become established as part of the accepted critical response to Kahlo's texts. For example, they can be read in the catalogue that accompanied the 2005 Frida Kahlo retrospective at Tate Britain (Emma Dexter and Tanya Barson (eds), *Frida Kahlo* (London: Tate, 2005)). All the critical work included in this catalogue is concerned with moving beyond what it regards as simple autobiographical criticism, and offering an account of Kahlo as a political painter. Yet, to my mind, the arguments put forward do not move beyond the kind of reductive autobiographical readings that are the apparent target of their criticism. For example, in her contribution, entitled 'Frida Kahlo: the fabric of her art', Gannit Ankori initially sets out to argue against those who read Kahlo's work as 'merely "autobiography in paint"' (Gannit Ankori, 'Frida Kahlo: the fabric of her work', in Emma Dexter and Tanya Barson (eds), *Frida Kahlo*, pp. 31–46, p. 31). Yet, of Kahlo's attempted abortion, and subsequent miscarriage, Ankori writes that such 'unmediated and dramatic encounters with the forces of life and death, maternity and morality, experienced viscerally through the body . . . determined the course that Kahlo's art was to follow' (p. 32). Each of these critics relies on the notion that

Kahlo's texts offer any reader access to the non-linguistic, unmediated truth of the artist's experience and that this experience can then be understood as authoring those texts. I would argue, therefore, that these critics share Lindauer's reliance on the conventions of autobiographical criticism as much as they do her desire to break from them. (See for a biography of Frida Kahlo: Hayden Herrera, *Frida: a Biography of Frida Kahlo* (New York: Harper & Row, 1983).)

2   Lindauer, *Devouring Frida*, p. 170.

3   Lindauer, *Devouring Frida*, p. 2.

4   Lindauer, *Devouring Frida*, p. 45.

5   Lindauer, *Devouring Frida*, p. 179.

6   Lindauer, *Devouring Frida*, p. 179.

7   Emma Dexter, in 'The universal dialectics of Frida Kahlo', in Emma Dexter and Tanya Barson (eds), *Frida Kahlo* pp. 11–30, makes a connection between this notion of 'shifting signifiers' and Kahlo's political thought. Dexter claims that Kahlo: 'Innately as well as intellectually was drawn to seeing life as a series of dialectical struggles, which in her later years, under the influence of Eastern religions such as Buddhism, Taoism and Hinduism, developed into a more complex philosophy of the oneness of the universe, where dialectics are superseded by harmony, by Yin and Yang in balance.' (p. 12). Thus, shifting signifiers are a reflection of Marxist thought and inform a later religious understanding. Dexter's arguments often reflect those set out in this chapter. However, I would argue that the history that Dexter constructs ('dialectics are superseded by harmony') is one that needs to be read in more detail. For Dexter, the struggle of oppositional meaning ends with the two parts being recognised as a perfectly balanced whole. The idea here is, I think, that 'complexity' arises from seeing that oppositional identities cannot be separated from each other. Ying, in this sense, cannot be known as itself. Yet, despite this, I would argue that the problem of shifting signifiers, as put forward in this chapter, remains. Dexter suggests that Yin and Yang cannot, on their own, be self-present and that, because of this, any identity is always made up of both elements. Yet, within Dexter's analysis, Yin can, somehow, at some stage, always correctly be identified as Yin. It is the possibility of this identification that I wish to question. Everything is made up of Yin and Yang apart from Yin and Yang.

If a narrative of final harmony emerging from oppositional struggle can suggest that the identity in question is structured through irresolvable difference, it can also be used as a way to stabilise that identity. It is worth stating that it is at the point in Kahlo's life where her mature, 'complex' thought arguably leads her through dialectical struggle to a state of 'permanent', harmonious synthesis, that she most thoroughly advocates Stalinism. Dexter only briefly mentions this second discourse, and does not connect it to any of the others.

8   Lindauer, *Devouring Frida*, p. 44.

9   Lindauer, *Devouring Frida*, p. 44.

10   Lindauer, *Devouring Frida*, p. 44.

11   Lindauer, *Devouring Frida*, p. 45.

12   Lindauer, *Devouring Frida*, p. 44.

13 Lindauer, *Devouring Frida*, p. 40.

14 Lindauer, *Devouring Frida*, p. 45.

15 Lindauer, *Devouring Frida*, p. 40.

16 Lindauer, *Devouring Frida*, p. 45.

17 Lindauer, *Devouring Frida*, p. 44.

18 Lindauer, *Devouring Frida*, p. 46.

19 Lindauer, *Devouring Frida*, p. 159.

20 Lindauer, *Devouring Frida*, p. 159.

21 There are three occasions when facial hair is named. There is a discussion of the 'Frida-look' (Lindauer, *Devouring Frida*, pp. 158–63), the idea of exaggerated hair (p. 171) and the idea of the nurse in *My Nurse and I* (1937) having Kahlo's eyebrows (p. 97).

22 Lindauer, *Devouring Frida*, p. 171.

23 Lindauer, *Devouring Frida*, p. 44.

24 Lindauer, *Devouring Frida*, p. 46.

25 Lindauer, *Devouring Frida*, p. 45.

26 Lindauer, *Devouring Frida*, p. 44, referring to: Robin Richmond, *Frida Kahlo in Mexico* (San Francisco: Pomegranate Books, 1994).

27 Ankori, 'Frida Kahlo: the fabric of her work', p. 42.

28 Lindauer, *Devouring Frida*, p. 40.

29 Lindauer, *Devouring Frida*, p. 45.

30 Lindauer, *Devouring Frida*, p. 44.

31 Lindauer, *Devouring Frida*, p. 171.

32 A reading of Lindauer's reading of *The Little Deer* (1946) would help expand this particular reading of jewellery, as well as the broader reading of *Self-Portrait with Cropped Hair* (1940) offered in this chapter: 'In it Kahlo is portrayed with a male deer's body, with testicles and antlers, but wearing a dainty, feminine earring. In essence, she is a bisexual hybrid, a masculinized female, thereby defying patriarchal prescriptions' (Lindauer, *Devouring Frida*, pp. 72–3). Again, we have the idea of the detachable feminine, the idea of body hair being associated with the 'masculine', a one-to-one association between the artist Frida Kahlo and the half-animal figure, and an idea of a figure that refuses gender classification being grounded in the notion of 'she'.

33 Lindauer, *Devouring Frida*, p. 45.

34 Lindauer, *Devouring Frida*, p. 44.

35 Lindauer, *Devouring Frida*, p. 44.

36 Lindauer, *Devouring Frida*, back cover.

37 Lindauer, *Devouring Frida*, p. 49.

38 It is precisely this inability that finally links Lindauer's work to that of Ankori and Dexter and Barson (see also: Tanya Barson, '"All art is at once surface and symbol": a Frida Kahlo glossary', in Emma Dexter and Tanya Barson (eds), *Frida Kahlo*, pp. 55–79.

39 Lindauer, *Devouring Frida*, p. 45.

40 Lindauer, *Devouring Frida*, p. 40.

41 For a rigorous reading of issues of presence and absence in terms of frenzy and repose, see Sigmund Freud, 'From the history of an infantile neurosis (The "Wolf Man")', in *Penguin Freud Library*, vol. 9, trans. James Strachey (London: Penguin, 1991, originally published in 1918), pp. 227–345.

42   Lindauer, *Devouring Frida*, p. 96.

43   Lindauer, *Devouring Frida*, p. 44.

44   Lindauer, *Devouring Frida*, p. 44.

45   Lindauer, *Devouring Frida*, p. 171.

46   Lindauer, *Devouring Frida*, p. 171.

47   Lindauer, *Devouring Frida*, p. 46.

48   See Stephen Thomson, 'Sleepwalking into modernity: Bourdieu and the case of Ernest Dowson', *Criticism*, 41: 4, (Fall 1999), 495–512, for a detailed engagement with this question.

Index